Atlas of Vernacular Architecture of the World

Atlas of Vernacular Architecture of the World

Atlas of Vernacular Architecture of the World

Marcel Vellinga, Paul Oliver and Alexander Bridge

First published 2007 by
Routledge, 2 Park Square, Milton Park, Abingdon, Oxon, OX14 4 RN

Simultaneously published in the USA and Canada by
Routledge, 270 Madison Avenue, New York, NY10016

Routledge is an imprint of the Taylor & Francis group, an informa business

© 2007 Marcel Vellinga, Paul Oliver and Alexander Bridge
Typeset in Calisto by
Alexander Bridge

Additional typesetting by
Florence Production Ltd, Stoodleigh, Devon

Printed and bound in Great Britain by
Scotprint, Haddington.

British Library Cataloguing in Publication Data
A catalogue record for this book is available from the British Library

Library of Congress Cataloging in Publication Data
A catalog record for this book has been requested

ISBN10: 0–415–41151–3
ISBN13: 978–0–415–41151–6

Contents

Advisory Board and Consultants

Advisory Board

Jeffrey Cook[†]
Giles Darkes, Oxford, United Kingdom
Roderick J. Lawrence, Geneva, Switzerland
Maurice Mitchell, London, United Kingdom
Geoffrey Payne, London, United Kingdom
Susan C. Roaf, Oxford, United Kingdom

Consultants

Lana Al-Shami, Oxford, United Kingdom
Reed: Technologies

Simon J. Bronner, Harrisburg, USA
Horizontal log construction: Diffusion
Outbuildings: Barns

Hennie de Clercq, Johannesburg, South Africa
Used and manufactured: Corrugated iron

Philip Drew, Annandale, Australia
Tents: Membraneous and armature

Sriram Ganapathi, Madras, India
Ventilation and cooling: Middle East and Southwest Asia

Patricia E. Green, Kingston, Jamaica
Conservation: Open air museums

Antonio Guerreiro, Paris, France
Community and multi-family houses

Oscar Hidalgo-Lopez, Bogota, Colombia
Bamboo: Availability and use

Richard Howl, Edinburgh, Scotland
Plans: Courtyard

Adriaan de Jong, Arnhem, The Netherlands
Conservation: Open air museums

Borut Juvanec, Ljubljana, Slovenia
Stone construction: Wet and dry

Anthony D. King, Bristol, United Kingdom
Bungalow: Diffusion

Ronald G. Knapp, New Paltz, USA
Plans: Courtyard

Jiři Langer, Roznov, Czech Republic
Conservation: Open air museums

Léo Legendre, Paris, France
Community and multi-family houses

Helen Mulligan, Cambridge, United Kingdom
Underground Architecture: Cave, pit and semi-subterranean

John Norton, Lauzerte, France
Roofing: Thatch

Susan C. Roaf, Oxford, United Kingdom
Ventilation and cooling: Middle East and Southwest Asia

Harmut Schmetzer[†]
Bamboo: Availability and use

Roxana Waterson, Singapore
Symbolism: Botanical Metaphor

Reem Zako, London, United Kingdom
Plans: Courtyard

Acknowledgements

The idea to make an atlas that maps vernacular building traditions on a world scale has been around for a good many years. In 1987, the United Nations International Year of Housing the Poor, Paul Oliver first drafted a proposal to compile an *Atlas of the House*, indicating how such a publication, recording the distribution of vernacular resources, technologies and forms from around the world, would be of use to all those involved in the fields of housing, architectural history, geography and conservation. Editorial work on the *Encylopedia of Vernacular Architecture of the World* (EVAW) initially postponed the realisation of the proposal. However, because the compilation of an *Atlas of Vernacular Architecture of the World* would allow for comparisons that had been beyond the scope of EVAW, the idea was taken up again after the publication of EVAW in 1997. The allocation of QR (quality related) funding by the then School of Architecture at Oxford Brookes University allowed the project to start in September 2000. An Arts and Humanities Research Council Research Grant secured the continuation of the project in 2003, while a Bridge Funding grant by Oxford Brookes University allowed for its finalisation at the end of 2006. We are greatly indebted to the Arts and Humanities Research Council and Oxford Brookes University for their significant financial support.

Throughout the years, various people have offered invaluable advice, help and assistance in terms of both the management of the project and its academic scope. At Oxford Brookes University, special thanks are due to Sarah Taylor, John Glasson, Mike Jenks, Katie Williams, Helena Webster and Ros Mackay, all in the School of the Built Environment, whose invariable support made it possible for us to continue working on the project in a time of much uncertainty and organisational change. The advice and suggestions offered by members of staff in the Oxford Brookes Department of Cartography has been equally essential to the completion of the project. We are grateful to Roger Anson, Susie Hart and Teresa Gwilt for their assistance, and in particular would like to thank Advisory Board member Giles Darkes, whose thoughtful advice on the management of the cartographic production process and help in bringing us into contact with Taylor and Francis have been much appreciated. Invaluable academic input was received from our former colleagues in the International Vernacular Architecture Unit, including Valerie Oliver, Lindsay Asquith, Rosemary Latter and Antonia Noussia, and from the many students on the MA and PhD programmes run by the Unit, in particular: Lana Al-Shami, Ellen Andersen, Mariana Correia, Keith Daly, Colm Dunphy, Argus Gathorne-Hardy, Richard Howl, Yenny Gunawan, Dimitris Ioannidis, Sarika Jhawar, Regina Lim, Pratima Nimsamer, Martin Nissim, Rawiwan Oranratmanee, Ram Sateesh Pasupuleti, Anthony Reid, Brinda Shah, Siraporn Sihanantavong, Widya Sujana and Viviana Vivianco. Our warmest thanks go to them all.

Many people outside Oxford Brookes University have been of great help by offering advice on the structure of the atlas, by commenting on draft versions of the maps, and by ensuring that the aims and results of the project were disseminated. Our sincere thanks first of all go to the members of the international Advisory Board and to the expert Consultants listed elsewhere, without whose invaluable input it would have been difficult to compile many of the maps. Sadly two of them, Jeffrey Cook and Harmut Schmetzer, have not lived to see the work in print. Caroline Bundy's enthusiasm, interest and help has been crucial in the early stages of the project and has helped to define the scope and direction of the work. Our thanks also go to Nezar AlSayyad and David Moffatt of the International Association for the Study of Traditional Environments and to Warren Hofstra of the Vernacular Architecture Forum, for enabling us to publicise the project and its aims and objectives.

The scholars and students who supplied information additional to that available in EVAW are numerous and include: Ximena Vilela Ampuero, June Anderson, Syed Iskandar Ariffin, Neil Aulton, Danielle Bégot, Annette Bethke, Soukanh Chithpanya, Iuliana Ciotoiu, Miles Danby, Ann Dehennin, Rita Demmerle, Gaudenz Domenig, Roy Ellen, Maria Graça Fish, Stephen Fokke, Nerva Fondeur, Angela Froelich, Ali Gabban, Angela García, Gerda Gehlen, Chew Chang Guan, Lennox J. Hernandez, Stephen Hugh-Jones, Emma Jane, Michael Jessamy, Lloyd Kahn, Christien Klaufus, Diane M. Konrady, Edward C. Lee Tang, Heide Leigh-Theisen, Christine H. Mack, Trevor Marchand, Kathy Martin, Isaac Meir, Joanne Mol, Vianna Murday, Carolyn Murray-

Wooley, Maureen Otwell, Pat O'Donnell, Helen O'Mahony, Szabolcs Patai, Geoffrey Payne, Cecilia Berrocal Perez-Albela, Kate Pirie, Silvia Renacsova, Alberto Saldarriaga Roa, Nigel Sadler, Cyril Joseph Saltibus, Silvia de Schiller, Andrei Serbescu, Judith Sheridan, Simron Jit Singh, Gay Soetekouw, Marion Steffens, Fernando Vegas, Ulrik Westman and Mauricia Windsor. Our sincere thanks go to them all and to all those whom we may have forgotten to list here. Special thanks are due to Zita van der Beek and Patricia Green for their invaluable help on the Open Air Museums map.

In conclusion we would like to thank Caroline Mallinder, Kate McDevitt, Neil Warnock-Smith, Georgina Johnson and Andrew Watts at Taylor & Francis, for their interest in the field of vernacular architecture studies and for helping us bring the project to completion.

Alex Bridge, Paul Oliver and Marcel Vellinga,
Oxford, November 2005t

Introduction

Introduction

Vernacular architecture and its study

Vernacular architecture comprises the dwellings and all other buildings of the people. Related to their environmental contexts and available resources, they are customarily owner- or community-built, utilising traditional technologies. All forms of vernacular architecture are built to meet specific needs, accommodating the values, economies and ways of living of the cultures that produce them. They may be adapted or developed over time as needs and circumstances change (Oliver 1997 and 2003).

As an academic field of interest, vernacular architecture has been subject to much neglect. Until well into the twentieth century, the vast majority of research and teaching in the fields of architecture and architectural history has been concerned with formal, monumental and prestigious architecture that, designed by master builders or professional architects, signifies power, status, wealth or, most often, all of these together. In comparison to the palaces, cathedrals, seats of government or temples of the great and mighty of this world, both past and present, the traditional, non-formal and non-monumental houses, barns, shrines, stores and granaries that represent the vernacular traditions of the world for a long time seemed less significant. As a result, vernacular architecture has been systematically omitted from most histories or encyclopaedias of architecture. Although incidental references to vernacular buildings may be found, or even brief entries (Oliver 2004), most architectural reference works still pay attention principally to monumental historic architecture or commercial, public or transport structures built in the International Style of the twentieth century (for example Kostof 1985; Cruickshank 1996; Neal 2000; Moffett 2003).

Nonetheless, despite this continuing academic and professional neglect, it is clear that, at the beginning of the twenty-first century, the vast majority of the peoples of the world still live, work and worship in vernacular buildings. Although estimates vary and actual numbers are not available, the vernacular is today believed to make up between 90 and 98 percent of the world's total building stock (Oliver 2003; Rapoport 2006). Most of these vernacular buildings are to be found in countries in the so-called 'developing' world (that is, large parts of Africa, Asia and Latin America), where traditional economies, social structures and cultural values have on the whole been more persistent, due to a more recent advance of the combined processes of modernisation, urbanisation and globalisation. In the more developed countries of Europe and North America, where these transformation processes took place at an earlier date, the vernacular is less predominant, many traditions having given way to more specialised and mechanised ways of construction that have resulted in forms of popular architecture exemplified by expansive suburbs and commercial buildings related to food, transport and entertainment. Nonetheless, even in these countries, the vernacular still makes up a significant (and often increasingly valued) part of the inherited built environment, whilst some vernacular building traditions have proved themselves remarkably tenacious.

However, even though vernacular traditions are today numerous and widespread, in many parts of the world their survival is threatened. During the second half of the twentieth century in particular, the steady processes of modernisation, urbanisation and globalisation have exerted increasing pressure on traditional cultures throughout the world, leading to widespread and often radical changes in social and economic structures, the erosion of local cultural values and, with respect to the built environment, the internationalisation of architectural practices, forms and materials. In the process, many vernacular traditions have become associated with the past, underdevelopment and poverty, leading to the perception of vernacular buildings as obstacles on the road to progress rather than as works of architecture that are well-adapted to local cultures, economies and environments. In turn, this has led to the abandonment and replacement of many distinctive and unique vernacular buildings. In many areas, the destruction caused by natural disasters and human conflict only adds to the peril of the vernacular, as buildings are ravaged and whole communities are forced to abandon their homes and migrate. Today, the threats facing the vernacular as a consequence of rapid development seem best exemplified by the situation in China, where rapid economic growth is resulting in the wholesale destruction of vernacular traditions at a truly unprecedented speed and scale (see Knapp 2000; Knapp and Lo 2005).

In the case of China, the local population for the most part seems unsentimental about the rapid destruction of vernacular buildings, viewing it as the necessary, if unfortunate, accompaniment to modernisation (Knapp 2000: 332). This attitude may well be shared by many peoples throughout the world, as examples abound of cases in which, in trying to emulate western standards of living, vernacular traditions (some of which had been handed down for hundreds of years, or even longer), seem to have been willingly sacrificed. But there are also examples in which modern changes have been resisted, as well as many instances in which growing concerns about the destruction of the vernacular have led to the establishment of conservation and restoration programmes. Such efforts have taken various different forms, including the establishment of open air museums, the listing of indi-vidual buildings and the designation of entire settlements as heritage sites. The regeneration of vernacular traditions for reasons of cultural identity and pride is also increasingly noted (Figure 1). In many (though certainly not all) cases, the tourist potential of the vernacular plays an important part. In spite of prevalent negative attitudes, the vernacular has always had a romantic tourist appeal. Similarly, it has always served as a source of inspiration for architects, many of whom have expressed admiration of its functionality or aesthetic qualities. In recent years, the environmental appro-priateness of the vernacular has been added to its appeal, as lessons taught by the vernacular have increasingly come to be regarded as essential to the develop-ment of sustainable architecture.

Figure 1: Ancestral houses (tongkonan) under reconstruction, Tana Toraja, Sulawesi, Indonesia. Photograph: Paul Oliver.

The predicament of the vernacular and the contrasting attitudes towards it are reflected in the historic development of the field of vernacular architecture studies. Despite a slow start, this international and interdisciplinary field has grown significantly during the last few decades of the twentieth century. Early studies of vernacular architecture, going back to the late nine-teenth century, were often carried out by architects and antiquarians or, in the case of non-western traditions, by western missionaries, travellers and colonial officials. In general, these studies focused on the documenta-tion, classification and naming of historic or traditional building forms, materials and styles, many of which, it was believed, were destined to disappear due to the destructive influences of industrialisation, urbanisation and colonialism. Though often used as a means to criticise contemporary architectural practice, little attention was generally paid to the cultural context of the traditions concerned. This situation changed during the late 1960s, when a number of seminal publications indicated the importance of studying the vernacular in its historic and cultural context (Oliver 1969; Rapoport 1969). Published in a time of rapid modernisation and social change, these studies provided a major research impetus and helped to raise more awareness of the need to document and understand building traditions that, in many instances, were threatened in their survival.

The international study of vernacular architecture received a further impetus during the 1980s with the estab-lishment of international networks like the International Association for the Study of Traditional Settlements (IASTE), the International Association for People-Environment Studies (IAPS) and the Vernacular Architecture Forum (VAF), each of which has since been organising regular interdisciplinary conferences on the subject. Consequently, research into the vernacular has steadily expanded, resulting in an increased knowledge and understanding of a great variety of vernacular traditions, both in the western and non-western world. Today, the national and disciplinary representation of scholars involved in the field is diverse. This diversity has resulted in a variety of emphases in terms of research interest and methodologies, as well as in the way in which the ver-nacular is defined, and does in fact make it difficult to speak of a field of vernacular architecture studies in the singular. Different discourses exist, with some scholars focusing on the documentation, classification and under-standing of historical, rural and often pre-industrial building heritage (e.g. Upton and Vlach 1986; Pattison, Pattison and Alcock 1992), whilst others pay more attention to the ways in which the design and meaning of vernacular buildings change within the context of contemporary processes of modernisation and globalisation (e.g. AlSayyad 2001; 2004). In recent years, interest in the way in which the knowledge and skills of vernacular builders may be actively integrated into contemporary design has also grown (Asquith and Vellinga 2006). All discourses have produced important and sometimes pioneering studies, and continue to enrich our understanding of the vast field of vernacular studies.

An Atlas of Vernacular Architecture of the World

In 1997, the growing interest in and understanding of vernacular traditions worldwide resulted in the publication of the *Encyclopedia of Vernacular Architecture of the World* (EVAW) (Oliver 1997). Focusing on vernacular traditions from around the world and bringing together the work of more than 750 scholars from over 80 countries, EVAW is a reflection of the development and state of research up until that moment and has been said to help to define vernacular architecture as an accepted field of study in its own right (Rapoport 2006). The aim of EVAW was to provide a comprehensive reference work for international vernacular architecture studies. Such a work had not been published up to that date, most studies of the vernacular having been published in dedicated journals, conference proceedings or monographs, whilst those architectural reference works that had been published focused, as noted above, on western and, incidentally, Oriental or Indian historical and modern architecture. EVAW tried to give as balanced a coverage of the world's vernacular architecture as available research permitted, endeavouring to be representative whilst recognising that it could never be comprehensive. At the same time as it aimed to document vernacular traditions from around the world, it also acknowledged the diversity of concepts and disciplinary approaches to the subject (Oliver 1997).

In the attempt to synthesise past writings with then current research on both specific vernacular traditions and the development of the field of vernacular architecture studies in general, a specific framework for EVAW was created that allowed for a presentation of the data in a logically integrated and related form. Hence, the work has been divided into two parts. Part One (Volume 1), *Theories and Principles*, deals with some of the theoretical aspects of the study of vernacular architecture and moves from conceptual and methodological issues to some general cultural traits and environmental contexts. Part Two (Volumes 2 and 3), *Cultures and Habitats*, considers these general principles within specific cultural and societal contexts. The building traditions concerned have been classified within their cultural and environmental contexts, rather than by nation, seeing that in many cases they extend beyond political boundaries or vary widely within one country. In turn, the individual cultures and societies have been located within their geographical, political and wider culture area context, so as to reflect cross-cultural affinities and relationships. Because of the difficulties, in many instances, of obtaining comprehensive and reliable historical information, the scope of EVAW has been restricted to vernacular architecture that has been in use during the twentieth century.

In drawing attention to the richness, diversity and ingenuity of the world's vernacular building traditions, EVAW represented what had been learned about vernacular architecture during the twentieth century. All together it discusses the vernacular traditions of over 2000 different cultures, in all continents, documenting and analysing the dwellings, outbuildings and social and religious architecture of a large variety of communities, ranging from tribal nomadic hunter-gatherer and pastoralist groups to more complex peasant and industrialised societies. Despite its extensive scope, EVAW is not, and cannot be, complete in its coverage. To a large extent this is a result of the fact that it is generally very difficult to define how many cultures there are in the world, or indeed what defines one culture as distinct from another. More specifically, varied geographic and political circumstances, specialised disciplinary backgrounds and the personal interests of many of those working in the field have meant that the vernacular traditions of some peoples or regions have been studied with much enthusiasm and in great detail, whilst those of others have hardly been studied at all, or have only just come to our notice. The geographical spread of research in the field of vernacular architecture studies is unequal in the extreme and in a very real sense therefore, the entries in EVAW reflect where the lacunae in our knowledge are located.

In addition to not being comprehensive in terms of its coverage, EVAW does not specifically focus on the cross-cultural or geographical comparison of vernacular traditions. The first volume includes entries that deal with cultural, environmental and architectural aspects that influence vernacular architecture in general, but volumes 2 and 3 are focused on the documentation and analysis of the specific traditions of distinct cultures or locations. In part this restriction is pragmatic and the result of the specific framework that has been adopted, but again it reflects the nature of the field of vernacular architecture studies in general. On the whole, research has been regionally focused, with national, regional or cultural boundaries setting the limits of much of the work that has been done. Still, many vernacular traditions, or specific aspects of them, are in fact not restricted to individual cultures or regions, but may be found in much larger geographic areas, frequently crossing the boundaries of nations, culture areas or, in some cases, even continents (Figure 2). The cross-cultural relationships, patterns and developments that these wider geographical distributions reveal have not received as much attention as the specific characteristics or dynamics of individual traditions, even though they are essential to our understanding of the traditions concerned. Although various comparative studies have been published, both at a regional and global scale, the study of the singularities and commonalities of traditions and of the way in which these have developed, diverged or converged over time and in space is still largely overlooked in the field of vernacular architecture studies.

To complement the information collated in EVAW, the *Atlas of Vernacular Architecture of the World* (AVAW) has been compiled, presenting the information assembled in EVAW in a cartographic form. Mapping building forms and plans,

Figure 2: Sun-dried bricks, Sjarjah, United Arab Emirates. Sun-dried brick is used throughout large parts of the world, especially in hot and dry areas. Photograph: Marcel Vellinga.

resources, technologies and service systems at a global scale, AVAW specifically focuses on the geographical distribution and cross-cultural comparison of the vernacular traditions of the world. Applying a cartographic approach to the study of vernacular architecture, AVAW contributes to our understanding of the world's vernacular building traditions from a thematic rather than a culturally or regionally specific point of view and provides a geographic documentation that so far has been lacking in the field of vernacular architecture studies. In documenting aspects of the vernacular at a global scale, it helps us to visualise the major gaps in our knowledge and understanding. Moreover, it is hoped that AVAW will be of comparative and analytical use, as the maps (and combinations of them) may indicate specific cross-cultural trends, relationships or anomalies that were not known or obvious before, due to the tendency of much vernacular research to focus on the culturally or regionally specific. As such, they may give rise to new hypotheses and questions, and stimulate new research efforts.

AVAW constitutes a different way of representing what we have learned so far about the vernacular architecture of the world. It documents the diversity and interrelationship of vernacular traditions from a comparative perspective, in a way that augments the information collated in EVAW. Paying attention to the geographical distribution and contiguity of particular traditions, it enables us to learn more about the way in which architectural aspects relate to national, cultural and ethnic identities, as well as to environmental contexts. Indicating both what we know and what we do not know about the vernacular architecture of the world, AVAW also points to potential new areas for recording and research. As such, it is hoped that it may prove of use to all those interested in the responsible and sustainable utilisation of resources, the conservation, restoration or regeneration of architectural heritage, or the design and provision of culturally and environmentally appropriate housing.

Vernacular architecture and maps

The second half of the twentieth century has seen the publication of an ever-increasing number of thematic atlases. Many of these thematic atlases are simultaneously aimed at academic and popular markets, serving as general reference works that aim to provide introductory and, frequently, global perspectives on specific subject matters. So, for example, there are atlases on topics as diverse as the Roman world, disappearing languages, water and natural disasters (Cornell and Matthews 1982; Wurm 1996; Clarke 2004; McGuire et al. 2004). In addition to these relatively general thematic atlases, there are also those that are more expressly academic, focusing on specific subject matters in greater detail. Examples include atlases on food crops, embryology and climate change (Bertin et al. 1971; Freeman and Bracegirdle 1963; Henderson-Sellers and Hansen 1995). In these cases, the atlases are meant to be research tools rather than general reference works and the potential audience is consequently more limited. A common characteristic of both kinds of atlases is an emphasis on the use of maps to communicate the information concerned, although it should be noted that the degree of this emphasis varies per atlas. Indeed, some atlases might perhaps have been more accurately called encyclopaedias, as the maps are clearly secondary to the written text and, often, to the illustrations.

Interestingly, despite the obvious popularity of the thematic atlas as a medium, the number of atlases that deal with architecture is relatively limited (e.g. Bagenal and Meades 1980; Beazley 1984). Besides, those that have been published mainly belong to the category of atlases in which the emphasis is not so much on maps, but on other means of communication (Phaidon 2004). The only thematic atlas that so far deals with vernacular building traditions is *Afghanistan: An Atlas of Indigenous Domestic Architecture* by Albert Szabo and Thomas Barfield (1991). Published two years after the Soviet withdrawal from the country, this work aimed to serve as a documentation of the variety and richness of the vernacular heritage of Afghanistan, much of which by the late 1980s had been obliterated by various modernist government policies and subsequent decades of war. Focusing on building traditions as diverse as tents, caves and fortified farms, the core of the atlas is formed by drawings, including elevations, plans and cutaway perspectives, accompanied by brief descriptive texts and, occasionally, black-and-white photographs. Twenty-nine black-and-white maps, of standardised design and size, serve to indicate the geographic distribution of the building types concerned (Figure 3). In combination with the drawings, texts and illustrations, the maps provide a comprehensive documentation of Afghan vernacular architecture before the wars, adding a geographic dimension to other works on the subject (e.g. Hallet and Samizay 1980).

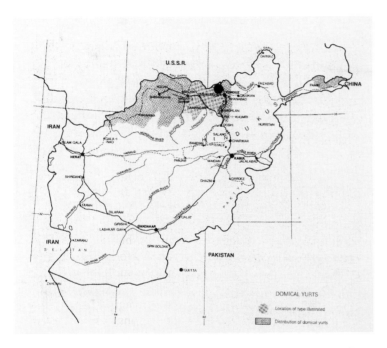

It can be argued that, in a time when thematic atlases abound, the exceptional status of Szabo and Barfield's work is a reflection of the marginal position that the study of vernacular architecture still occupies, despite the increasing interest noted above. However, it also seems to represent a remarkable disregard for the use of maps among the growing community of scholars that do work in the field. Although maps have long been an important research tool in related disciplines like archaeology and cultural geography, they have not been able to secure an equally prominent position within the interdisciplinary field of vernacular architecture studies. On the whole, the techniques of recording and analysis of vernacular scholars are restricted to descriptions, architectural drawings, plans, photographs and, in recent years, video (Oliver 1997). Whether a study appears in the form of a book or journal article, whether its focus is on a particular region or culture, or on a specific building type or technology, maps are only rarely included to communicate

Figure 3: 'Distribution of domical yurts (Turkmen, Uzbek, Central Asian Arab, Kirghiz)', in A. Szabo and T.J. Barfield, Afghanistan: An Atlas of Indigenous Domestic Architecture (Austin: University of Texas Press, 1991). Reprinted by kind permission of the authors.

information or illustrate arguments. Admittedly, plans of buildings or settlements in relation to their natural and built surroundings are regularly made, but their focus is generally on individual buildings or settlements. Maps that show the distribution or diffusion of resources, building types or technologies in an individual country, on a continent or across the world are relatively rare. Even in the works of some cultural geographers, the only maps included are general reference maps that serve no purpose other than indicating the locations of the places, cultures or architectural features that are dealt with. Strikingly, this disregard has not yet been altered by the rapid development and increased availability of new digital means of communication, including relatively cheap desktop mapping programmes or more sophisticated Geographical Information Systems (GIS) (Dorling and Fairbairn 1997; Slocum 1999; see, however, Ford, El Kadi and Watson 1999, for a recent discussion of the potential use of GIS systems for the study of vernacular architecture).

This is not say that maps have not been used at all in the field of vernacular architecture studies. Various studies can be identified that rely on the use of maps to support the arguments relating to location, density or movement put forward in the text. In many cases these studies have been carried out by cultural geographers concerned with the typological identification, classification and distribution of particular types or features in specific periods or regions, or by scholars interested in issues of spatial and temporal diffusion and the question of how and why particular traditions have undergone changes during historic processes of migration. Whether by chance or not, many of these studies refer to European or American vernacular traditions. Ronald Brunskill, for example, in his many works on the British vernacular (1981, 1985, 1997), regularly uses distribution maps to show vernacular regions or variations in location and density. Likewise, Allen Noble uses quantitative maps to chart the distribution and diffusion of barn types in the Northeast of the United States (Noble 1984a and b)(Figure 4), whilst Smith (1975) charts the distribution of different types of cruck frames in England and Wales. On a larger geographic scale, Philip Drew (1979) and Torvald Faegre (1979) use maps to illustrate the distribution of tent types in North America, the Middle East, and East and Central Asia. In a similar vein, Hugo Houben and Hubert Guillaud (1994) employ maps to indicate the global distribution and diffusion of various earth construction technologies.

A particularly well-known and influential study in which maps have been used to support hypotheses about housing regions and the geographic and temporal diffusion of vernacular building types, is Fred Kniffen's 'Folk housing: Key to diffusion' (1986)(Figure 5). Based on almost thirty years of field research into American vernacular traditions, particularly those of European origin, Kniffen distinguishes three 'source areas' or 'cultural hearth zones' along the East coast of the United States: New England, Middle Atlantic and Lower Chesapeake. Applying the concepts of 'initial occupance' and 'dominance of contemporary fashion', he attempts to trace how, in the eighteenth and nineteenth centuries, house types diffused westward from these source areas through the migrations of European settlers. To illustrate his argument he has drawn his hypothetical 'hearths' and routes of diffusion on a (by his own admittance very generalised) map of the eastern United States, which he compares with distribution maps of American 'community areas' and dialects to try to validate his hypotheses.

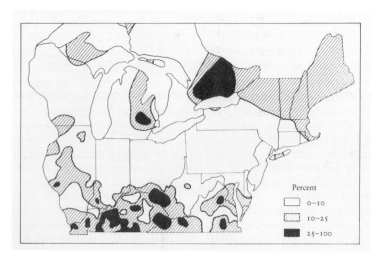

Figure 4: 'The percentage of crib barns to all barns', in A.G. Noble, Wood, Brick and Stone: The North American Settlement Landscape, vol. 2: Barns and Farm Structures (Amherst: University of Massachusetts Press, 1984). Reprinted by kind permission of University of Massachusetts Press.

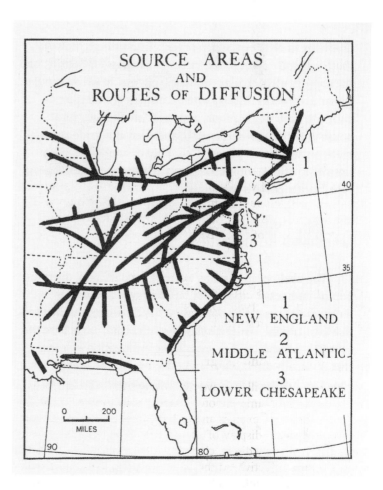

Figure 5: 'Source areas and routes of diffusion', in F.B. Kniffen, 'Folk housing: Key to diffusion', Annals of the Association of American Geographers, 55 (4): 549-577 (1965). Reprinted by kind permission of Blackwell Publishing.

Although Kniffen's study has proved highly influential, diffusionist studies of this kind are nowadays relatively rare, especially with regard to the study of traditions in the so-called developing world. Similar types of maps that chart, for example, the spread of flat-roofed adobe houses from Mexico to the southwestern United States or the diffusion of wood construction in the eastern United States have been published (West 1974, Kniffen and Glassie 1986).

Although maps therefore have been employed as tools in the field of vernacular architecture studies, most of them are small and relatively crude in terms of their cartographic design. Indeed, some maps, such as Brunskill's (1997) maps of British house types or Knapp's (2000) map of Chinese courtyard houses, are sketches rather than finished products, whilst many others do not portray any data other than the distribution or diffusion of the building traditions concerned. Even though they may have been important in the research process and the development of hypotheses, as is clearly the case with regard to Kniffen's map, they have not been chosen as the primary medium to communicate the results. In most cases, descriptions and, frequently, photographs, plans and drawings are still dominant, the maps mainly serving to illustrate and explain arguments that are made in the texts that they accompany. Maps that are intended to 'speak for themselves', with little or no commentary or other visual support, do exist, as in the case of Christopher Tunnard and Henry Hope Reed's map of three-storey dwellings in New England (1956) or John Prizeman's map of regional variation in stone construction in Great Britain (1975)(Figure 6). In these cases, the cartographic design of the maps is generally more elaborate and thought-out. Interestingly, however, these maps are frequently found in books or atlases that focus on the general cultural geography of particular countries or ethnic groups, where maps of 'shelter'

Figure 6: 'Regional variation in stone construction in relation to ethnic divisions and rainfall in Great Britain', in J. Prizeman, Your House: The Outside View (London: Hutchinson, 1975). Reprinted by kind permission of Mark B. Prizeman.

or 'rural house types' are sometimes included alongside similar maps on settlement patterns, clothing or languages (e.g. Harvey 1966; Davies 1971). Their use by scholars in the field of vernacular architecture studies appears to be more restricted.

Communication and geographical visualisation

The limited, mainly illustrative use of maps in the field of vernacular architecture studies is unfortunate. As is obvious from the examples noted above and the analytical employment of cartography in other disciplines, maps are eminent tools to express and interpret information of a geographic nature. As symbolic representations that facilitate the visual display of spatial data, they have the capacity to communicate geographic information in a way that is visually direct, clear and often (depending on factors such as the resolution of data and the cartographic design) effective. At the same time, moreover, as recent writings in the field of cartography and geography have shown (MacEachren and Monmonier 1992; Slocum 1999), maps may be more than a mere means to communicate data, seeing that they also have the ability to help the map-maker and reader gain new insights, raise new questions and hypotheses, and open up new areas for future documentation and research. Maps may reveal patterns and relationships that may not be apparent unless they are drawn on paper. As media for *geographic visualisation* as well as *communication*, they are therefore potentially of great value and use to academics, including those working in the field of vernacular architecture studies. Allowing for the visual representation of patterns of distribution, density and diffusion at, potentially, any geographic scale, maps allow us to cross the national and cultural boundaries that until now have set the limits of so much work in the field. Besides, in addition to recording and documenting existing traditions, maps may enable us to explore the complex inter-relationships between vernacular architecture and cultural, environmental and geological factors; facilitating comparisons and, in doing so, visualising previously unobserved patterns, relationships, trends or anomalies.

Until now, many published maps dealing with vernacular architecture have focused on the communication of data regarding particular countries, cultures or culture areas. Given the regional focus of much of the work in the field, this restriction should come as no surprise. Indeed, it would be quite understandable if the building forms, resources or technologies that have been mapped were only to be found in the country or culture area concerned. Quite frequently, however, the traditions concerned are encountered in other places as well, crossing national or cultural boundaries. For example, the distribution of domical yurts, black tents and sun-dried brick walls charted by Szabo and Barfield (1991) extends well beyond the present-day political borders of Afghanistan. Their extensive dispersal is related to the complex cultural history of Central Asia, which for thousands of years has acted as a stage for commerce, wars, migration and religious dissemination, resulting in a complex cultural constellation in which some traditions are found across several national borders, whilst others are restricted to small isolated regions only. Clearly, an overview of the overall distribution of yurts, black tents and sun-dried bricks may have told us more about the origins, historic development and meaning of these traditions than a limited focus on their distribution within the borders of Afghanistan. Similar observations can be made with regard to, for instance, Noble's maps on crib and raised three-bay barns (1984b), each of which can be found outside the north-eastern part of the United States; or for M.E. Harvey's map of rural house types (1966) (Figure 7), including circular huts with thatched conical roofs, in Sierra Leone. In all cases, the maps fail to indicate that the political boundaries which define them do not, in fact, necessarily coincide with the cultural and architectural ones represented on them.

Notwithstanding these examples, however, maps that go beyond the confines of national or cultural borders and focus on the distribution of particular vernacular traditions at a cross-cultural, international level have been published.

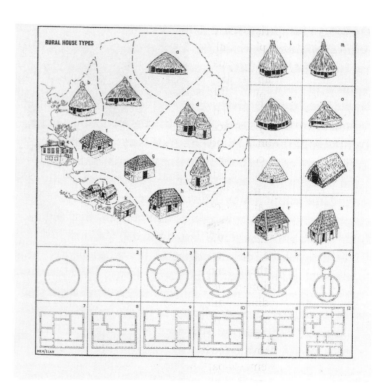

Figure 7: 'Rural house types', by M.E. Harvey, in J.I. Clarke (ed.), Sierra Leone in Maps (London: University of London Press, 1969). Reprinted by kind permission of Continuum International Publishing Group.

One good example is Harold Driver's maps on the vernacular traditions of Native American groups in North and Central America (1961) (Figure 8). The maps, which are accompanied by illustrations and descriptions, bridge the borders of Canada, the United States, Mexico and the Central American countries, showing the distribution of various kinds of Native American house and tent types before 'contact' with European settlers. Another good example is provided by Philip Drew's maps of, once more, nomadic tent types (1979). In some of these maps, such as the ones on black tents in the Middle East and tent types in northern Eurasia, cultural and national borders are clearly bridged and an overall picture is presented, the geographical limits of which are defined by the traditions concerned rather than by a predetermined cultural or national focus. The same applies to the maps on the distribution and diffusion of earth technologies in Houben and Guillaud (1994).

A map that deserves a special mentioning in this respect is Peter Andrew's map of Middle Eastern nomadic tent types (1990) (Figure 9). Designed by a cartographer rather than the author himself, this map shows the location and relative density of various tent types, divided into several kinds of 'framed' (armature) and 'velum' (frameless, membranous) tents, some of which are further distinguished on the basis of the materials used as cover (e.g. felt, goat hair, palm matting). The map not only shows general distribution patterns, but indicates where particular types have definitely been found ('observed'); where they may probably be found; and where they have been common in living memory, but are now no longer in use. In addition, arrows are used to indicate the migration routes covered by the peoples who use the tents, a distinction being made between routes that are carried out periodically and those that take place only occasionally. The names of the various groups are included on the map, as are, in certain areas, the locations of tribal boundaries. Further background is given that helps to show how various typological, cultural, geological and national boundaries sever different regions or coincide with them. These include national borders, watercourses, differences in altitude and the locations of towns and cities. Together with Andrew's two-volume *Nomad Tent Types in the Middle East* (1997), the map provides a unique and authoritative documentation of the diversity of tent structures in the region. If the books add to the map by providing detailed descriptions and illustrations of the various types of tents, the map equally contributes to the books by showing complex distribution and movement patterns that would be difficult to communicate in written form.

The exceptional status of Andrew's map in terms of its level of detail, cartographic design and, to some extent,

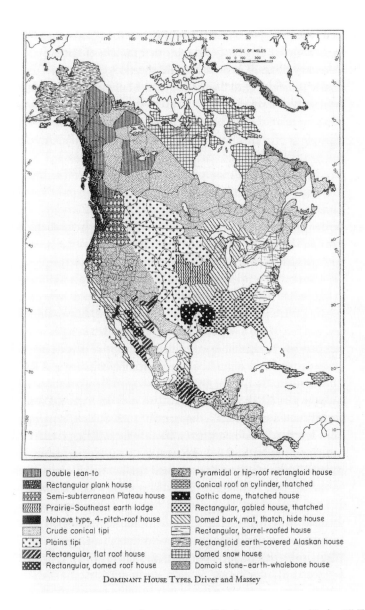

Double lean-to
Rectangular plank house
Semi-subterranean Plateau house
Prairie-Southeast earth lodge
Mohave type, 4-pitch-roof house
Crude conical tipi
Plains tipi
Rectangular, flat roof house
Rectangular, domed roof house
Pyramidal or hip-roof rectangloid house
Conical roof on cylinder, thatched
Gothic dome, thatched house
Rectangular, gabled house, thatched
Domed bark, mat, thatch, hide house
Rectangular, barrel-roofed house
Rectangloid earth-covered Alaskan house
Domed snow house
Domoid stone-earth-whalebone house

DOMINANT HOUSE TYPES, Driver and Massey

Figure 8: 'Dominant house types (Native American)', in H.E. Driver, Indians of North America (Chicago: University of Chicago Press, 1961). Reprinted by kind permission of University of Chicago Press.

scale, underlines the assertion that maps have not been able to secure a firm methodological position in the field of vernacular architecture studies. Although, as noted above, the scarcity of maps and atlases on architecture, including the vernacular, is particularly marked, this disregard for maps seems related to a fairly common ignorance among both scholars and the general public of the power of maps, and of the skills and knowledge needed to make or read them. Although architectural drawing is generally part of the curriculum of architects, cartographic education is not, nor has it generally been taught to anthropologists, sociologists, conservationists, architectural historians or others involved in the study of vernacular architecture. Indeed, mapping does not generally receive as much attention in education as reading and writing, despite the fact that graphic images, and not in the least maps, are playing an ever more influential role in our lives today (Monmonier 1991). Such an awareness of the potential and use of maps would also help reveal the power relations that are involved in cartographic representation. Often, maps are thought of as objective, ever more accurate representations of reality, a notion that is easily enhanced by their frequent association with up-to-date technology. But, in truth, as recent writings on cartographic representation have made clear, they are as selective and subjective as any other means of communication (Harley 1988 and 1989; Monmonier 1991).

In comparison with Andrew's map, most other maps of vernacular architecture, both the nationally and the cross-culturally focused ones, are very crude, generalised and simplified. The vast majority of them are in black-and-white, using outlines, simple symbols or shading to indicate the locations or diffusion of the architectural features concerned, often on a relatively small scale. To a large extent this generalised quality may be helpful (indeed, even necessary in thematic mapping), since the inclusion of too much information would make it very difficult to read and interpret the maps (Slocum 1999). Yet, in some cases, the level of simplification is so high that their actual usefulness in raising the reader's understanding of the geography of the traditions concerned is minimal. For an extreme example, Henry Glassie's (1975) maps on the distribution house types in Louisa County in Middle Virginia only consist of a few lines, triangles, squares and circles which, without any information on the location and names of towns, rivers, roads, and so on, do not add much to our knowledge of the building types concerned, except for giving a very general idea about where we may be able to find them (Figure 10). Similar remarks can be made with regard to Harvey's (1966) map of rural house types in Sierra Leone (Figure 7), Brunskill's (1997) maps of houses and cottages in Britain or Faegre's (1979) maps of black tents and yurts. In all cases, a generalised picture of the location of particular traditions is

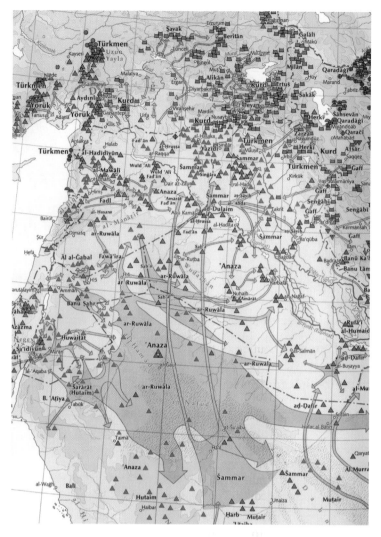

Figure 9: A section of TAVO A IX 5, by P.A. Andrews (Wiesbaden: Dr. Ludwig Reichert Verlag, 1990). Reprinted by kind permission of Dr. Ludwig Reichert Verlag.

presented, while the actual location of their boundaries remains vague and uncertain.

Although this generalised and crude nature of most maps is undoubtedly related to a lack of cartographic education, a more fundamental problem is an absence of data. Although it will in many instances be possible to show general distribution patterns of vernacular forms, services or resources, it is very difficult to get to a level of detail at which regional variations or differences in relative density can be portrayed, simply because the geographic information needed to do so is often not available. In the case of Andrew's map, the information has been gathered over a period of some twenty years. Similar databases may perhaps exist on other subjects, but generally speaking our knowledge of vernacular building traditions is not sufficiently thorough to allow for the compilation of equally detailed maps. For many parts of the 'developing' world in particular, our knowledge is scattered and partial. In many cases the focus has been restricted to particular regions because the necessity for documentation in other areas has not been recognised, or the opportunities to do research have not occurred because of their inhospitable or isolated nature. Ronald Knapp (1997: 45) notes that, beyond Europe and North America, our understanding of the geography of vernacular traditions is very limited. But even in those parts of Europe and North America where long-standing and intensive research efforts have led to the availability of more comprehensive sets of data, as in England or the north-eastern United States, the mapping of vernacular traditions in any great detail is still a difficult exercise.

Taken together, the restricted focus on specific cultures or countries, the crude and generalised nature of existing maps, and a lack of comprehensive data sets have tended to limit the usefulness of maps of vernacular architecture. Nonetheless, even though the absence of sufficient geographic information clearly limits the pos-

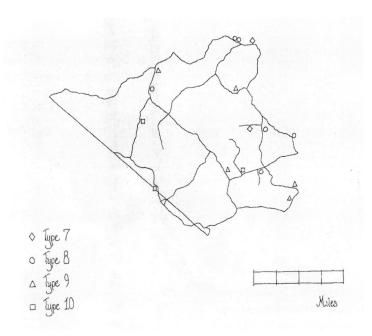

◇ Type 7
○ Type 8
△ Type 9
□ Type 10

Miles

Figure 10: 'Distribution of types 7, 8, 9, 10', in H. Glassie, Folk Housing in Middle Virginia: A Structural Analysis of Historic Artifacts (Knoxville: University of Tennessee Press, 1975). Reprinted by kind permission of University of Tennessee Press.

sibilities of compiling detailed distribution maps, it is possible to approach the difficulties involved from a more constructive point of view. For if the making of maps is regarded as an explanatory analytical process, rather than a mere means to communicate data, the maps that are made can be valuable in showing us what we already know about the geographic distribution, diffusion or density of particular traditions, and what information is still missing or incomplete. In other words, by attempting to chart, for example, the availability and use of resources, the distribution of service systems or the diffusion of building forms and technologies, we may be able to identify the 'white spots' on our conceptual world map of vernacular building traditions; the lacunae in our knowledge and understanding of the resources, service systems and technologies concerned. At the same time, by comparing the data we have with geographic information of a different (for instance climatic, geological or political) kind, we may be able to recognise and identify previously unno-

ticed relationships, patterns or anomalies. In so doing, we may use the maps to indicate new areas for recording and research, treating them not just as media for *communication*, but as tools for *geographic visualisation*; that is, as valuable means to gain insights in geographical gaps, patterns, relationships and contexts that are otherwise not known or not immediately obvious.

Research and cartographic design

As noted above, the maps in AVAW aim to do exactly this. However, the problem of a lack of data has also been a major issue with regard to the compilation of AVAW. Visualising geographic patterns, connections and developments using a Geographic Information System (GIS) has not been possible, for instance, simply because the comprehensive data sets that would be needed to map resources, forms or services on a global scale are not available in the field of vernacular architecture studies. Detailed data sets can sometimes be found on a national or regional level, but even in those cases the information is often not quantified, nor are exact locations always known. With a few notable exceptions, the maps in AVAW are therefore qualitative rather than quantitative, attempting to indicate patterns of distribution and diffusion on the basis of data that has been accessible in discursive or visual form. This means that the boundaries that are drawn on the maps are not always completely accurate in terms of their geographical positioning, nor are they necessarily as rigid as the lines may sometimes suggest. Also, they point out where particular features may be found, but do not (unless specifically indicated) make statements about their density or their dominance in relation to other features. Nonetheless, as symbolic depictions, they are representative in the sense that they indicate what is currently known about the distribution or diffusion of a particular vernacular tradition. What is shown, in effect, is what is known or, rather, what has been recorded in the course of the twentieth century. As such, the principle of geographic visualisation may still apply, seeing that the maps can give us a good indication of the areas, both geographical and thematic, where research has or has not yet been carried out, or where certain anomalies or relationships seem to exist that had not been realised or been clear before.

The main source of information for AVAW has been EVAW. Aiming to document and visualise what is known about the vernacular architecture of the world, AVAW is first of all meant to be a cartographic representation of the data collated in EVAW. Hence its thematic coverage to a large extent corresponds to that of EVAW, whilst its scope is restricted to those traditions that have been in use during the twentieth century. Although this limitation means that the maps may not always be fully representative, seeing that additional information from other sources may not necessarily have been included, it has been unavoidable to restrict the scope in this way. On the whole, research into the geography of the vernacular architecture of the world has been so limited and uneven that, in many cases, EVAW turned out to be the only source of information available. Publications that deal with the vernacular architecture of regions larger than countries or individual cultures do exist (e.g. Denyer 1978; Waterson 1990; Knapp 2003), but they are still relatively rare and do on the whole not give much geographical information. Information for individual cultures is more easily accessible, but again it is scattered, making it difficult to consistently document the use of a particular feature on a global scale. Nonetheless, where additional information has been found in available literature, this has been included. On the whole it has not been possible to initiate new research, though in a number of cases new information from the field has been included. In most cases, draft versions of the maps have been sent to specialist consultants, who have commented on their accuracy and detail, ensuring that the picture portrayed on the maps conforms to our current knowledge and understanding.

The problem of the availability of data and the fact that maps are symbolic representations raise some important design issues. Cartographic design involves the application of established generalisation techniques (such as selection, classification, simplification and symbolisation) to geographic information, resulting in the generation of a two-dimensional model of reality: a map. Central to the entire process is the issue of scale. Ideally, the scale of a map would be dictated purely by the density of information required for the map to make its point (for example, if we need to differentiate between, say, three settlements, the map scale should be such that the symbolised settlements do not merge on the page; if we need to differentiate between three houses in one of those settlements, a larger scale is required so that the symbolised houses do not merge). However, based on the extent of coverage and, in the case of an atlas, the size of the page, a compromise is usually necessary. Once scale has been established, any topographic or thematic data selected for inclusion, must be clearly symbolised in relation to the given scale.

When a theme is added to a topographic base map, the ideal source data are consistently high in resolution, clear in definition, dense in detail and easily processed for symbolisation. However, during the compilation of AVAW, it has often been the case that very dense, high-resolution data sets have been available for some regions, whilst only very limited and sparse, low-resolution information has been available for other regions. A good example is the distribution of log construction, which has been very well documented for the eastern United States, but has been studied in much less detail in Europe, Russia and Siberia, or in those parts of Australia and Latin America where log buildings can be found. Rather than seeking to mask this inconsistency and balance the page, it is intended that, where possible, the chosen point, line and area symbols reflect the true nature of the available data. Thus, isolated, singular points should appear isolated and singular, generalised boundaries should appear generalised, and blurred areas should appear blurred.

Structure and contents

Like EVAW, AVAW is not comprehensive in its coverage. The inclusion of a theme has been dependent on whether mapping it would contribute to our understanding of it, as well as on its mappability and the availability of data. Hence some themes that would seem to be of much interest have not been included, either because the data needed is not available, or because it has proved difficult to represent the data in cartographic form. Conversely, some maps focus on traditions that are well-known and have been documented in great detail. Although it may seem that these maps do not necessarily add to our understanding of the traditions concerned, they have been included because the data has been accessible and because the maps may still reveal patterns or relationships that so far have not been considered. On the whole, care has been taken to be as thematically and regionally comprehensive and varied as possible. The work has been divided into two Parts, *Contexts* and *Cultural and Material Aspects*, with Part 2 being subdivided into six major Sections.

Part 1, *Contexts*, contains maps that literally set the context for the more specific thematic maps in Part 2. Climate, the availability of water, geology and vegetation are environmental aspects that affect the nature of vernacular traditions and influence their distribution and diffusion. Social and cultural traits like population density, economy, religion and language have a similar influence and relate closely to environmental aspects. Political boundaries are important as a point of reference, though the nature of vernacular traditions is better understood in the context of cultures and culture areas. Together, the maps in Part 1 act as reference maps that may be consulted when trying to understand the more specific thematic maps in Part 2.

Part 2, *Cultural and Material Aspects*, contains maps that focus on the distribution and, in some cases, diffusion of specific vernacular traditions. The first Section, *Materials and Resources*, includes maps on the use of a variety of important vernacular resources, including natural ones such as timber, earth and bamboo, and manufactured ones like fired brick and corrugated iron. Some of these materials have been mapped in relation to their availability.

The maps in Section Two, *Structural Systems and Technologies*, link up with those in Section One, focusing on the specific ways in which resources may be employed. Timber-framed walling, dry stone construction and thatching are among the technologies featured in this section.

Section Three, *Forms, Plans and Types*, includes distribution maps of a variety of forms, plans and types that are commonly encountered in the vernacular. Circular plans, roof forms and courtyards feature alongside pile dwellings, community houses and the well-known 'suburban vernacular', the bungalow.

The maps in Section Four, *Services and Functions*, focus on services that allow for a building to function effectively, such as cooling systems and smoke vents, as well as on building types that are used for purposes other than housing. Examples in this Section include chimneys, barns and mills.

Section Five is devoted to *Symbolism and Decoration*. It includes maps that deal with the various means by which houses may be embellished, as well as with the ways in which meanings may have been symbolically expressed. Roof finials and coloured wall decorations are among the themes included in this Section.

Finally, Section Six, *Development and Sustainability*, focuses on a number of social, cultural and environmental processes that have a bearing on the future transmission, development and sustainability of vernacular traditions. Population growth, deforestation and conservation efforts are among the processes mapped.

All the maps are accompanied by other means of representation. In all cases, these include brief texts communicating useful background information that is difficult to portray in cartographic form (e.g. definitions, meanings, attitudes or preferences), but which makes it easier to understand the patterns and relationships shown on the maps. In a number of instances, drawings have been included for the same reason. Because the data portrayed on the maps has mainly been drawn from EVAW, and seeing that more detailed and elaborate background information on the themes mapped is generally available in EVAW, cross-references to related entries in EVAW have been included in the *References* Section. References to other sources of information that have been used in the compilation of the maps have also been briefly listed in this section and, in a complete form, in the *Bibliography*.

In combination, the texts, drawings and cross-references ensure that the maps are more than examples of 'vernacular housespotting', i.e. the gathering of data on locations and distribution patterns for the sake of recording only (Oliver 1969). As noted before, although documentation is an important aim of AVAW, the mapping of vernacular traditions for AVAW has been regarded as a tool rather than an end in itself. For, to map traditions just for the sake of recording would offer information but no hypotheses; data but no meaningful conclusions. It is hoped that the maps collated in AVAW do offer such hypotheses and conclusions, and that they will raise questions that may help to further our knowledge and understanding of the rich variety of vernacular architecture in the world.

Part 1
Contexts

Rice Fields, Java, Indonesia. *Photograph: Paul Oliver*

Contexts

No one knows exactly, or even approximately, how many buildings there are in the world, but estimates of well over a billion have been made, based largely on the numbers of people that are housed, and the stores, workshops and services that are necessary to sustain their lives and occupations. Of these, perhaps eighty per cent, or even a higher proportion, are vernacular: 'the architecture of the people' and not of the wealthy or the elite. Vernacular structures are not designed by architects or other professional designers, but are constructed by communities, by families, or are self-built by their owners. They are built and occupied in lands and territories which may be traditionally those of the owners' cultures and inheritance, or which are identified today with nations.

The contexts in which vernacular traditions exist and survive are various: some relate to political divisions, others may be conditioned by religion, or by language and the capacity to interact with other societies. Fundamental to the potential for survival and development are the economies, or work and occupations that people undertake. These in turn influence the population densities of regions, and are largely dependant on the soils, the vegetation, the prevailing climatic conditions and the water supplies that support life. Much of human settlements reflects the physical geography of the land on the one hand, and cultural influences on the other. These physical and cultural contexts are summarised in the following introductory maps, which bear upon the many aspects of vernacular architecture, in all continents and culture areas.

Nations

GREENLAND

RUSSIAN FED.

U.S.A

C A N A D A

ICELAND

U
KI

REPUBLI
OF IRELAN

**UNITED
STATES
OF AMERICA**

PORTUGA

MORO

MEXICO

THE
BAHAMAS

CUBA

JAMAICA HAITI

DOMINICAN
REP

Tropic of Cancer

WESTERN
SAHARA

MAURITANI

BELIZE
GUATEMALA HONDURAS
EL SALVADOR NICARAGUA
COSTA RICA PANAMA

DOMINICA
ST VINCENT ST LUCIA
GRENADA BARBADOS
TRINIDAD & TOBAGO

SENEGAL
THE GAMBIA
GUINEA-BISSAU GUINEA

SIERRA LEONE

LIBERIA

VENEZUELA GUYANA
SURINAME
COLOMBIA FRENCH GUIANA

Equator

ECUADOR

BRAZIL

SAMOA

PERU

BOLIVIA

PARAGUAY

Tropic of Capricorn

C
H
I
L
E

URUGUAY

ARGENTINA

A.	Andorra
AL.	Albania
AR.	Armenia
AUST.	Austria
AZER.	Azerbaijan
BAH.	Bahrain
BEL.	Belgium
B.H.	Boznia-Herzegovina
BUR.	Burkina
CR.	Croatia
CYP.	Cyprus
CZECH R.	Czech Republic
HUNG.	Hungary
LEB.	Lebanon
LUX.	Luxembourg
MA.	Macedonia
MOL.	Moldova
NETH.	Netherlands
QUA.	Quatar
R.F.	Russian Federation
SL.	Slovenia
SLOVA.	Slovakia
S.M.	Serbia and Montenegro
SWI.	Switzerland
U.A.E.	United Arab Emirates
U.S.A.	United States of America

Topography

ARCTIC OCEAN

SCANDINAVIA

L. Ladoga

SIBERIA

Ural Mtns.

West Siberian Plain

Yenisey

Lena

Ob

Stanovoy Ra.

North Euopean Plain

Volga

A S I A

L. Baikal

Kamchatka

Carpathians

Caspaian Sea

Aral Sea

Amur

Alps

Danube

Elbrus

Caucasus

L. Balkhash

Altai

Gobi Desert

Apennines

Tigris

Elburz Mts.

Tian Shan

Pamirs

Kunlun Shan

Qilian Shan

KOREA

Euphrates

Hindu Kush

K2

Plateau of Tibet

Yangtze

Libyan Desert

ARABIA

Sulaiman Mts.

Himalaya

Mt. Everest

CHINA

PACIFIC

ara

Nile

Thar Desert

Ganges

INDO-CHINA

INDIA

RICA

Ethiopian Highlands

Mekong

OCEAN

L. Chad

L. Turkana

Congo

Congo Basin

L. Victoria

Kilimanjaro

INDIAN

BORNEO

L. Tanganyika

NEW GUINEA

L. Malawi

Zambezi

MADAGASCAR

OCEAN

Kalahari Desert

AUSTRALIA

Great Victoria Desert

Darling

Great Divide

Murray

OCEAN

Water

Reference to settlement virtually implies access to fresh water. Indeed, it can be argued that it is the prime factor in determining where people live, for human beings cannot survive more than a few days without drinking water. This the sea does not provide, but freshwater lakes, some of great size, have been the focus of numerous settlements. These have included fishing economies, often with whole villages built on piers in the water, and some with 'floating villages' on rafts or artificially made islands. However, it is the rivers that have been most important in the location of communities. Flowing from higher altitudes, often as tributaries to larger rivers, the source springs, the narrow brooks and the flowing streams gain more water as their flow is determined by gravity and defined by features in the topography.

Essential as water is to human life, it is also of fundamental importance to animal life, whether wild or domesticated. The routes of pastoral nomads with flocks of goats or herds of cattle, are largely conditioned by the location of water supply, whether this is from brooks and streams, rivers, lakes or man-made wells. In many such instances there can be fish, with consequent choice of settlements close to these as sources of food as well as of water. To increase the opportunities for fishing and to claim the fishing grounds, numerous cultures build dwellings on piles and stilts, raising the floors above tidal and flood levels.

Some regions' rivers attract dangerous animals, such as water snakes, alligators and crocodiles, so many rivers have to be treated with great caution. Others are subject to infestation by mosquitoes and insects, with the consequence that settlements in many areas are not necessarily located directly by the rivers, but are within daily reach of them. The major rivers eventually spill into the seas and the oceans and it is notable that villages and towns have sprung up at the river mouths, or points of entry, which have become important focuses of trade, and may also have a regular flow of fresh water sufficient to meet the needs of urban populations.

In many instances the waters accumulated with the flow of the rivers from the high ground through the valleys of plains, often augmented by the additional waters of tributaries or waterfalls from precipitous heights, are discharged at the river mouths in immense quantities. The volume of water released into the sea or the ocean in every second of time is measured in cubic meters. Although the figures have to be simplified and are subject to seasonal variation and sometimes flooding or total inundation, the waters of the Nile are discharged at a rate of a thousand cubic meters per second. Yet those of the Amazon reach an astronomic hundred thousand cubic meters per second, while the confluence of the Ganges and the Brahmaputra discharges at a still greater rate into the Bay of Bengal. This, moreover, is a region which is

subject to exceptionally heavy rain, the average annual rainfall being over a hundred inches, occasioning the severe flooding to which it is subjected every year. In much of the world the rainfall is seasonal, which means that there may be long dry periods.

Run-off, or the quantities of water drained off the land and feeding the rivers, can be a better indicator of the water that is available to the inhabitants of the territories through which the rivers flow. The map reveals the massive discharge of some rivers and the small amount available in others, which can indicate severe flood risk. Thus the Mississippi flow is 19,000 cubic meters per second; that for the Ganges is above 25,000, but the flow of the Amazon is 120,000. All this has bearing on the location of settlements, and the density of the population that they can support.

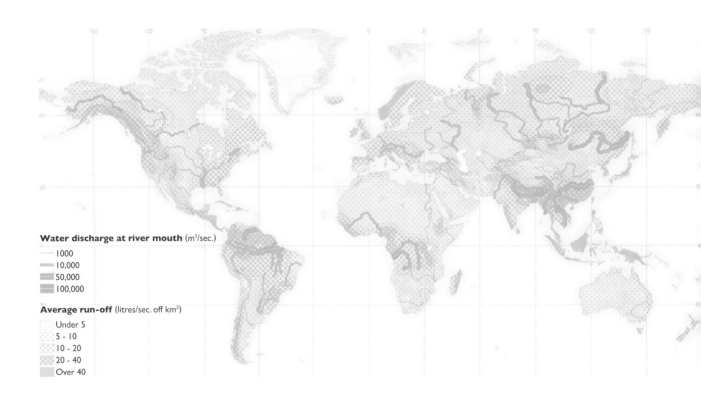

Water discharge at river mouth (m³/sec.)

- 1000
- 10,000
- 50,000
- 100,000

Average run-off (litres/sec. off km²)

- Under 5
- 5 - 10
- 10 - 20
- 20 - 40
- Over 40

Climate

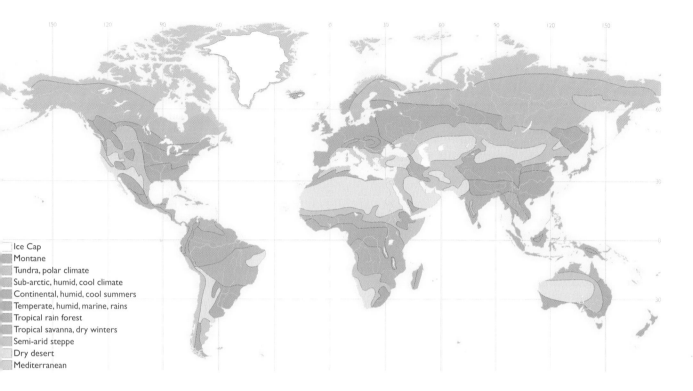

Ice Cap
Montane
Tundra, polar climate
Sub-arctic, humid, cool climate
Continental, humid, cool summers
Temperate, humid, marine, rains
Tropical rain forest
Tropical savanna, dry winters
Semi-arid steppe
Dry desert
Mediterranean

Of environmental factors, the climate plays an important part in building. Although the desire for the defence of the family or of society, and the preservation of individual or collective privacy, are reflected in the need for buildings in most cultures, a major factor in their design is their response to prevailing climatic conditions. For cultures in different parts of the world the nature of this emphasis varies: for some it may be protection from excessive heat or undue exposure to solar radiation that influences design; for others it may be the weight and penetration of precipitation, whether this be rain, hail or snow. Some regions in the world are subject to hurricanes and wind storms, while further regions may have periods of bitter cold. These climatic conditions may constitute seasonal distinctions which are experienced with comparative regularity, but others can be diurnal and not so readily anticipated.

Whether the climate is steady and changing regularly over time, or unpredictable and sudden in its occurrence and effects, the impact of the climatic variations has to be accommodated in the buildings of most cultures. Sometimes a product of extreme climate, most notably snow among the Inuit, may be employed as a building or other resource. But in the majority of instances the building offers shelter from the discomforts of certain climates, and in many cases from excessive exposure to the heat of the sun or to monsoon rains. Simple devices

have been developed in desertic areas for the internal cooling of buildings by the use of loggias or courtyard shade, but others may be more ingenious, such as the gathering of cool breezes at roof-top level with wind scoops, and channelling them to cool and humidify the interiors of houses.

Privacy may be retained even with large windows, these being screened to admit light but designed to reduce solar gain and penetration. In other regions, such as those of the humid tropical belt, cooling may be effected by roof forms which may be designed to provide air circulation and ventilation. Alternatively, these may be achieved by raising the buildings on piles, although pile structures are also employed as a means of living above rising damp - or mosquitoes.

In addition to seasonal changes and regular climatic extremes, many architectural traditions are subject to the destructive forces of natural hazards. Prone to damage or demolition from swollen rivers or oceanic flooding, or from tropical storms, gales and high winds, countless vernacular buildings have been destroyed over the last century. But many have been saved or reconstructed, sometimes by the reuse of the materials or the acquisition of others. Some vernacular traditions, such as those on a number of island sites in Oceania, survive violent climatic conditions and storms

by virtue of their elasticity or open-sided walls, while others in regions with heavy timber or stone may have been constructed so that they resist or accommodate such impacts.

Apparently increasing in their intensity in the early twenty-first century, the severity of climatic extremes may be induced by human intervention. Atmospheric changes, shifting seasons, violent winds, rising high temperatures and other alterations in the global climates may well be the result of pollution occasioned by the extensive consumption of fossil fuels. The climatic regions that are identified here are those that have been relatively consistent over time, and with which the cultures in the respective regions have learned to cope in their building design and construction. Climate has a profound bearing on all living flora and fauna, and rising temperatures are causing a degree of melting of arctic and antarctic ice, which may well have devastating effects as water levels rise. The consideration of their implications on architecture if trends towards global warming are likely to continue is essential.

Vegetation

Naturally growing vegetation in various forms is widely used in building. Among these, the most accessible are the grasses. Within the broad classification of the grasses, the monocotyledon botanical family, which includes the bamboos and palms, provides widely distributed resources. Because of its strength and flexibility, bamboo is a commonly employed vernacular building material, the species of which are now believed to comprise close to a thousand varieties. Although conventional timber joints cannot be made in bamboo, it is extensively used for light structures, various methods of jointing having been developed.

Split, or otherwise adapted, palms are used for many building purposes, being flexible and tensile. With a variety in excess of 2500 species, palms vary considerably in their strength and reliability in differing climates and conditions. Palm leaves are widely used for thatching and can also be woven to form panels for roof cladding, or as components in walls and fences. Coconut palms in particular, have strong, fibrous stems and these are variously employed for lashings, weaving or the making of cordage. Hemp palms can also be made into, ropes, cords or twine.

Conventional grasslands cover large areas of all continents, being the fundamental ground cover vegetation of the Argentine pampas, the North American prairies, the African savannas and the Asiatic steppe, as well as of substantial proportions of the temperate forest regions of north-western Europe and south-eastern China. These grasslands are important in such regions in providing pasture for animals, and ground cover for lands which lie fallow between periods of cultivation. Certain grasses, such as wheat, rye and barley, are cultivated on a large scale for the production of flour, but their stems are also extensively used for the thatching of roofs, generally in the dried state of straw.

Vegetation at the largest scale is, of course, in the form of trees, from which are derived the timbers which constitute much of the construction of buildings in all continents. The gymnosperms, or 'evergreens', are the coniferous timbers which are classified as softwoods, and are principally found in the northern hemisphere in a forest belt across North America and Eurasia, south of the frozen soils of the tundra. Many conifers grow to a great height and their regular diameters make them easily workable, but they are less durable than the deciduous timbers, which include oak, elm, beech, birch and ash. These broadleaf varieties, or angiosperms, are found in the temperate forests. Closer to the equator are the tropical rain forests of South America, West and Central Africa, and Southeast Asia. Here grow the hardwoods such as mahogany and teak.

Timbers are subject to rot, as they can readily absorb water, and they can also be host to insects, notably the termites. They are vulnerable to fungi, and most dangerously, to fire. Consequently, timber has to be selected with skill and used with clear knowledge of its properties. But these, most societies using wood have long acquired. Logs of wood, as found de-barked or trimmed, have been extensively employed in horizontal log constructions in well-forested parts of the world, while timber frames have provided the basic structural elements of many buildings, being constructed of softwoods or hardwoods as these have been available.

While wood is essential for the sustainability of the vernacular, the reckless felling and selling of timbers on the international markets, particularly of the tropical hardwood varieties, has led to serious problems of deforestation.

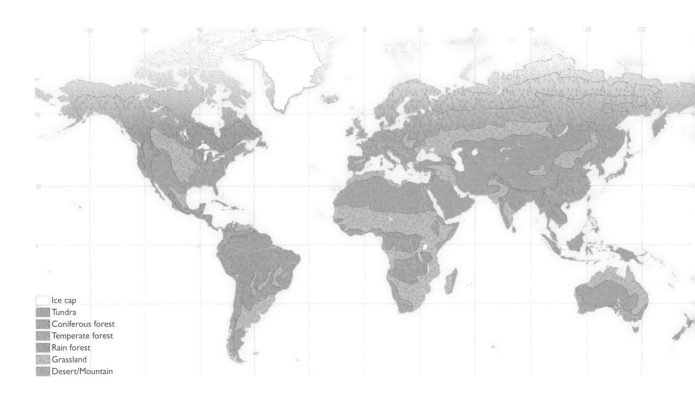

Ice cap
Tundra
Coniferous forest
Temperate forest
Rain forest
Grassland
Desert/Mountain

Soils

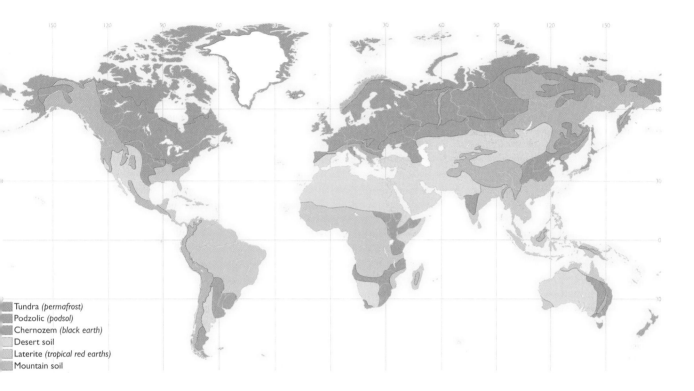

Tundra *(permafrost)*
Podzolic *(podsol)*
Chernozem *(black earth)*
Desert soil
Laterite *(tropical red earths)*
Mountain soil

Whatever their differences may be, all vernacular architecture traditions are located within environmental contexts. For some nomadic peoples these may vary. But for the majority, the sedentary cultures, their environments are largely consistent, at least as far as certain material resources are concerned.

It has been estimated that over half of the world's buildings are built of earth or clay, either in its raw state or transformed by water, admixtures and compression. Soils are essentially decomposed rocks, which have been eroded and weathered over immeasurable time, their constituents of gravel, sand, silt and clay being of different particle size, and their concentration in differing proportions largely accounting for the diverse range of soil types. The degree of water in the soil affects its plasticity, some very dry soils being unsuitable for building, while the water content is important when the material is to be compacted.

Soils are often forced, or daubed, into the interstices of wattle walls while others may be applied as plaster. Some clays may be moulded into the forms desired or they may be pounded in layers, being packed in moveable box frames and tamped using the 'rammed earth' technique. Others may be formed as blocks, often with straw or another stabilising material, and dried by exposing to the sun, to make 'sun-dried bricks', while suitable clays may be moulded in blocks and then fired as bricks in kilns.

The composition of the specific soil will have a bearing on its performance and utilisation. Soil types differ widely in various parts of the world, with the laterites and tropical red soils being especially suitable for building, as they harden when exposed to the sun. They are to be found in West Africa and in south India where they are extensively used for building, and also in central Africa. Laterites are also prominent in Amazonia and Brazil, and Columbia and the north coast of South America, in Southeast Asia and in southern China. However, they are not always used for the main building structure in areas where timbers are accessible, being frequently employed as a daub.

Red soils are often found in proximity to the darker, 'black earth' chernozem soils which are prevalent in southern Africa, Argentina and the western half of south India, where they too are extensively used. Desertic soils which are predominant in Australia, in the Sahara and North Africa, in the Arabian peninsula and further east to much of Central Asia and the north-western part of China, as well as the North American south-west, have a high sand content, although often of a fine grain. Mixed with water they can be moulded into adobe blocks, which may be further stabilized with the addition of lime or bitumen.

Podzolic soils, or podsols, constitute another widely distributed class of soils, and are found almost exclusively in the northern half of the globe, being dominant in much of Europe and Siberia, and the northern half of North America. They are generally fertile and may support large forests, but the clay is malleable and used for such layered construction as the French pise-de-terre and the 'cob' construction of Devon in England. Mountain soils, being close to the rock in its natural state and not decomposed, are seldom used for building, while the soils of the tundra are effectively rendered useless for building purposes because of the presence of permafrost. Yet, to most statements concerning earth as a building material there are exceptions, for soils are of many different types. One of these is loam, a combination of clay and sand, often with decaying vegetable matter, which lends itself to hollowing in order to make cave dwellings.

Economy

All families, social groups, cultures and nations have to survive by the organisation of their labour, and their utilisation, production and consumption of resources. For some who have a subsistence economy only, this means the support solely of the group. For others, producing in quantities above their needs, their labours may lead to a surplus, with which they may trade. For still more, it may result in a market economy for which the ultimate objective may be one of financial gain. Vernacular architecture traditions exist in all such categories, although probably least in the latter, essentially urban, contexts.

Subsistence economies at their most basic are those of 'hunter-gatherers', who rely upon the obtaining of natural resources for consumption, such as leaves, berries, fruits, fish animals or birds; gathering some, hunting for others. Their dwellings may be similarly based on what is available, and subject to a short period of use as movement to other resources becomes necessary. Such cultures are now few, but they are present in every continent.

Nomadic cultures that comprise pastoralists, customarily follow specific routes while moving their herds of cattle, camels, goats or sheep to new pastures. Many such nomadic groups transport their shelter with them, in the form of tents of skin or woven cloth stretched over light frames, which can be assembled on arrival and rapidly dismantled

when departing, some animals generally transporting the components between sites. Transhumant cultures may move their animals to specific fresh pastures, while former pastures recover. In such cases a permanent base and a semi-permanent one for the transhumant herders may be constructed.

By far the majority of non-urban cultures are sedentary, or not nomadic, with economies deriving from the land. Subsistence economies based on small-scale crop cultivation may enable many cultures to survive, but not thrive. Agriculture, notably with the growing and harvesting of wheat, rice, other cereal crops, vegetables and fruit, constitutes the widest economic distribution, and extensive farms may produce surpluses that can be marketed. But in many desertic, montane, arid and water-deficient regions such farming is seldom possible. The raising of cattle, sheep, swine and herds or flocks of other domesticated animals as well as birds such as fowl and geese is widespread, the kinds of livestock farmed being largely conditioned by the nature of the market.

Farmhouses and farm buildings, including barns and granaries, stables and byres, dovecotes and outbuildings, while differing widely in form and capacity, constitute a large proportion of the world's vernacular buildings. In peasant or market economies, such buildings are commonly used to store and process surplus agricultural products, including grains,

rice, fruit, vegetables and animal feed. Varying greatly in size, form, location and structural system, they are also frequently used to house farm machinery and livestock.

In recent decades, the integration of nomadic and agricultural societies into national and international market economies has been rapid. This integration is exemplified by, for example, the widespread diffusion of monetary systems of exchange, changes in the size and ownership of landholdings, and transformations in agricultural production. Industrial and service economies, based on the mass production and provision of goods, are now dominant throughout various parts of the world. Vernacular architecture survives in many of these areas, but its continuity is often under threat.

With the growth of mono-crop cultivation on a large scale, for example of cotton or sugar cane, and the ever-increasing expansion of agribusiness, many cultures, in large parts of the world, have suffered the loss of their traditional economies. Their people have either become employees of international business concerns or they have been forced to migrate to the cities in search of jobs, in order that their former rural families can survive. These developments have a large impact on the use and meaning of vernacular traditions and raise many questions regarding their development and sustainability.

- Agriculture
- Hunting, Gathering, Fishing
- Pastoralism
- Ranching
- Forestry
- Industry

Population

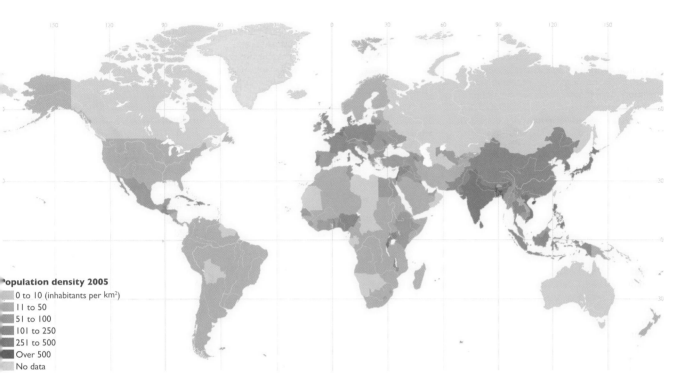

Population density 2005
- 0 to 10 (inhabitants per km²)
- 11 to 50
- 51 to 100
- 101 to 250
- 251 to 500
- Over 500
- No data

In abbreviated usage, vernacular architecture constitutes the buildings of, and by, the people. It follows therefore, that where there is a vernacular tradition there are the people that maintain it, and where there are people one may find vernacular buildings. Although families may live independently of others in dispersed settlements, especially when their economy is based on farming, there is a general tendency for members of one or even several clans to live together in clusters, or hamlets. Mutual support, greater protection, sharing of skills and reduction of time spent in travelling and marketing encouraged the forming of villages, with populations numbered in hundreds. As market centres became established and businesses began to flourish, towns developed with populations measured in thousands, and increasingly, in tens of thousands. Many of these became nodal towns with rural villages and districts converging on them.

Although the patterns differed with various cultures, the fundamental relationship of the rural areas to the towns became consistent, some towns growing in size and importance as they became cities. True, there have been cities since the earliest Egyptian Dynasty, the Mesopotamian cities of Sumer and the Indus Valley civilisation of Harappa and Mohenjo-Daro – all existing in the fifth millennium before the present. Notable for their buildings of authority and worship their dwellings were

otherwise relatively modest, the people protected by city walls. Cultures in most regions of the world, and in all periods, have had seats of power, whether aristocratic, military, religious or in trade, frequently becoming the capital cities of nations.

Such dispersal of the rural areas and concentration in the towns and cities had an impact upon population distribution and densities. Many cities developed ports at river mouths, where they acted as national and international trade centres, while others grew in prominent situations on the rivers inland. The exploration and discovery of cultures in other parts of the world was encouraged, particularly by European countries, eventually leading to the colonisation of other continents. Incentives for migrants to engage in large-scale agriculture, ranching, mining and manufacturing were considerable, as were the exploitation of the resources of the newly established colonies, and of their indigenous populations.

Since the Industrial Revolution of the eighteenth and nineteenth centuries, the world has become increasingly, if unevenly, urbanised. Cities have frequently become the seats of industry, with mass housing 'for the workers' contrasting with the vernacular of rural cultures. All this has had an impact on vernacular traditions which nevertheless, in view of these influences and interventions, have survived

to a remarkable degree. Often they persisted in the regions of lower density, the climates and conditions being inimical to the colonists, but the damaging effect upon their traditional economies has forced many rural people to move to the cities.

By the end of the first decade of the twenty-first century we are witnessing the world's urban populace equalling or exceeding that of the non-urban, or rural population. Millions of migrants have been drawn to the cities, but with fewer job opportunities than anticipated, and consequent desperate poverty, most are found living in the squatter settlements that extend beyond the urban periphery. Self-built dwellings constructed largely of waste materials are regarded by some as being representative of new, urban vernacular traditions, whether these are the barriadas of Peru, the gecekondus of Istanbul and Ankara, or the favelas of Rio de Janeiro.

Language

Fundamental to the distinctions and the similarities, to the borrowings, the influences and the diffusion of ideas that have occurred, are the means of communication between humans, of which spoken language is the most significant. Reference to linguistic clusters and their global distribution, not only helps in the definition of cultural groups but also accounts in part for the commonalities in their building traditions. Communication between cultures has taken many forms apart from language, even though it is largely dependant on it.

Exploration of the globe, detailed penetration of remote (to the explorers) regions and continents, and experiments on determining where in the world's vast oceans, these newly discovered lands might be, over the centuries have led to its mapping. Most marked has been the mapping of the sites of human settlements, but the nature of the latter has been determined by the conjunction of many of the features already noted. Much of the exploration has been driven by curiosity, much more by the exploitation of resources and still more by the drive to make contact with, and sometimes to conquer, the peoples of other lands.

Language, as a means of communication taking particular forms and structures, can be said to be a cultural product rather than being one that reflects race and ethnicity. Even as a cultural product it does not define the culture

that uses it, for the peoples throughout the world that speak English, Spanish or French, for instance, may have no ethnic links with the nations with which they were originally associated. And these were profoundly influenced, and their speech shaped, by former dominant peoples such as the Romans and the Saxons. Many languages were introduced by armies and immigrants to the regions where they are now spoken, among the most notable examples being the related languages of the populace of Finland and Hungary, which derive from a Uralic language spoken by a Siberian people. In excess of 6500 languages have been identified and documented throughout the world, with some regions, such as New Guinea, having literally hundreds in use in their restricted territories.

Around a dozen linguistic clusters have been classified that embrace the majority of the world's languages, but certain of these, most notably the Indo-European cluster, include a number of languages which reveal common elements that are several thousand years old. Spoken by over half the population of the world they seem, in customary usage, to be distinguished and separate, although the spread of Empire and the movement of peoples to the Americas, particularly in the nineteenth century, established the prevalence of the languages spoken by the colonists and eventually, by the colonised.

In spite of the complexities of language classification, even a simplified map as presented here, reveals connections that may be reflected in traditional architectures. So, for instance, the coherence of the Austronesian languages relates closely to the nature of certain architectural forms of insular Southeast Asia, but also indicates a connection with language use in the African off-mainland island of Madagascar, confirming a trans-Indian Oceanic link.

Within the languages as spoken there are often emphases or preferences from their inheritance. Gaelic for instance in the British Isles, which lead to differences in customary usage. There can also be marked differences in local speech, which may include the terminology and grammatical structures involved, and the accents that prevail. Together, these may constitute distinct dialects, or regional variants of the standard language use, which may be reflected in the training of craftsmen and in the work of builders. Although these may be too local to include in a world map, their prevalence and influence on regional vernacular architecture should be acknowledged.

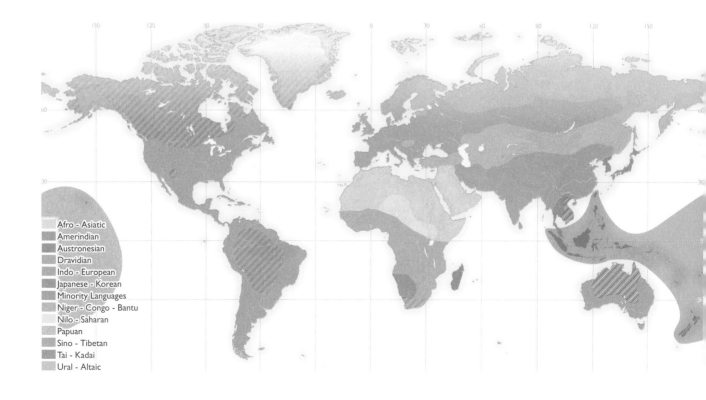

Afro - Asiatic
Amerindian
Austronesian
Dravidian
Indo - European
Japanese - Korean
Minority Languages
Niger - Congo - Bantu
Nilo - Saharan
Papuan
Sino - Tibetan
Tai - Kadai
Ural - Altaic

Religion

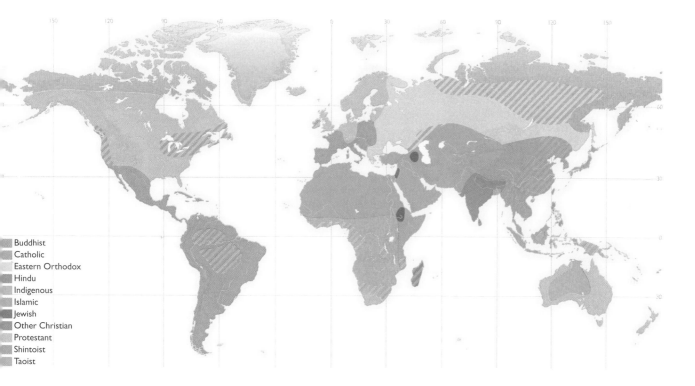

Buddhist
Catholic
Eastern Orthodox
Hindu
Indigenous
Islamic
Jewish
Other Christian
Protestant
Shintoist
Taoist

Among the oldest and most significant of motivations for cultural complexes to influence others has been the desire to spread religious beliefs. This has not been merely by contact, but by evangelism, by 'holy wars' and by the dominance of certain faiths. Probably the oldest surviving religious belief system is shamanism, with evidence of related rock paintings dating back to the Upper Paleolithic era. Shamanism may have originated in Siberia and spread from the Artic to the Americas, and also by way of Asia to Australasia. Shamanist rituals are trance induced and the shamans, or priests, seldom build a structure except as a place for keeping ritual objects, although in cold climates some shamans such as those of the Evenki of Siberia perform their rituals in tents. Seeking to make contact with the souls and spirits of the 'upper' and 'lower' worlds, the concept of the pole or 'tree of life', the axis mundi, is also associated with shamanist practice.

Animism, or the belief in spirits and a living soul in creatures and plants or, in some cases, in all phenomena, also relates back to the earliest beliefs of humankind. It is rigorously adhered to by many cultures, such as the Dogon of Mali. Among some cultures animism can evolve as polytheism, or the worship of multiple deities, such as is the case in the Hindu religion, predominantly in India but spread in the past, throughout southeast Asia. Reincarnation is a

significant Hindu tenet, with a good life spent in a low caste in the present, rewarded with birth into a higher caste in the next life. Sacred shrines erected to Brahma, Vishnu, Shiva and other deities attract large numbers of pilgrims.

Two and a half millennia ago, the monotheistic teachings of Gautama Buddha of Nepal, with his doctrine of the Four Noble Truths, and of ultimate beatitude or Nirvana, split from Hinduism, and permeated throughout Asia where Buddhist temples and stupas, or shrines, are numerous. In the Middle East the growth of the religions deriving from the teachings of Abraham and of later prophets, including Jesus Christ and Mohammed, led to the founding of Judaism, Christianity and Islam and their eventual diffusion world-wide. More confined to specific cultures are other religions, such as the Indian Sikhism and the Japanese Shinto, although few of these are mapped here.

The doctrines of the more widely diffused religions, and particularly those that are monotheistic, have led to the widespread use of temple structures for the worship of the deity, or deities. In Judaism this takes the form of the synagogue, which may vary in size in accordance with the prevalence of the Jewish religion in specific areas. Although the best-known mosques in the Middle East are magnificent in their design and dimensions, many ver-

nacular mosques are to be seen in the Islamic settlements of North Africa and the Maghreb. Among the most distinctive are the adobe and moulded clay churches of the savanna grasslands and the Sahel regions of West Africa, while the tiered mosques of Southeast Asia are also notable.

For the Christian religion, worship is customarily in parish churches and in the larger, generally urban, cathedrals of the bishops. Many Anglican churches were of Catholic origin being subsequently occupied by Protestants following the Reformation. Many Methodist, Baptist, Quaker and other persuasions worship in smaller chapels and meeting houses, some of which are justifiably regarded as vernacular. So too, are the impressive horizontal log construction Protestant and Reform churches of the Ukraine, Belarus and Eastern Europe, the Orthodox churches of Russia, the timber-framed churches of the Baltic and the Nordic stave churches.

Culture

Asia, East and Central

I.1   Arctic Asia and Siberia
I.2   Central Asia and Mongolia
I.3   China, North and Korea
I.4   China, South
I.5   India, Northeast, and Bangladesh
I.6   India, Northwest and Indus
I.7   India, South and Sri Lanka
I.8   Japan
I.9   Kashmir and West Himalayas
I.10 Nepal and East Himalayas
I.11 Thailand and Southeast Asia

Australasia and Oceania

II.1   Australia
II.2   Indonesia, East
II.3   Indonesia, West
II.4   Malaysia and Borneo
II.5   Melanesia and Micronesia
II.6   New Guinea
II.7   Philippines
II.8   Polynesia and New Zealand
II.9   Taiwan

Europe and Eurasia

III.1   Alpine
III.2   Baltic and Finland
III.3   British Isles
III.4   Central Europe
III.5   Gallic
III.6   Germanic
III.7   Lowlands
III.8   Nordic
III.9   Russia
III.10 Ukraine, Belarus
       and Eastern Europe

Mediterranean and Southwest

IV.1   Arabian Peninsula
IV.2   Asia Minor and Caucasus, South
IV.3   Balkans
IV.4   Eastern Mediterranean and Levant
IV.5   Iberian Peninsula
IV.6   Insular Mediterranean
IV.7   Italian Peninsula
IV.8   Mesopotamia and Plateau
IV.9   North Africa and Maghreb

I.1

I.1

I.1

I

I.2

I.2

I.3

I.8

I.9

I.10

I.4

I.6

I.5

II.9

I.11

I.7

II.7

II.4

II.2

II.6

II.5

II.3

II

II.1

II.8

III.2

III.8

III.9

III.6

III.4

III.10

IV.3

II.1

IV.7

IV.2

IV.6

IV.4

IV.8

IV.9

IV.1

VII.7

VII.6

VII.3

VII.2

VII.1

VII.10

VII.5

VII.11

VI

VII

Latin America

Amazonia and Brazil, Northeast

Andes and West Coast

Argentina and Gran Chaco

Brazil, South

Caribbean Islands

Colombia and North Coast

Mexico

Yucatán and Central America

North America

VI.1 Arctic, Canadian and Sub-Arctic

VI.2 Canadian Borderlands

VI.3 East and Northeast

VI.4 Midwest and Lakes

VI.5 Prairie Plains

VI.6 South

VI.7 Southwest

VI.8 West and Pacific

Sub-Saharan Africa

VII.1 East Africa

VII.2 Equatorial and Central

VII.3 Ethiopia and the Horn

VII.4 Guinea Coast

VII.5 Madagascar and Islands

VII.6 Nigerian Plateau

VII.7 Nile and Sudan

VII.8 Sahara and Sahel

VII.9 Savanna Grasslands

VII.10 South Central

VII.11 Southern Africa

Part 2
Cultural & Material Aspects

Harvard House, Stratford-upon-Avon, United Kingdom. *Photograph: Paul Oliver*

Cultural & Material Aspects

Throughout the world vernacular traditions have evolved in diverse environmental and cultural contexts, but the traditions take forms that have been further conditioned by regional and local factors. Among these are the raw materials and natural resources available in a region, which are seldom used without informed selection and the transformation of their nature by the application of appropriate building technologies. The kinds of construction may reflect the way of life followed; nomadic peoples frequently raise tents, which can be subsequently dismantled. However, most cultures are sedentary, constructing their permanent buildings by means developed over centuries, and sometimes diffused over continents.

Customarily, the building forms are Platonic, i.e. primary, but employed in combinations and in arrangements or plans that relate to the needs of the societies concerned. All cultures desire that their buildings provide shelter and security, and the majority will require efficient servicing, which may depend on the prevailing climate and on the nature of the economy by which life is supported. Sometimes these have led to the construction of functional outbuildings and mills. Domestic vernacular architecture may be enriched by decoration and a society's values expressed by the symbolic connotations of plans, structures or details. Pressures of unprecedented scale are being exerted on vernacular traditions by natural disasters, by exploitation of natural resources, and by the demands of urbanisation, raising major issues concerning the conservation and development of vernacular traditions.

Materials & Resources

Town house, Landis Valley, Pennsylvania. *Photograph: Marcel Vellinga*

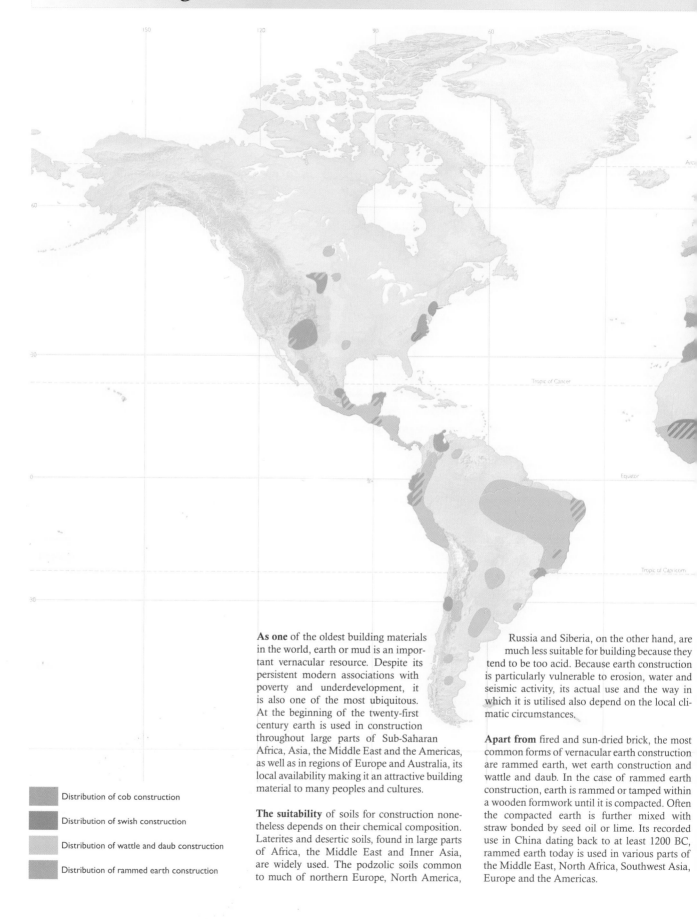

Distribution of cob construction

Distribution of swish construction

Distribution of wattle and daub construction

Distribution of rammed earth construction

As one of the oldest building materials in the world, earth or mud is an important vernacular resource. Despite its persistent modern associations with poverty and underdevelopment, it is also one of the most ubiquitous. At the beginning of the twenty-first century earth is used in construction throughout large parts of Sub-Saharan Africa, Asia, the Middle East and the Americas, as well as in regions of Europe and Australia, its local availability making it an attractive building material to many peoples and cultures.

The suitability of soils for construction nonetheless depends on their chemical composition. Laterites and desertic soils, found in large parts of Africa, the Middle East and Inner Asia, are widely used. The podzolic soils common to much of northern Europe, North America,

Russia and Siberia, on the other hand, are much less suitable for building because they tend to be too acid. Because earth construction is particularly vulnerable to erosion, water and seismic activity, its actual use and the way in which it is utilised also depend on the local climatic circumstances.

Apart from fired and sun-dried brick, the most common forms of vernacular earth construction are rammed earth, wet earth construction and wattle and daub. In the case of rammed earth construction, earth is rammed or tamped within a wooden formwork until it is compacted. Often the compacted earth is further mixed with straw bonded by seed oil or lime. Its recorded use in China dating back to at least 1200 BC, rammed earth today is used in various parts of the Middle East, North Africa, Southwest Asia, Europe and the Americas.

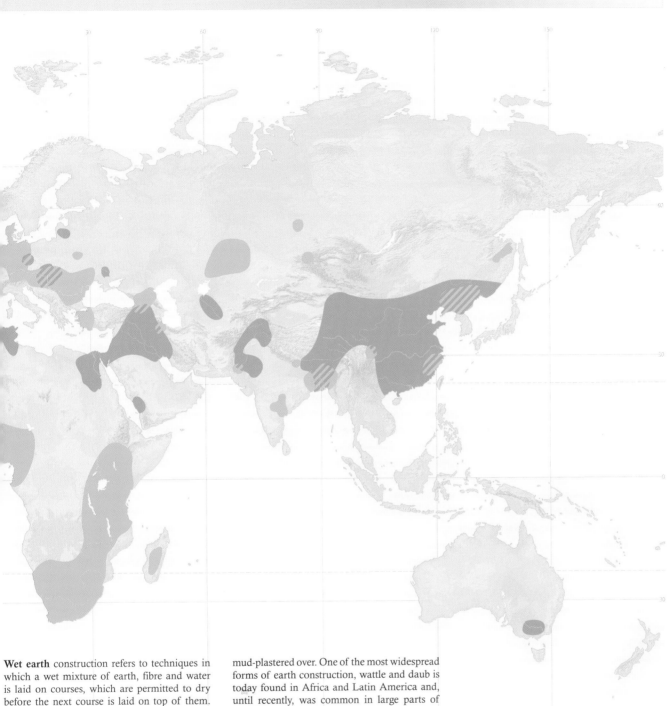

Wet earth construction refers to techniques in which a wet mixture of earth, fibre and water is laid on courses, which are permitted to dry before the next course is laid on top of them. Variations of this form of earth construction are mainly found in West Africa, where it is commonly referred to as swish, and in parts of Europe and the United States, where it is known as cob. The balance of aggregates in swish and cob varies with the composition of soils and may comprise small stones, gravel, sand and silt.

In the case of wattle and daub construction, earth is plastered onto a framework of interwoven wattles made of timber, bamboo or branches. Often used in timber frame buildings, the earth daub is forced into the interstices to make the wattle infill weather resistant; the whole is then mud-plastered over. One of the most widespread forms of earth construction, wattle and daub is today found in Africa and Latin America and, until recently, was common in large parts of central and north-western Europe.

During the last few decades of the twentieth century, the academic and professional interest in earth construction has grown, exemplified by the establishment of a number of research institutes, the regular organisation of exhibitions and international conferences, and the existence of an extensive body of literature. As a result, earth is increasingly considered as an appropriate and sustainable building resource, offering both economic and ecological advantages over manufactured materials, such as steel and concrete.

Problems nonetheless remain regarding its use and integration into modern building practice. Firstly, not all types of earth are suitable for building. Secondly, because of its physical characteristics, earth is highly vulnerable to erosion, water and certain natural hazards, especially earthquakes. Thirdly, because soils are needed for agriculture and pasture, the uncontrolled use of earth for construction may have an adverse affect on vital economic support systems. In order to assess the sustainability of earth construction, further and continued research is needed.

Sun-dried brick: diffusion

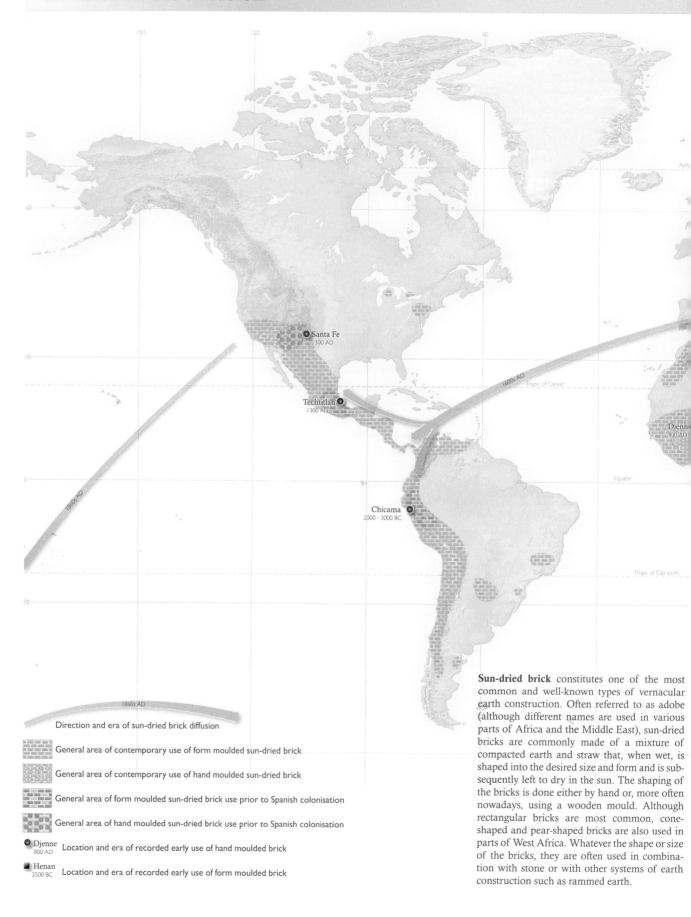

Santa Fe
300 AD

Techtitlan
1300 AD

1600s AD

Tropic of Cancer

Djenne
800 AD

Equator

Chicama
2000 - 3000 BC

1860s AD

Tropic of Capricorn

1860s AD

Direction and era of sun-dried brick diffusion

General area of contemporary use of form moulded sun-dried brick

General area of contemporary use of hand moulded sun-dried brick

General area of form moulded sun-dried brick use prior to Spanish colonisation

General area of hand moulded sun-dried brick use prior to Spanish colonisation

Djenne
800 AD   Location and era of recorded early use of hand moulded brick

Henan
2500 BC   Location and era of recorded early use of form moulded brick

Sun-dried brick constitutes one of the most common and well-known types of vernacular earth construction. Often referred to as adobe (although different names are used in various parts of Africa and the Middle East), sun-dried bricks are commonly made of a mixture of compacted earth and straw that, when wet, is shaped into the desired size and form and is subsequently left to dry in the sun. The shaping of the bricks is done either by hand or, more often nowadays, using a wooden mould. Although rectangular bricks are most common, cone-shaped and pear-shaped bricks are also used in parts of West Africa. Whatever the shape or size of the bricks, they are often used in combination with stone or with other systems of earth construction such as rammed earth.

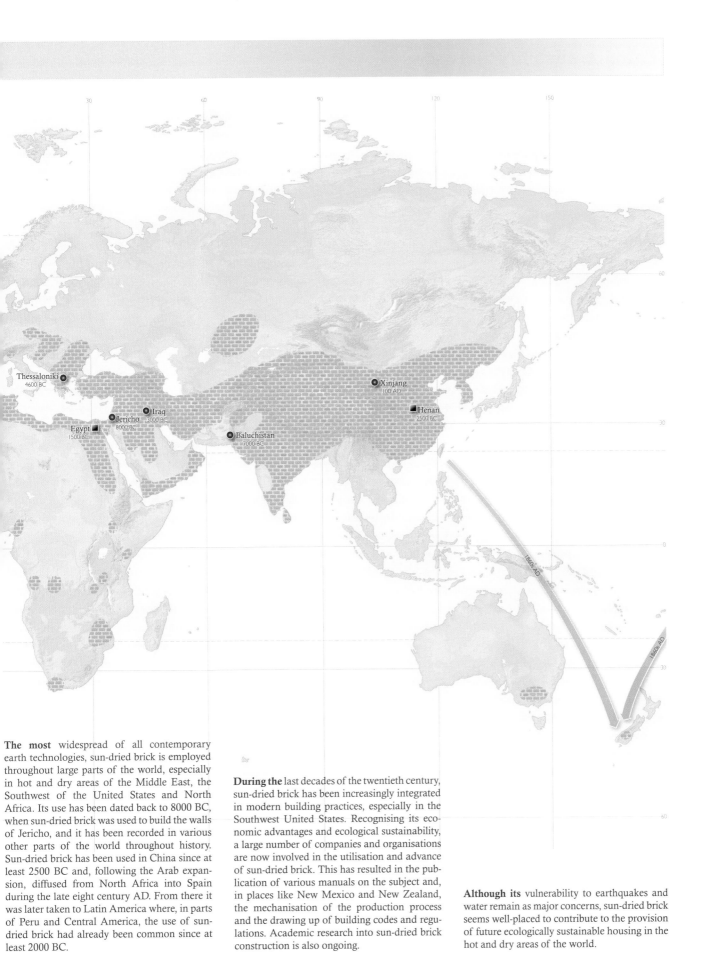

The most widespread of all contemporary earth technologies, sun-dried brick is employed throughout large parts of the world, especially in hot and dry areas of the Middle East, the Southwest of the United States and North Africa. Its use has been dated back to 8000 BC, when sun-dried brick was used to build the walls of Jericho, and it has been recorded in various other parts of the world throughout history. Sun-dried brick has been used in China since at least 2500 BC and, following the Arab expansion, diffused from North Africa into Spain during the late eight century AD. From there it was later taken to Latin America where, in parts of Peru and Central America, the use of sun-dried brick had already been common since at least 2000 BC.

During the last decades of the twentieth century, sun-dried brick has been increasingly integrated in modern building practices, especially in the Southwest United States. Recognising its economic advantages and ecological sustainability, a large number of companies and organisations are now involved in the utilisation and advance of sun-dried brick. This has resulted in the publication of various manuals on the subject and, in places like New Mexico and New Zealand, the mechanisation of the production process and the drawing up of building codes and regulations. Academic research into sun-dried brick construction is also ongoing.

Although its vulnerability to earthquakes and water remain as major concerns, sun-dried brick seems well-placed to contribute to the provision of future ecologically sustainable housing in the hot and dry areas of the world.

Palm used for thatching purposes

Palm used for walling purposes

Palm used for framing purposes

Distribution of palm species (coconut, cohune, date, doum, sago and nipa)

Palms or Palmaceae are employed for a variety of vernacular building purposes throughout large parts of Latin America, Africa, Southeast Asia and the Pacific. Palm timber may be used in the construction of roof frames, as is the case in most of northern and western Africa, where palm beams frequently act as supports for the flat earth roofs that are common in the area. The use of palm leaves for thatching purposes is widespread throughout all areas where palm is employed, while in some places (such as Oman and parts of the Caribbean) the fronds of the leaves may also be used to clad walls. Finally, palm fibres may be used to make ropes and cords for lashing.

Comprising over 2500 species, the natural distribution of palms (which are essentially tropical plants) is limited to an area between latitudes 40'N and 40'S. They can grow at altitudes of 300 meters but mostly flourish at sea level, often lining coasts and bays. Their variety in terms of strength, size and durability is large, but many palms are characterised by tall, unbranched and often straight stems topped by a fan-form crown of branches and leaves. Though others may sometimes be used as well, coconut, palmyra, cohune, date, doum, sago and nipa palms are most commonly employed in vernacular architecture, with certain species dominating in particular localities (e.g. the date palm in the Middle East or the sago palm in New Guinea).

Though it is the most important plant to be used in vernacular architecture, the employment of palm is not a given fact, nor will its application necessarily be the same in all parts of the world where it is found. Its actual use is influenced by the specific qualities of the particular species found in a locality, as well as by the availability of other suitable building resources. Besides, in some cultures the use of palms for construction purposes is restricted because the plants are highly valued for the fruits, shade and other products that they can provide.

Although a widespread vernacular building resource, palms are not without their disadvantages. The surfaces of the stems are often so hard that nails cannot be driven into them, whilst they are also unsuitable for conventional joints. At the same time they can often not be carved, nor can they be trimmed or planed into planks. Palm thatch is also vulnerable to decay and insect attack, as well as to fire. As a result, it is often being replaced by more modern materials such as concrete and corrugated iron.

Timber: technologies

Combining tensile and compression strength with elasticity, timber provides one of the most important vernacular building materials in the world. Throughout history, its durability and ease of workability have made it a resource that has been widely used for a variety of architectural purposes, including the construction and cladding of frames, walls and roofs. Today, in spite of rapid global deforestation and increased competition from manufactured resources, timber is still widely employed in large parts of the world as a structural and cladding material, as well as for the making of furniture, doors and shutters, fences and stairs.

A large variety of timbers is used in vernacular architecture. Coniferous trees or gymnosperms are mainly found in cold and temperate climates and are easily workable because of their height and diameters. Deciduous timbers such as oak, beech, birch and elm are found in temperate and subtropical climates, as well as in the tropical parts of Latin America, Africa and Southeast Asia. Apart from the trunks of trees, branches, twigs, roots, bark and leaves of trees may be used for vernacular building purposes. Trees may also be employed to provide shade or to direct or deflect breezes and winds.

A well-known vernacular timber technology is horizontal log construction. Generally found throughout the heavily forested areas of Europe, Asia and North America, as well as in isolated parts of Latin America and Australia, log con-struction is characterised by the use of timbers that are laid horizontally, using the mass and dead weight of the wood rather than its tensile properties. A variety of joints has been developed to secure and interlock the logs, such as the double saddle notch, the double V notch and the double square notch. Providing solid and well-insulated walls, log construction was once widely employed to construct houses, fortresses, barns and mills, but its use has steadily decreased since the nineteenth century. Nonetheless, substantial log structures, some up to five or six storeys in height, can still be found in use throughout Russia, eastern and central Europe, and North America.

Apart from log construction, timber is also widely employed in the construction of structural frames. Exploiting the tensile strength of timber rather than its mass, timber framed buildings are constructed on the post and beam principle, in which the beam transfers vertical loads to its supporting posts. Today used virtually throughout the world, apart from those areas where timber is scarce or log construction prevails, timber frames are generally lighter and easier to construct than log buildings, and require less timber for their production. Various kinds of timber framing exist, some of which are distinctive to particular cultures or countries.

Apart from structural uses, timber is frequently used for cladding purposes. Long and thin slats of wood, cleft or sawn from logs and called shingles or shakes, are used to clad roofs or walls in Europe, the Americas, Africa and Asia, providing a weatherproof surface that can shed rain or snow. Bark, the external sheath of trees, is extensively used to construct or insulate walls and roofs in the arctic regions, as well as in parts of Africa, East and Southeast Asia, and Australia. Timber planks or boards, again cleft or sawn from logs, are used to clad walls throughout large parts of Southeast Asia, Europe and North America.

At the beginning of the twenty-first century, the environmental and social implications of rapid deforestation constitute a major challenge for the global community. Well-informed management of forests, including careful selection, cropping and felling, is needed to ensure the continuous sustainable exploitation of timber as a building resource. Taking into account the long and widespread application of timber in vernacular architecture, it would seem that much can still be learned from traditional timber construction practices. More research is needed, however, to assess the role that vernacular knowledge, skills and practices may play in this respect.

Timber framing and log construction

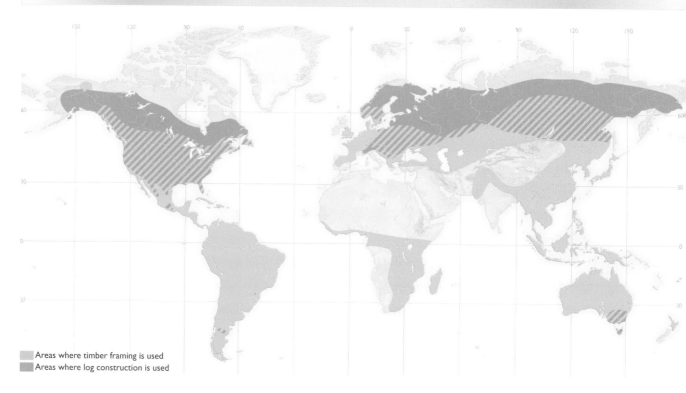

Areas where timber framing is used
Areas where log construction is used

Timber cladding

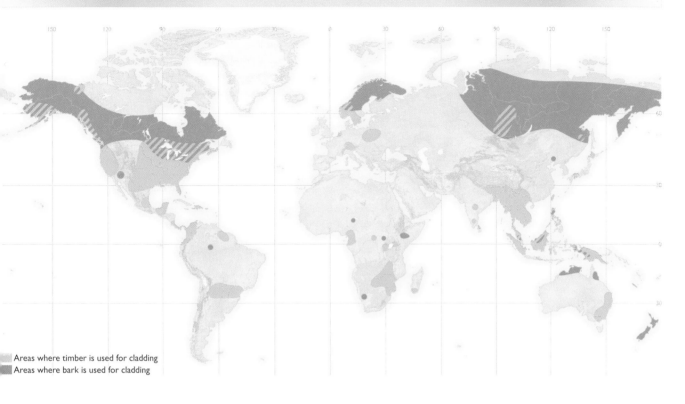

Areas where timber is used for cladding
Areas where bark is used for cladding

Examples of log construction joints

Double saddle notch log construction

Double v notch log construction

Double square notch log construction

Bamboo: availability and use

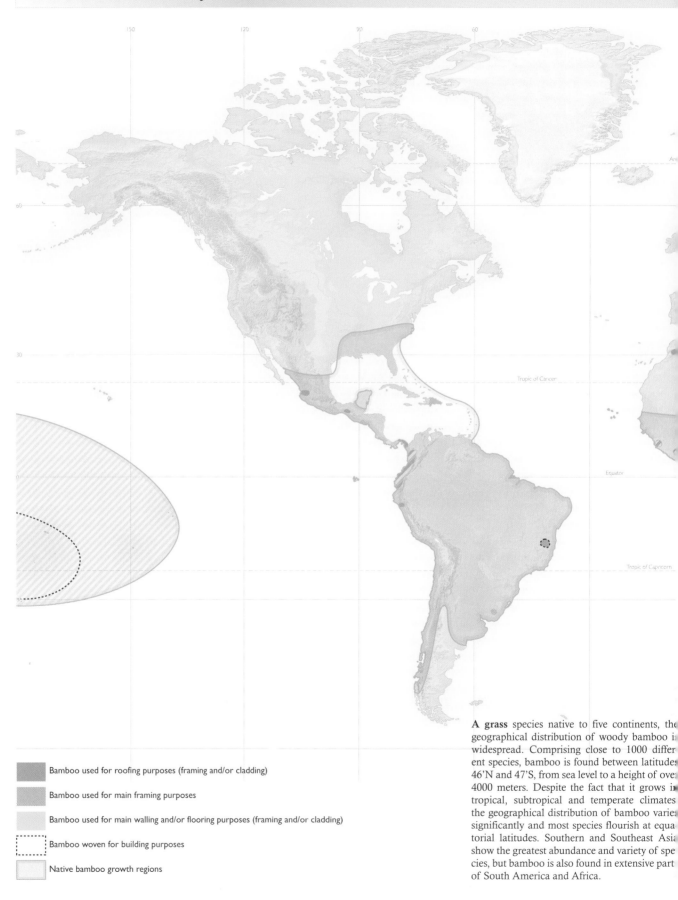

Bamboo used for roofing purposes (framing and/or cladding)

Bamboo used for main framing purposes

Bamboo used for main walling and/or flooring purposes (framing and/or cladding)

Bamboo woven for building purposes

Native bamboo growth regions

A grass species native to five continents, the geographical distribution of woody bamboo is widespread. Comprising close to 1000 different species, bamboo is found between latitudes 46'N and 47'S, from sea level to a height of over 4000 meters. Despite the fact that it grows in tropical, subtropical and temperate climates, the geographical distribution of bamboo varies significantly and most species flourish at equatorial latitudes. Southern and Southeast Asia show the greatest abundance and variety of species, but bamboo is also found in extensive parts of South America and Africa.

Bamboo is characterised by the fact that its natural length is divided into several hollow segments, which are separated by nodes that reinforce the resistance of the cane against splitting and buckling, and give the bamboo a high strength-to-weight ratio. Since it is fast growing and easily harvested, possesses a great tensile strength and can be worked with simple tools, woody bamboo has been used for vernacular building purposes by many peoples and cultures, for at least two millennia. Bamboo posts and beams, roofs, walls and floors are found in various regions of the world, including Polynesia, Southeast Asia, Africa and Latin America, sometimes in combination with other materials such as timber, grass or mud.

Because of its favourable material properties and the fact that it grows in areas that have some of the highest population growth rates in the world, bamboo seems set to play an important part in the future provision of ecologically sustainable and culturally appropriate housing. The economic and ecological benefits of bamboo in an age of unprecedented population growth, climate change, pollution and scarcity of resources are actively propagated in a large body of academic and semi-popular literature, as well as through the web-sites and activities of several bamboo societies.

Nevertheless, the intensity in which bamboo is currently used for building purposes, the ways in which it is applied and the techniques that are employed to do so vary considerably. There are discrepancies between its availability and actual use in large parts of the world, and there is a large geographic diversity in its application, both of which seem related to the particularities of different bamboo species and the availability of alternative resources in certain areas. In some parts of the world it is used for vernacular building purposes, even though it does not actually grow there as a native species. More research into these issues is needed to assess the potential of bamboo as a sustainable building resource for the future.

Reed used for matting purposes

Reed used for thatching purposes

Reed used for matting and thatching purposes

Reed used for structural purposes

Botanically classified as a grass species, reed can be found in all continents of the world. Being dependent on water, its distribution is nonetheless restricted to marshy and well-watered places and is especially dense in tropical areas.

Though their height and diameter can vary significantly, reeds generally have great flexibility and elasticity. Consisting of cylindrical hollow stems strengthened by nodes, their compression strength is nonetheless limited and, when uprooted, reed stems are insufficiently rigid to support their own weight. The application of reed in vernacular construction has therefore been mainly restricted to cladding purposes, though incidental examples of the structural use of reeds can be found.

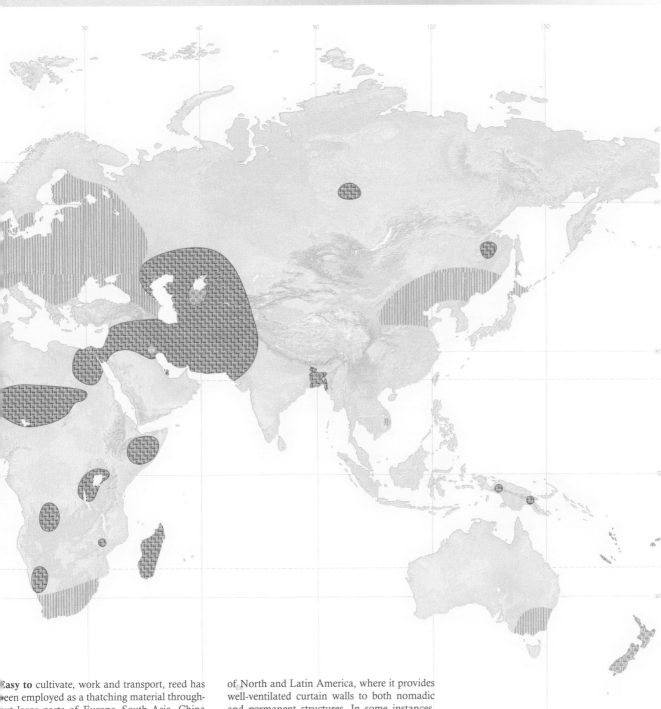

Easy to cultivate, work and transport, reed has been employed as a thatching material throughout large parts of Europe, South Asia, China and Japan, as well as in those parts of Australia, Latin America and Africa that have been settled by European immigrants. Because it is thick and insulates well, it may last up to eighty years without having to be replaced, making it one of the most durable thatching materials in the world.

Though a less common application than thatch, reed may also be used to weave mats. Reed matting is especially common in the Middle East, Southwest Asia and the Sahara region of Africa, as well as in scattered areas of North and Latin America, where it provides well-ventilated curtain walls to both nomadic and permanent structures. In some instances, the mats are daubed and plastered with mud, cement or lime.

Finally, when the stems are bundled and tied together, reed may be used for structural purposes. This is most famously done by the Ma'dan or Marsh Arabs in southern Iraq, whose houses and guest-houses are made of rows of arches of bundled reeds, clad with reed mats.

Although a proven vernacular building material, the use of reed has been in decline since the twentieth century. The popularity of reed thatch and matting has decreased in favour of inorganic materials such as corrugated iron, clay tiles, concrete and brick. The future of the unique buildings of the Ma'dan looks even more insecure, with recent accounts suggesting that little remains of the ancient tradition due to drainage projects and the political turbulence of recent years.

Nonetheless, reed continues to be cultivated in various parts of the world for thatching purposes and research is being carried out to increase its resistance to decay, fire and insects.

Used and manufactured: fired brick

Europe: Initially introduce to Europe by the Romans, fire brick has been mainly used fe monumental architecture durir the medieval period. Howeve having been recognised as durabl fire resistant and cheaper tha stone, it quickly became a part c the European vernacular during th late eighteenth century. Today it found throughout large parts of the continent, exhibiting a significant variety in terms of size, bonds and colour.

Americas: Not known by Native American groups, the vernacular use of fired brick was introduced to the Americas by European settlers from the seventeenth century onwards. Its contemporary use is widespread, if scattered, throughout both continents. Its initial employment reflecting the availability of suitable soils, the use of fired brick has declined in the United States during the twentieth century because of the increased popularity of concrete blocks.

Africa: Though suitabl soils, climates and supplie of fuel can be foun in various parts of th continent, the use c fired brick was unknow to sub-Saharan Afric before being introduce by European coloni powers. Initially it wa mainly used in public c religious buildings. Durin

Since the eighteenth century fired brick has beer an increasingly common vernacular buildin material throughout many parts of the world Though the technology dates back to prehistoric times, its use before the eighteenth century wa mainly restricted to public and religious build ings. Today fired brick is used for vernacula dwellings throughout Europe, China and Sout Asia, as well as in large parts of Africa and bot Americas, where it was introduced by Euro pean settlers. Mostly used for walling and, ir some cases, roofing, its use is mainly related t the availability of suitable soils and ample supplies of fuel.

Recorded use of continuous kiln

Recorded use of temporary clamp kiln

Contemporary use of fired brick as a vernacular building material

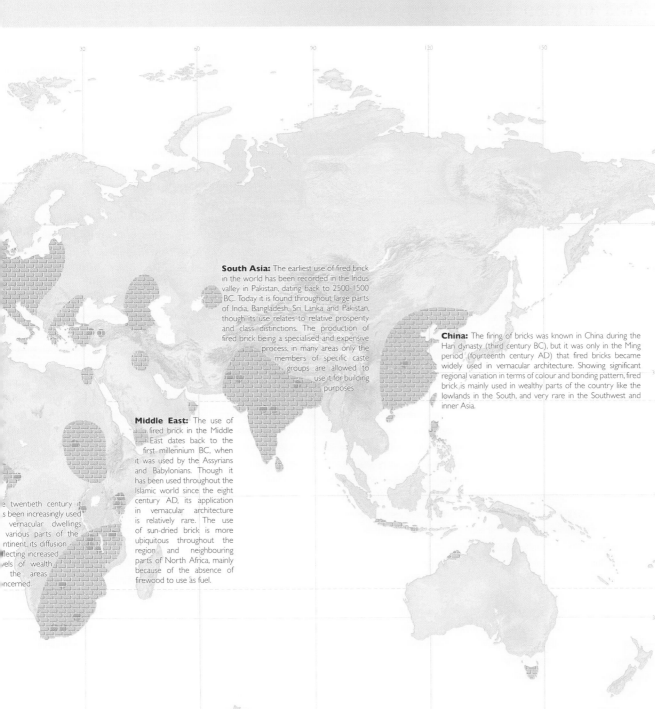

South Asia: The earliest use of fired brick in the world has been recorded in the Indus valley in Pakistan, dating back to 2500-1500 BC. Today it is found throughout large parts of India, Bangladesh, Sri Lanka and Pakistan, though its use relates to relative prosperity and class distinctions. The production of fired brick being a specialised and expensive process, in many areas only the members of specific caste groups are allowed to use it for building purposes.

China: The firing of bricks was known in China during the Han dynasty (third century BC), but it was only in the Ming period (fourteenth century AD) that fired bricks became widely used in vernacular architecture. Showing significant regional variation in terms of colour and bonding pattern, fired brick is mainly used in wealthy parts of the country like the lowlands in the South, and very rare in the Southwest and inner Asia.

Middle East: The use of fired brick in the Middle East dates back to the first millennium BC, when it was used by the Assyrians and Babylonians. Though it has been used throughout the Islamic world since the eight century AD, its application in vernacular architecture is relatively rare. The use of sun-dried brick is more ubiquitous throughout the region and neighbouring parts of North Africa, mainly because of the absence of firewood to use as fuel.

the twentieth century it s been increasingly used vernacular dwellings various parts of the ntinent, its diffusion lecting increased els of wealth the areas ncerned.

ired brick is an attractive building material to hose who can afford it because of its durability nd relative imperviousness, which make it par- cularly suited to areas with lots of wind and ain. Besides its resistance to fire makes it an ttractive alternative to timber. Because of the otential variety in brick size, colour and bond- ng system, it can also be used to create diverse ecorative patterns.

Despite these qualities, however, fired brick has ome significant disadvantages. Its production is elatively expensive, requiring specialised knowl- dge, labour and kilns, and consuming large uantities of fuel. As a result, in many areas in Africa, Asia and Latin America fired brick is only used by the wealthy, whilst unfired earth constitutes a more common building material. Besides, because of the physical changes that take place during the firing process, fired brick cannot be easily reconstituted.

Fired brick is commonly made of local clays, with the ultimate colour of the bricks depending on the chemical composition of the soil. In a ver- nacular context, the firing is carried out in kilns. In many parts of the world, temporary clamp kilns are used, which consist of truncated pyra- mids made of unfired bricks. Using firewood or coal as fuel, clamps are simple and cheap, but the quality of the bricks is uneven. More con- tinuous kilns, made of permanent walls and moveable chimneys, are used in China, India and parts of Africa. More cost effective, these kilns can produce higher temperatures and achieve greater fuel efficiency.

Though promoted by many governments and international aid organisations, the production of fired brick is in decline in many parts of the world. Its non-renewable nature, rising fuel costs and the increased popularity of materials such as concrete and cement raise serious ques- tions regarding the sustainability of fired brick in comparison to, for instance, sun-dried brick.

Used and manufactured: corrugated iron

1825 First production in Britain
1829 First use of the term
1829 Corrugated iron patented

1820s

1832 Used as roof and wall cladding for warehouses and sheds
1839 Hot-dip galvanising applied to resolve oxidation problem

1830s

1843 Used in galvanised form for roof cladding
1844 New production process allows greater production at reduced cost, resulting in large scale export from Britain
1845 Zinc coating patented
1849 First American manufacturers active during California Gold Rush

1851 Victoria Gold Rush (Australia); first criticisms in Australia about climatic inefficiencies
1856 First Australian manufacturer active

1850s

1860s
Productio
industrial
increases

ICELAND
1870s

BRITA
184

CALIFORNIA
1849

Tropic of Cancer

JAMAICA 1844
HONDURAS
1846
ST. LUCIA
1844

PANAMA
1853

Equator

PERU
1854

Rio De Janeiro
1850

Tropic of Capricorn

Santiago
1850

Buenos Aires
1855

Tierra del Fuego
1885

Despite the persistent notion that the vernacular is built of local and often natural materials, many vernacular resources are in fact manufactured and may have been transported over long distances before being applied. Others may have been used for different purposes before their application as building resource, including discarded waste products such as beer cans or tyres, that may still be put to good use as construction material. Though the use of such resources is commonly associated with informal ways of housing, many manufactured and used materials are and have long been used by vernacular builders.

One of the most well-know and ubiq uitous of all manufactured vernacula resources is corrugated iron. Commonl made of galvanised steel, sheet iron, aluminiun or asbestos-cement, corrugated lamina are use throughout the world, especially in the tropi cal and humid upland areas of Latin America Africa and Southeast Asia, as well as in mor temperate areas like North America, Europ and Central Asia. Widespread and popula since the late nineteenth century, but not alway well-adapted to local climatic circumstances corrugated iron embodies to many observers th perceived contamination and decline of vernac ular architecture during the twentieth century.

Santiago ● 1850 Date of first recorded use of corrugated iron (industrial or domestic) at key locations

Corrugated iron used as a vernacular building resource

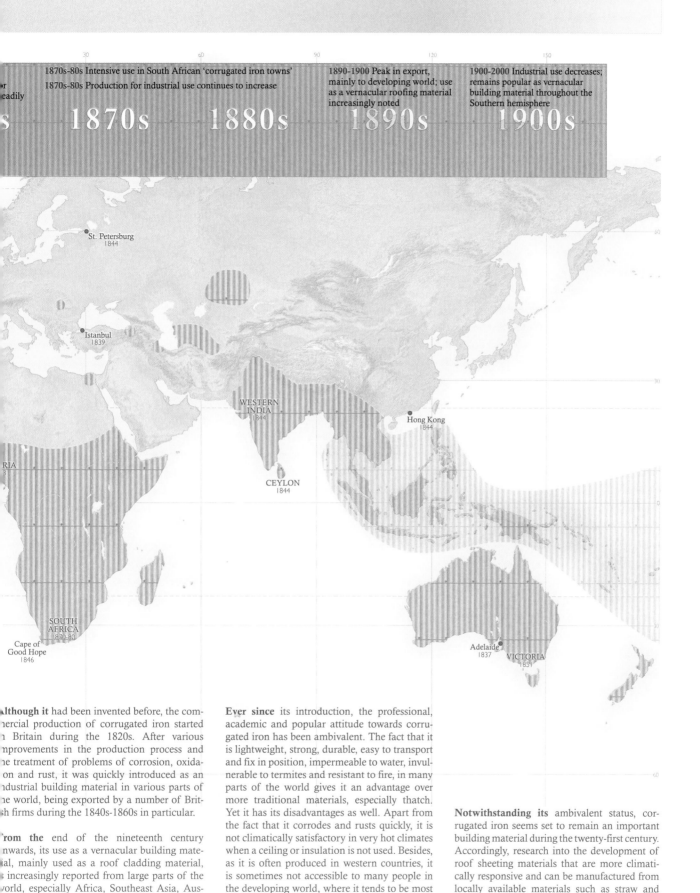

1870s-80s Intensive use in South African 'corrugated iron towns'

1870s-80s Production for industrial use continues to increase

1890-1900 Peak in export, mainly to developing world; use as a vernacular roofing material increasingly noted

1900-2000 Industrial use decreases; remains popular as vernacular building material throughout the Southern hemisphere

1870s   **1880s**   **1890s**   **1900s**

St. Petersburg
1844

Istanbul
1839

WESTERN
INDIA
1844

Hong Kong
1844

CEYLON
1844

SOUTH
AFRICA
1870-80

Cape of
Good Hope
1846

Adelaide
1837   VICTORIA
1851

Although it had been invented before, the commercial production of corrugated iron started in Britain during the 1820s. After various improvements in the production process and the treatment of problems of corrosion, oxidation and rust, it was quickly introduced as an industrial building material in various parts of the world, being exported by a number of British firms during the 1840s-1860s in particular.

From the end of the nineteenth century onwards, its use as a vernacular building material, mainly used as a roof cladding material, is increasingly reported from large parts of the world, especially Africa, Southeast Asia, Australasia and Latin America.

Ever since its introduction, the professional, academic and popular attitude towards corrugated iron has been ambivalent. The fact that it is lightweight, strong, durable, easy to transport and fix in position, impermeable to water, invulnerable to termites and resistant to fire, in many parts of the world gives it an advantage over more traditional materials, especially thatch. Yet it has its disadvantages as well. Apart from the fact that it corrodes and rusts quickly, it is not climatically satisfactory in very hot climates when a ceiling or insulation is not used. Besides, as it is often produced in western countries, it is sometimes not accessible to many people in the developing world, where it tends to be most intensively used.

Notwithstanding its ambivalent status, corrugated iron seems set to remain an important building material during the twenty-first century. Accordingly, research into the development of roof sheeting materials that are more climatically responsive and can be manufactured from locally available materials such as straw and timber, is ongoing.

Structural Systems & Technologies

Home construction, West Sumatra, Indonesia. *Photograph: Marcel Vellinga*

Tents: membraneous and armature

Membraneous (frameless) tents

1. Black tent, African (goat hair; sheep wool or camel hair)

2. Black tent, Arabian (goat hair; sheep wool or camel hair)

3. Black tent, Persian (goat hair; sheep wool or camel hair)

4. Black tent, Tibetan (yak hair)

Armature (framed) tents

5. Ridge tent, Inuit (timber, whalebone; caribou or seal skin)

6. Skin tent, Tuareg (goat skin, sheep skin)

7. Conical-cylindrical tent (reindeer skin)

8. Conical tent, Eurasian (chum)(reindeer skin, birch bark, rush, felt)

9. Conical tent, North American (tipi)(buffalo skin)

10. Conical Wigwam (birch bark)

11. Wigwam (birch bark, reed, grass)

12. Domical tent, Inuit (caribou or seal skin)

13. Trellis tent, Mongol (yurt)(felt)

14. Trellis tent, Kirgiz (yurt)(felt)

15. Frame and mat tent, African (bark, reed mats, palm mats)

Despite making up a relatively small proportion of the world's population, nomadic people who, for economic reasons, engage in periodic or cyclical movement, inhabit vast areas of the world, including the most inhospitable ones. The arctic regions of Asia and North America, the hot and arid deserts of North Africa and the Middle East, and the tropical rainforests of Sub-Saharan Africa, Latin America and Asia are home to a large variety of nomads, including hunter-gatherers, pastoral herders, travelling craftsmen and transhumant farmers. Often engaged in symbiotic relationships with neighbouring sedentary peoples, these nomads maintain their distinctive ways of life and traditions despite significant political pressures to sedentarize.

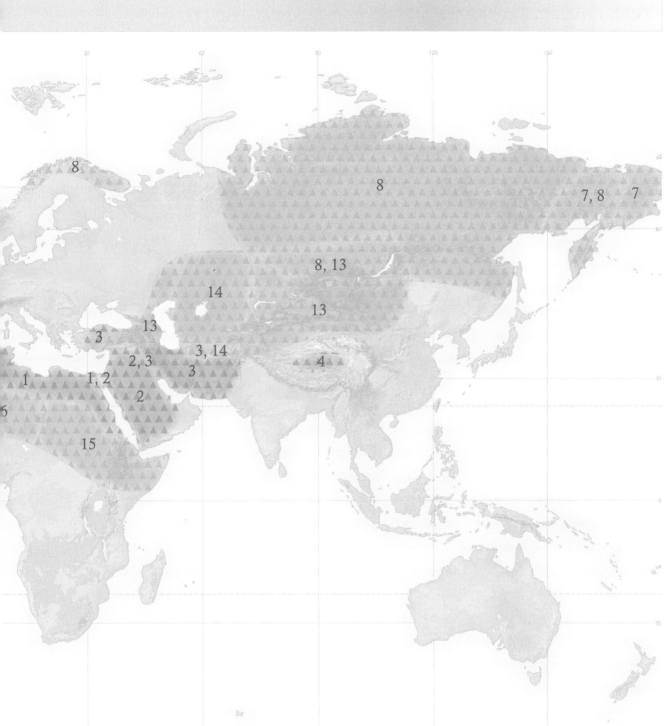

The rich diversity in nomadic cultures, that results from differences in local topography, climate, economy and history, goes hand in hand with an equally abundant variety of building forms. Although not the sole form of nomadic architecture (which also includes houseboats and wagons), tents are among the most widespread of nomadic structures, being used in large parts of Asia, Africa and, to a lesser extent nowadays, North America. Well-known vernacular tent types include the Central Asian yurt or ger, the native American conical tipi, and the 'black tent' of the North African and Middle Eastern deserts.

Varying greatly in terms of form, plan, size, materials, means of transportation and geographic distribution, tents may generically be characterised as structures that are designed to be easily erected, dismantled and transported. A structural distinction is commonly made between armature or framed tents (i.e. tents in which the load is carried by a structural frame) and membraneous or frameless tents (i.e. those where the covering membrane is the load-carrying structure). Both categories can be subdivided on the basis of form, materials and structural details, resulting in a large number of different tent types.

Whilst clusters of geographical distribution and diffusion can be distinguished, typological differences cannot always be directly related to ethnic or cultural divisions, and similar types of tents may sometimes be found among various peoples, distributed over vast areas of land, or different tent types within one ethnic group. The density of use may also vary within the clusters, and some tents are only used during particular seasons of the year or for specific purposes. The Native American tipi and wigwam, for example, continue to be periodically built for use at ceremonial community meetings.

Underground architecture: cave, pit and semi-subterranean

The map shows the world-wide distribution of underground structures, with symbols indicating location rather than quantity.

- Natural cave or cavity used for habitation and/or storage

- Newly excavated cave or significantly modified natural cave or cavity

- Constructed cave, consisting of a stone or brick vault covered with earth

- Pit dwelling, consisting of a pit courtyard surrounded by excavated rooms

- Natural cave or cavity, but the authenticity of use as habitation is subject to controversy

- Semi-subterranean (winter) dwelling, made of timber poles, logs or bone covered with wood, brush and earth

- Semi-subterranean dugout built by European settlers, dug into a hillside with stone or log walls and a timber and earth cover

- Industrially dug cave, adapted for use as habitation

Selected climatic regions

- Continental; humid, cool summers

- Semi-arid steppe

- Mediterranean

In places where the geology makes it possible, houses may be excavated into mountain slopes, rock faces or the earth. Generically referred to as underground architecture, such excavated structures include horizontally dug caves, vertically sunken pit dwellings and semi-subterranean structures with a dugout floor covered with logs, earth or stone.

Currently, there are about five million cave dwellings in the world, providing accommodation for some fifty million people. The majority of these cave dwellers or 'troglodytes' (approximately 80 per cent) live in the Yellow River region of China with another major, though rapidly reducing, concentration being located in the Mediterranean region. More scattered cave dwelling traditions are also encountered in parts of Africa and Latin America.

Although some natural caves are used for habitation, most contemporary cave dwellings have been excavated or are natural caves that have been substantially adapted. Offering good protection from extreme climates, their function may range from home to monastery and from hotel to storage place, and in some cases has changed significantly over time.

Underground dwellings are often found in hills or mountain sides, but they may also be excavated in areas with more open land. Pit dwellings, which consist of pits that act as courtyards around which living quarters are excavated, can be found in various parts of north Africa and China. In Shaanxi province in China, many underground dwellings are

constructed rather than carved, vault structures of stone or brick being covered with earth to acquire the same climatic advantages as actual excavated ones.

Though essentially a cultural expression, the distribution of underground architecture is largely conditioned by geology. The cave and pit dwellings in China have been excavated in loess, a fine sediment that is unsuitable for building because of its susceptibility to wind erosion, but which is easily excavated. Digging into the more compact layers of the deposits, use is made of its structural properties, whilst a greater availability of fertile land for agriculture is ensured. Other suitable soil types include limestone, sandstone and volcanic deposits, especially tufa/tuff.

Semi-subterranean dugouts, consisting of timber structures that are partially built underground, are found throughout vast areas of arctic Asia and America. Commonly having roofs covered with logs, planks, sod or earth, they are used as permanent winter dwellings by their nomadic owners, offering good insulation, warmth and protection from winds. Similar structures were also built by early European settlers on the North American Plains, and in a few parts of Africa and south-eastern Europe. Though some examples remain, most have been abandoned in the late nineteenth century.

Horizontal log construction: diffusion

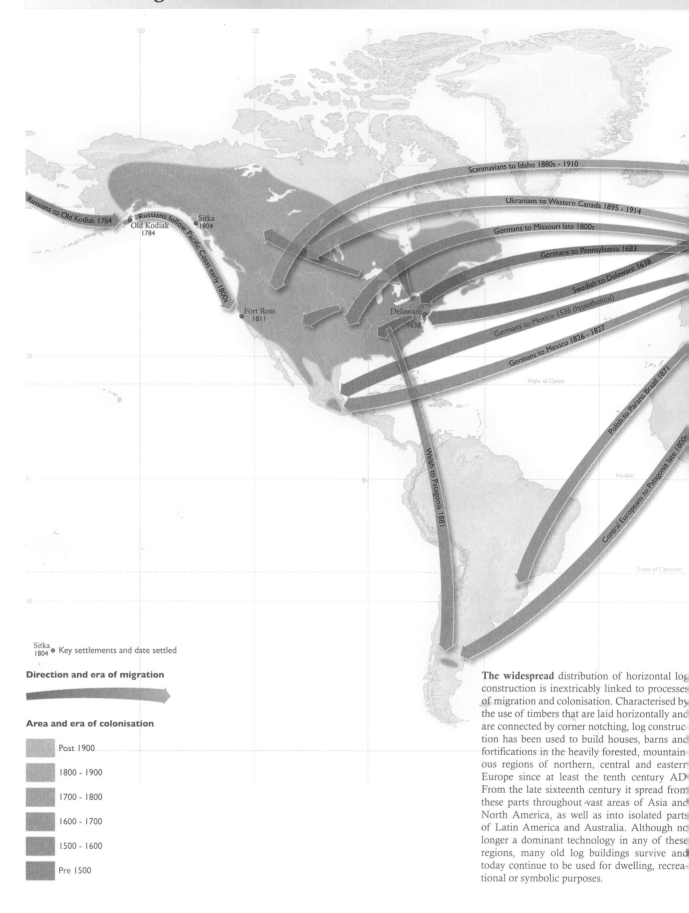

Scaninavians to Idaho 1880s - 1910

Ukranians to Western Canada 1895 - 1914

Germans to Missouri late 1800s

Germans to Pennsylvania 1683

Swedish to Delaware 1638

Germans to Mexico 1536 (hypothetical)

Germans to Mexico 1826 - 1827

Polish to Parana Brazil 1871

Central Europeans to Patagonia late 1800s

Russians to Old Kodiak 1784

Russians follow Pacific Coast early 1800s

Old Kodiak 1784

Sitka 1804

Fort Ross 1811

Delaware 1638

Welsh to Patagonia 1881

Tropic of Cancer

Equator

Tropic of Capricorn

Sitka 1804 ● Key settlements and date settled

Direction and era of migration

Area and era of colonisation

- Post 1900
- 1800 - 1900
- 1700 - 1800
- 1600 - 1700
- 1500 - 1600
- Pre 1500

The widespread distribution of horizontal log construction is inextricably linked to processes of migration and colonisation. Characterised by the use of timbers that are laid horizontally and are connected by corner notching, log construction has been used to build houses, barns and fortifications in the heavily forested, mountainous regions of northern, central and eastern Europe since at least the tenth century AD. From the late sixteenth century it spread from these parts throughout vast areas of Asia and North America, as well as into isolated parts of Latin America and Australia. Although no longer a dominant technology in any of these regions, many old log buildings survive and today continue to be used for dwelling, recreational or symbolic purposes.

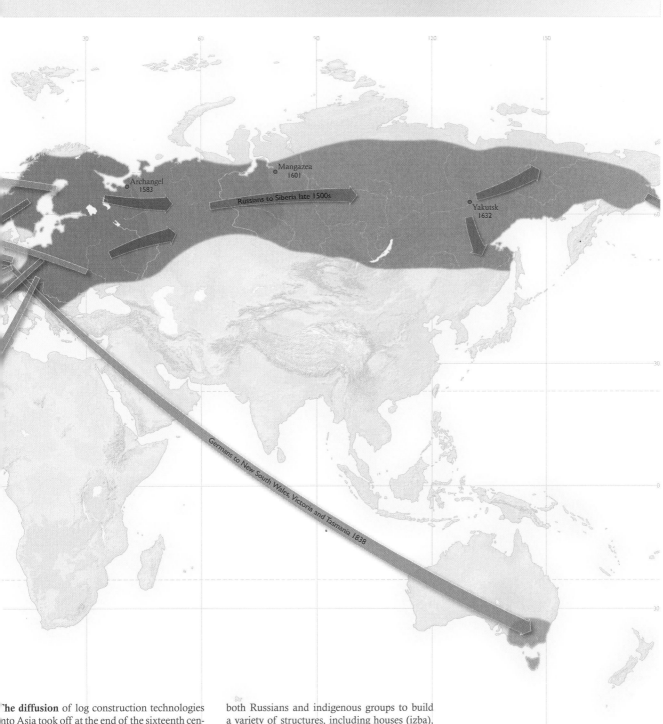

Archangel
1583

Mangazea
1601

Russians to Siberia late 1500s

Yakutsk
1632

Germans to New South Wales, Victoria and Tasmania 1838

The diffusion of log construction technologies into Asia took off at the end of the sixteenth century when various Russian expeditions crossed the Ural Mountains to explore and settle the vast stretches of land to the east. Colonisation and the subsequent diffusion of log construction was particularly rapid in the seventeenth century and culminated in the erection of Russian log fortifications in eastern Siberia, Alaska and California around the turn of the nineteenth century. Nowadays few of these early fortifications, strategically located along the waterways that served as transportation routes, remain. As a technology, however, log construction is still common throughout the region and used by both Russians and indigenous groups to build a variety of structures, including houses (izba), dugouts and barns.

The introduction of log construction to North America took place somewhat later, in the first half of the seventeenth century. Having initially been brought along by the Swedish and German immigrants who settled in the early colonies along the east coast, the technology was readily adopted by English and Scots-Irish colonists and quickly diffused throughout the eastern parts of the United States and Canada in the seventeenth and eighteenth centuries. Subsequently 're-introduced' intermittently by new settlers from Germany, Scandinavia and the Ukraine, it reached the west coast and Alaska in the course of the nineteenth century. Used to build fortifications, houses and barns, horizontal log construction proved a particularly fit technology in the heavily forested regions of the New World, even though its use was not restricted to timber-rich areas only. Although nowadays mainly associated with the cabins of early white settlers, building with logs was adopted by a number of Native American groups and has been used in various parts of North America until well into the twentieth century.

Corbelled stone structure/group of structures

Dry stone construction (no bonding used)

Wet stone construction (bonded with mortar)

Since prehistoric times stone has been a important building resource in large parts o the world. As a strong, durable, insulating an fire-resistant material, it has been employed i a variety of ways, using different technologie that depend on the type of rock used, the skil of the builders and the tools available to them Some stones may be used as they are foun naturally (rubble), whilst others require quarry ing and extensive working. Because of the tim and skills required, stone buildings have bee constructed by sedentary people only and hav often, though not exclusively so, been reserve for the wealthy.

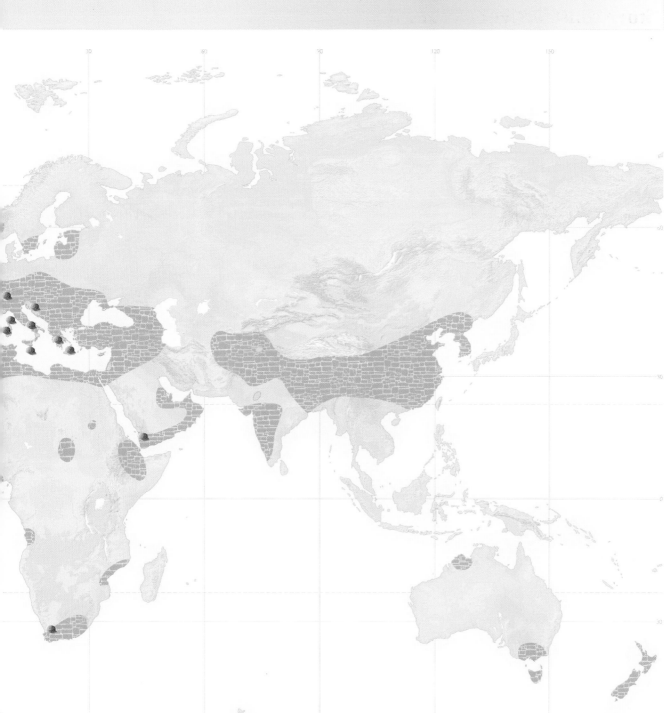

Nowadays, stone architecture can be found in various parts of the world where suitable rocks are easily accessible. Stone walls, roofs and foundations are common in the Mediterranean, southern China, the eastern United States and parts of Central Asia, whilst more scattered traditions of stone construction exist in parts of Africa, Latin America, Polynesia and northern Europe. However, despite its wide distribution and long pedigree, the use of stone as a vernacular building material is diminishing, even in those areas where it is easily available, as comparatively cheaper and more efficient materials like concrete have become more and more common.

Stone walls can be built with or without mortar. Mortared or 'wet' stone walling, in which a mixture of sand, lime and cement or earth is used to create a bond is most common and found in large parts of the northern hemisphere. 'Dry' stone traditions that do not involve the use of mortar often exist alongside wet traditions. Mainly used to build stone fences, dry stone construction allows walls to expand and contract with changes in temperature. It requires only a minimum amount of tools and does not deplete natural resources, as the stone can easily be re-used. Nonetheless, on a world scale and in comparison to wet stone construction, its distribution is restricted.

Apart from free-standing and retaining walls, dry stone structures, including dwellings, storage places, temporary shelters and bridges are found in small parts of Europe, North and Latin America, and Asia. One of the most distinctive dry stone traditions is the method of 'corbelling', in which stones are placed on top of each other without a bond, with each stone projecting inwards by a fraction of its depth beyond the layer below, creating a distinctive parabolic dome. Various kinds of corbelled stone structures can be found scattered throughout southern and western Europe in particular, raising questions about the origins and diffusion of the technology.

Walling: timber-framed

Walls are used to enclose space; they stake the boundaries of a building and provide privacy, whilst simultaneously offering protection from the elements by keeping out rain, wind and, depending on the climate, heat or cold. Various kinds of walls can be encountered throughout the world, differing in terms of function, material and structural characteristics. Mass walls, variously made of stone, timber or earth, achieve both structural stability and enclosure through the progressive accumulation of loads on top of one another. Curtain walls on the other hand, made of vegetal materials, animal skins or fabrics, are non-supporting and act solely to enclose space.

In large parts of western and central Europe, so-called timber-framed walling can be found. Dating back, in some cases, to the fifteenth century, timber-framed walls separate structural and space-enclosing functions, consisting of a timber frame made of a variety of jointed posts, beams, studs and braces, that can stand on its own and is enclosed with an infilling of wattle and daub, rubble or brick. Though considerable variety in scale, form and walling pattern exists, the spaces between the structural members are usually square or, in parts of England and France, tall and narrow (referred to as 'close studding').

In the majority of timber-framed walling buildings the walls form part of a 'box' frame. In box framed houses all posts, beams and braces are carefully jointed to produce a firm and stable structure in which each member carries an equal part of the load. Flexible in nature, the box frame allows for the building of wings, extensions and projecting storeys (jetties), and is found throughout western and central Europe. Especially widespread in medieval times, its use declined during the nineteenth century with the introduction of light weight machine-cut wooden structures.

Another structural system that may be combined with timber-framed walling is the 'cruck' frame. Found throughout large parts of the British Isles and in scattered areas of mainland Europe, a cruck consists of a pair of wooden blades, sometimes derived from a single tree-trunk, that are joined together at the apexes to support the ridge. Because the blades, which can be made of one piece of timber or be jointed, may rise from a timber sill or a stone wall, cruck frames do not necessarily combine with timber-framed walls. In those cases where they do, the walls provide only a partial load-bearing function.

Having originated in Europe, timber-framed walling has been diffused to parts of the United States, Brazil and Australia during the eighteenth and nineteenth centuries, thanks to the emigration of English and, in the main German settlers.

Cruck frame house, Herefordshire, England. *Photograph: Marcel Velling*

World

Direction and era of migration

Distribution of timber-framed walling

Box framed walling, close studding

Box framed walling, square panels

Cruck frame

Curtain walling: woven matting

Materials used for matting

- Bamboo
- Grass (elephant, marrow, sedge)
- Palm (coconut, sago, sugar cane, nipa)
- Pandanus
- Reed (water)
- Straw (rice, wheat, oat, barley, rye)

The term curtain wall refers to walls that are used for closure and separation rather than load carrying purposes. Such non-supporting walls may be made of leaves, bark or hides, but are also created from fabrics and prefabricated woven mats or panels. In contrast to mass walls made of logs, stone or earth, which add to the structural stability of the building as a whole, curtain walls serve solely to protect the inhabitants from the elements and to create an interior space that is secluded and private.

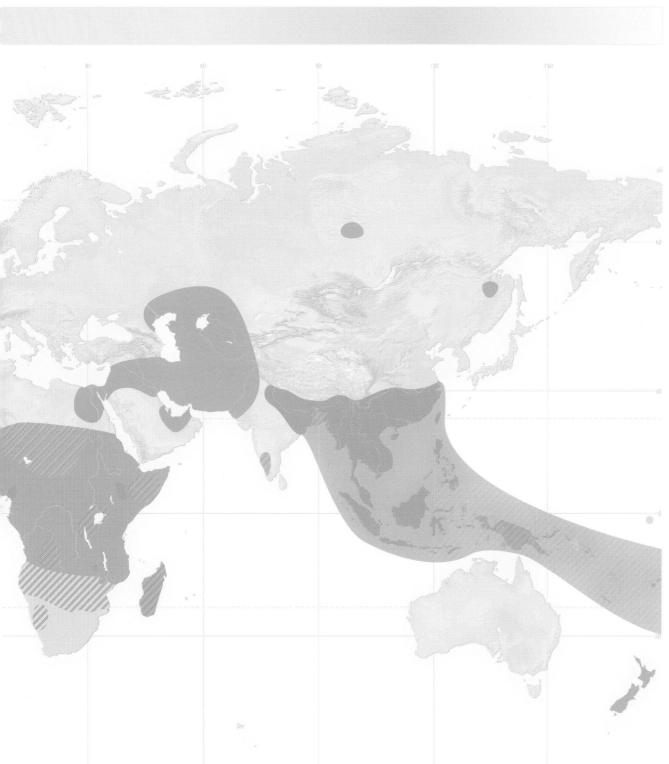

Curtain walls made of prefabricated woven mats can be found throughout large parts of the world. The matting is done with whatever materials are available locally. Bamboo is one of the most common matting materials, to be found throughout Southeast Asia, Madagascar and parts of Melanesia. Other widely used materials include palm leaves, which are used throughout Amazonia and large parts of Africa, and reed, which is common in the Middle East and Southwest Asia. Less common materials include grass, straw and pandanus.

The use of woven mats is closely related to economy. Being light and flexible, they are used by many nomadic and transhumant peoples to cover transportable shelters or tents. Often made by the women, they can be easily transported in periods of movement and allow for the closing and opening of spaces according to the seasonal requirements of function and climate. Woven mats used to cover structures are especially common throughout sub-Saharan Africa.

Though they are today frequently replaced by more durable materials like concrete and brick, woven mats are also widely used as curtain walls in more permanent houses. In these instances, climate seems to be an influencing factor. In hot and humid areas such as Amazonia, Southeast Asia and parts of Africa, woven mats of bamboo and palm are extensively employed, providing ventilation to the inhabitants by allowing currents of air to circulate through the building. In other climates, the use of woven curtain walls is far less common.

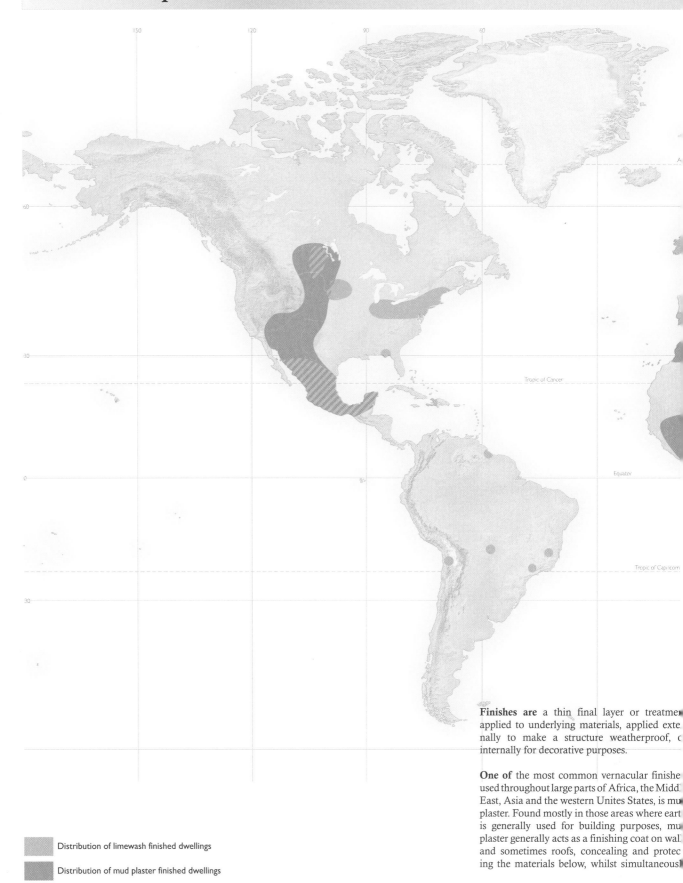

Distribution of limewash finished dwellings

Distribution of mud plaster finished dwellings

Finishes are a thin final layer or treatme▨ applied to underlying materials, applied exte▨ nally to make a structure weatherproof, o▨ internally for decorative purposes.

One of the most common vernacular finishe▨ used throughout large parts of Africa, the Midd▨ East, Asia and the western Unites States, is mu▨ plaster. Found mostly in those areas where eart▨ is generally used for building purposes, mu▨ plaster generally acts as a finishing coat on wal▨ and sometimes roofs, concealing and protec▨ ing the materials below, whilst simultaneous▨

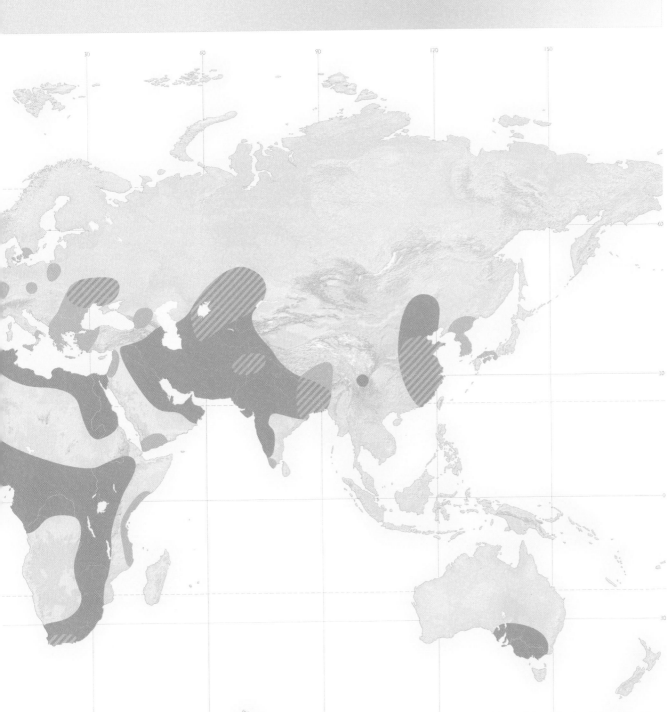

softening the contours of the buildings and enhancing their appearance. In some instances the mud plaster finish may be incised, moulded or coloured, either for decorative reasons or to assist the mud in drying, to prevent or conceal cracks, or to disperse concentrated flows of rain that might be harmful to the surface.

Regardless of the function or underlying material that is used (most notably sun-dried brick, but also bamboo, planks, reed, straw or timber logs), mud plaster almost always includes additives such as straw or animal dung to increase the cohesive properties of the plaster. Though regular replastering is often necessary, mud plaster has been noted to last up to ten or fifteen years, depending on the climate.

Another common finish, sometimes found alongside mud plaster, is limewash. Produced by burning limestone to yield quicklime, which is then diluted with water, limewash has been used as a decorative and protective finish throughout large parts of the United States, Europe and Asia, as well as along the East African coast. A diluted form of lime plaster, it basically is a means of transferring a thin layer of rock onto a wall in order to protect it. Allowing damp in a wall to evaporate without damaging it, limewash can be applied to earth, stone and timber walls. Although it can be durable, repeated limewashing is generally necessary to maintain the finish. To increase its water-resistance, the lime often needs to be mixed with additives such as tallow, casein or oil.

Though mud plaster and limewash have been in use for a very long time, the use of both has seen a steady decline during the twentieth century due to the introduction of modern materials like cement, which provide more convenient methods of achieving similar results. Nonetheless, both finishes are still widely used and, in the case of limewash, even making a sort of comeback.

Roof cladding: clay tiles, shingles and slate

Most vernacular buildings in the world are provided with roofs to protect the structure and its inhabitants from rain, snow, wind or sunshine. Because of the climatic impacts and the fact that roofs tend to form the largest single components which often visually dominate the appearance of buildings, the choice of roofing material is an important consideration. Throughout the world different materials have been used to clad roofs, the choice of which depends upon climatic considerations, the availability and nature of local resources, the function of the building and the size and form of the roof.

A common type of roof cladding, made of fired clay, is the tile. Clay tiles are believed to have originated in China and to have been subsequently introduced to the Mediterranean and Europe by the Romans. During the colonial period their use spread to other regions of the world where suitable clays, fuel and substantial roofing timbers are available. Today they are a common form of roof cladding in China, Europe and India, as well as in various parts of Latin America and Africa.

The shape of tiles is governed by the need to shed rainwater or snow. The interlocking or overlapping of the tiles is key to this process and is related to the pitch of the roofs on which the tiles are laid. Throughout the centuries, a variety of tiles has been used and developed, ranging from simple rectangular plain ones to the 'Spanish' half-truncated cones, the Chinese half-cones and the Dutch S-shaped pan tiles. Industrialisation brought the development of the 'Marseilles' and 'Bangalore' tiles, which have more complex series of indentations to improve the interlocking.

Shingles, or small thin pieces of timber cleft or sawn from a log and used in a similar manner to tiles, have a long history as cladding material in heavily forested parts of the world. Known to have been used by the Romans, they are today found throughout large parts of Russia, east and central Europe and the eastern United States, as well as in parts of Southeast Asia, Korea and Japan. In contrast to clay tiles, shingles (called 'shakes' in North America) are light in weight. They provide good insulation, but are less durable than clay tiles and are also easily inflammable.

A variety of tree species is used to make shingles. Most commonly fir or cedar are used, but oak or chestnut shingles are common as well. Shingles can be made fast and conveniently by driving an axe blade into the end grain of the timber, on the line of one of the rays which radiate from the centre in the heartwood. Although this cleaving of timbers using an axe or wedge was used widely in Europe and by early settlers and colonists in the United States, in time it has yielded to the production of sawn shingles. These sawn shingles have half the life-span of cleft shingles, whilst their appearance is markedly smoother and less textured.

A third common type of roof cladding is slate. Slate is a schistose rock, which is easy to split along natural planes of cleavage into plates and can be placed on roofs much like clay tiles or shingles. The advantages of slate are that it is durable, involves little processing, is relatively light in use and impervious to rain when well laid. The colour of slate may vary from green to purple or grey and imparts a uniform hue to the roof. Apart from roof cladding, slate has also been commonly used to clad walls, especially in areas where walls are persistently exposed to damp and rain.

Slate roofs can be found in parts of Europe, North America, Central Asia and Japan. In most regions, the slate is placed so that each succeeding layer overlaps the layer below by two-thirds its length, thus producing a double thickness over the entire roof.

Clay tiles

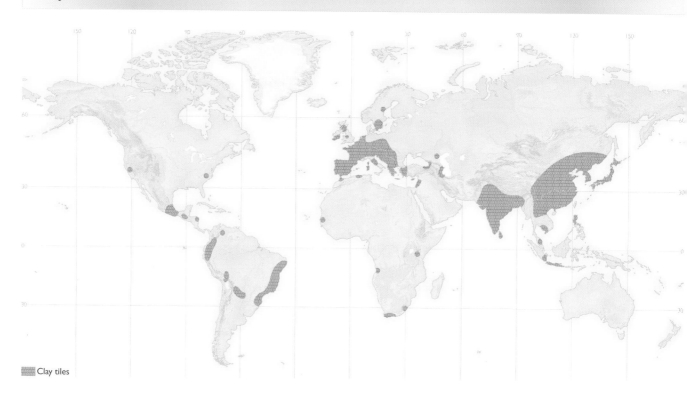

Clay tiles

Shingles

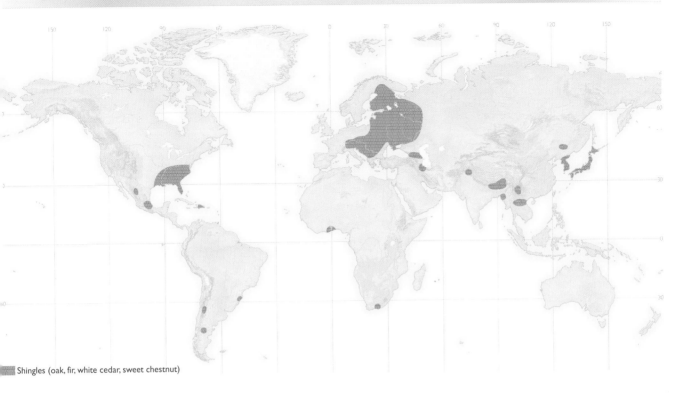

 Shingles (oak, fir, white cedar, sweet chestnut)

Slate

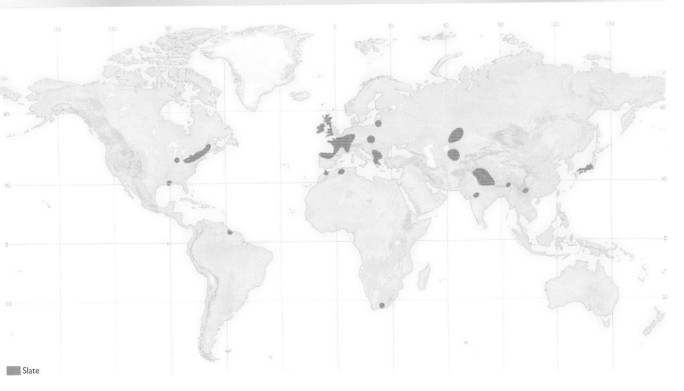

Slate

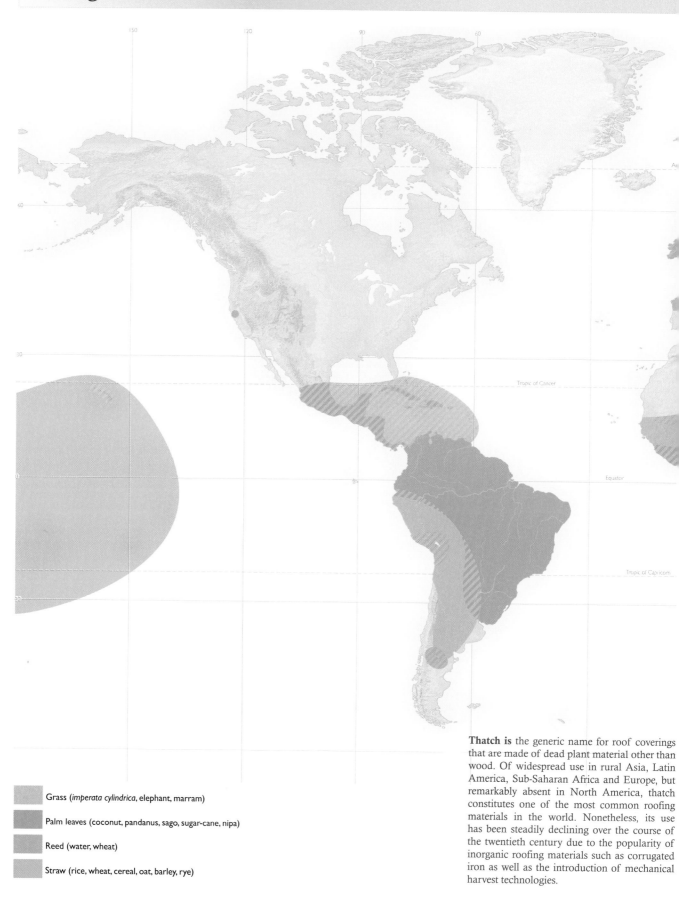

Grass (*imperata cylindrica*, elephant, marram)

Palm leaves (coconut, pandanus, sago, sugar-cane, nipa)

Reed (water, wheat)

Straw (rice, wheat, cereal, oat, barley, rye)

Thatch is the generic name for roof coverings that are made of dead plant material other than wood. Of widespread use in rural Asia, Latin America, Sub-Saharan Africa and Europe, but remarkably absent in North America, thatch constitutes one of the most common roofing materials in the world. Nonetheless, its use has been steadily declining over the course of the twentieth century due to the popularity of inorganic roofing materials such as corrugated iron as well as the introduction of mechanical harvest technologies.

Almost any vegetable material can be used to provide thatch, but grass, reed, straw and palm are among the most common ones. The choice of material largely depends on what resources, technologies and skills are available. Grass and palm leaves are most intensively used in Latin America, Sub-Saharan Africa, Southeast Asia and Polynesia, whilst straw and reed are common in Europe, South Asia, China and Japan, as well as in those areas elsewhere settled by European migrants. Among some peoples, combinations of materials are used.

Although reports on the durability of the resources used for thatching may vary or even be contradictory, depending it seems on local climatic and geographic circumstances, water reed is generally regarded as one of the strongest materials, lasting up to eighty years without having to be replaced. Similar life expectancies are noted for palm fibre thatched roofs, but thatch made of palm leaves often lasts no longer than two to five years. The most widely used grass is imperata cylindrica, which, like cereal straw, has a life span of about twenty-five to thirty years.

Depending on the materials used, various thatching techniques can be employed. The thatch may be applied directly to the roof structure in tied or nailed bundles, or it may be applied using prefabricated woven mats or panels. The thickness of thatch roofs varies, depending on the materials and technologies used, the climate and the socio-economic context. Although dampness, fire and excessive exposure to the sun constitute major problems, thatch roofs have the advantage (for example over corrugated iron or tile ones) that they are relatively cheap to make and use locally available and renewable resources that can easily be reused (e.g. as fuel).

Forms, Plans & Types

Primary forms: conical, cylindrical, cubic and domical

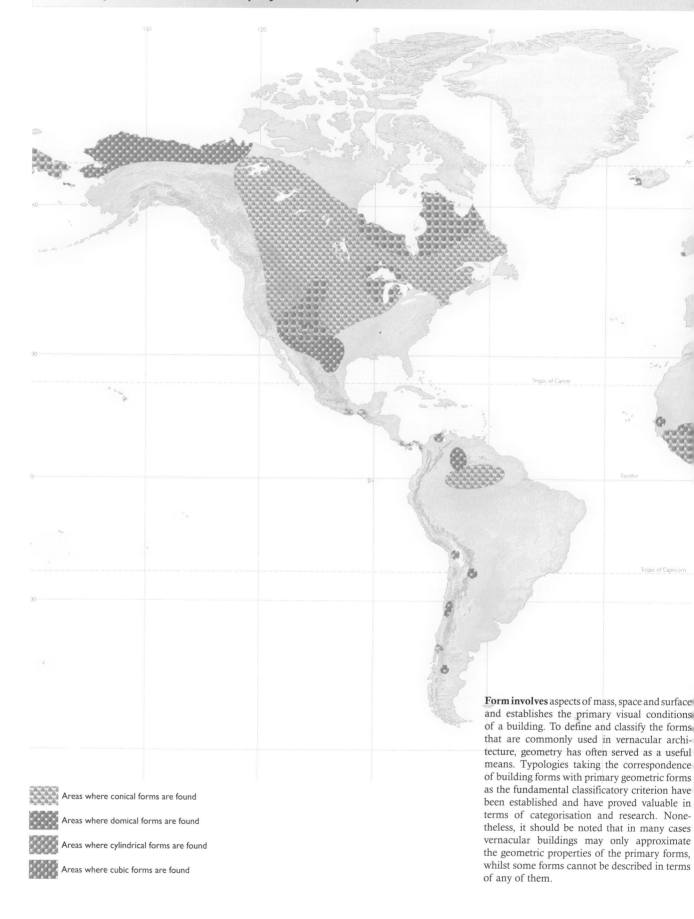

Areas where conical forms are found

Areas where domical forms are found

Areas where cylindrical forms are found

Areas where cubic forms are found

Form involves aspects of mass, space and surface and establishes the primary visual conditions of a building. To define and classify the forms that are commonly used in vernacular architecture, geometry has often served as a useful means. Typologies taking the correspondence of building forms with primary geometric forms as the fundamental classificatory criterion have been established and have proved valuable in terms of categorisation and research. Nonetheless, it should be noted that in many cases vernacular buildings may only approximate the geometric properties of the primary forms, whilst some forms cannot be described in terms of any of them.

Though more can be identified, four primary forms appear most regularly in vernacular building. One of most widespread is the cone, consisting of a circular plan and inwardly inclined surfaces that terminate in a single point. Found both as a roof form and as an undifferentiated structure (i.e. one in which there is no visual exterior distinction between the wall and roof), it is used throughout large parts of the Unites States, Africa and Asia, as well as in parts of Latin America, Southeast Asia and the Middle East.

Equally widespread, again in differentiated and undifferentiated form, is the dome, which is mainly found in the Mediterranean, Africa and Central Asia, as well as in parts of North America. Assuming a variety of profiles, including hemispherical or parabolic, the dome encloses the greatest amount of space with the least amount of surface area, making it an efficient means of spanning interior space.

The cylinder, generated by a vertical straight line rotated about a vertical axis, is often found in combination with the cone. Able to withstand substantial external and internal lateral forces, it is commonly used in structures such as windmills and store houses, and is found throughout large parts of Europe and Africa, as well as in isolated parts of Asia and Latin America.

A final primary form found in vernacular architecture is the cube. Creating buildings that are square in plan, have a height nearly equal to their length and are flat roofed, its distribution is nonetheless less widespread than that of the other forms. It is mainly found, often in aggregate form, in parts of the Mediterranean and Africa, and in isolated parts of the American Southwest and Central Asia.

The reasons to employ one form or another are complex and varied, and involve the interplay of factors such as climate, topography, function, technology, culture and resources. Each of these factors may affect the form, but none of them is the sole determinant.

Roof forms

Roofing represents one of the biggest challenges to vernacular builders. Especially when a large space needs to be covered, skills and knowledge of forces are required, as well as a good understanding of the nature of the materials used and the problems of ageing, damage and rot that they involve. Because of differences in resources, climate and culture, different vernacular roofing forms and systems have developed around the world.

The most widespread form of roofing is the pitched or gable roof. Consisting of two sloping sides that meet at a ridge and terminate at the gable end, it is found throughout most of the world, except for parts of Africa, the Middle East and East Asia. Comprising either a straight or a curved ridge, pitched roofs generally occur where wood is plentiful, helping to shed rainwater or provide shade by means of overhanging eaves.

Though less common than the pitched roof, the hipped roof is another widespread form of roofing that is used throughout large parts of Europe, the Americas and Asia. The hipped roof is characterised by a plane that slopes down to an eave on all sides. With or without a ridge, covering a rectangular or square plan, it has the advantage that all walls of the building can be of the same height, whilst the roof can be clad over the whole surface.

In regions with a shortage of wood or where timbers are valued for their shade or fruit, such as the Mediterranean, North Africa and the Middle East, masonry vaults may be found. Built of stone, earth or fired brick, vaults are used to create roofs as well as the ceilings of cellars and cave dwellings. Though less common, barrel vaults made of timber and clad with thatch have also been recorded in various parts of the world.

Pitched roof

Hipped roof

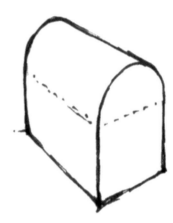

Vaulted roof

Pitched

▨▨▨ Distribution of pitched roof dwellings

Hipped

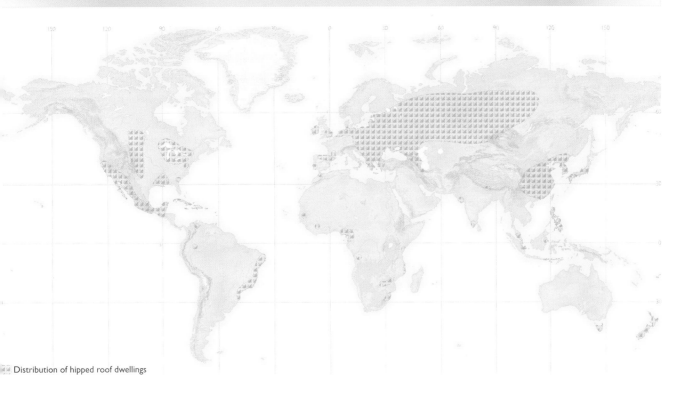

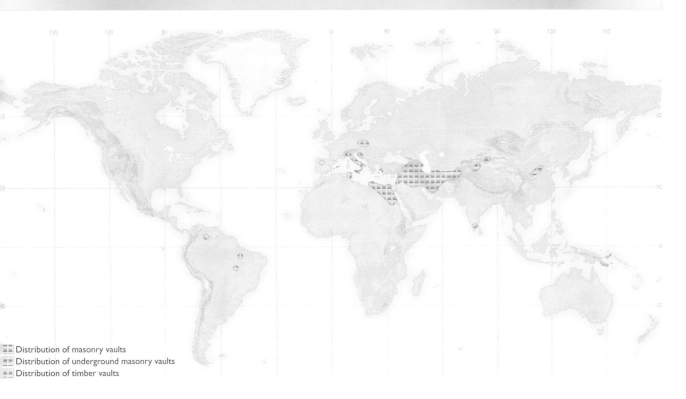 Distribution of hipped roof dwellings

Vaulted

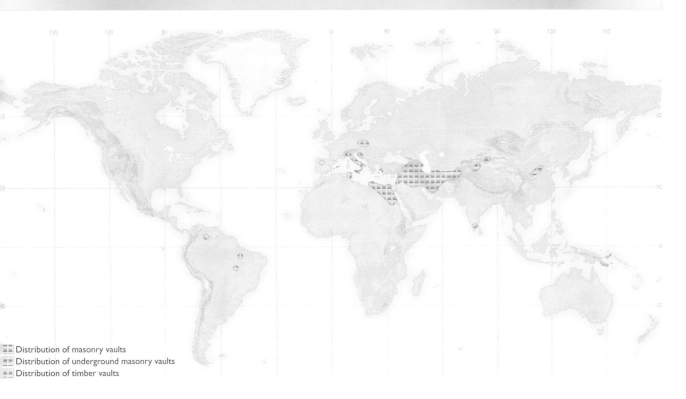

 Distribution of masonry vaults
 Distribution of underground masonry vaults
 Distribution of timber vaults

Roof forms: flat

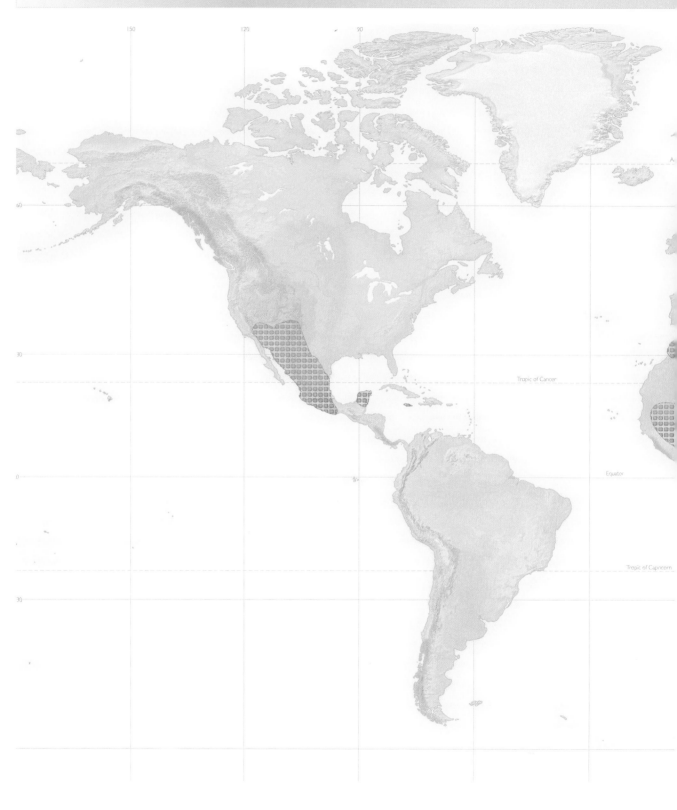

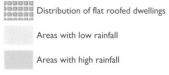 Distribution of flat roofed dwellings

Areas with low rainfall

Areas with high rainfall

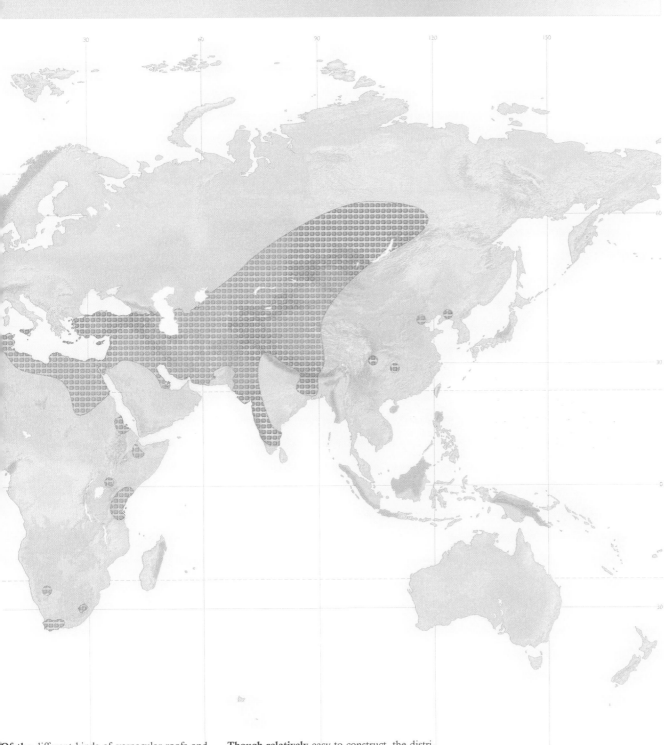

Of the different kinds of vernacular roofs and spans found throughout the world, flat roofs are the easiest to construct. Though wall plates or braces may need to be used in cases where the span is great, flat roofs are commonly constructed by laying timber or palm beams on supporting walls. The beams are then overlaid with joists, brushes, mats and planking and, frequently, a layer of earth. The beams, which have to carry the enormous weight of the earth roofs, are often inserted into the supporting walls and are thus kept in tension.

Though relatively easy to construct, the distribution of flat roofs is less widespread than that of pitched and hipped roofs. This fact mainly seems related to climatic influences. In contrast to most other roofs and spans, flat roofs do not enable rainwater to be easily thrown off. They are therefore mainly found in areas where precipitation of rain or snow is relatively low, such as the Middle East, the Mediterranean islands and northern Africa, as well as the Southwest of the United States and the West African savannah grasslands.

Apart from the clear relationship to levels of precipitation, vernacular flat roofs are often advantageous in hot climates because they reduce the indoor temperature increase from solar gain, having been made of compact layers of earth and allowing as few surfaces as possible to directly face the sun. They also radiate heat at night and are therefore often used for sleeping, as well as for daily activities such as drying fruit and airing clothes and bedding, or for movement from one dwelling to the next.

Plans: circular

A plan is the layout of a building at ground level. As a graphic representation it represents the shape and relative arrangement of space within a building, and can be used to indicate spatial organisation, social relationships and hierarchies, as well as aspects of construction and structure. Different kinds of vernacular plan type can be identified, which sometimes may be combined in complex arrangements, including the square, apse, rectangle and circle. Their occurrence is influenced by environmental and cultural factors, as well as the capabilities and constraints of construction materials and technologies. Some plans, like the square or rectangle, can be found in all parts of the world. The distribution of others plan types, like the apse, is more restricted.

The circular plan is found in various regions, and is especially widespread in Africa. Circular plans are common to a great variety of building types, including single-room houses in west, east and southern Africa, tents structures like the North American tipi or the central Asian yurt, and agricultural buildings such as mills, granaries, grain elevators and barns. In most cases, the circular plan is of a freestanding, single-room building, but in some cases, especially in Sub-Saharan Africa, a number of circular building may combine to form a circular cluster or com pound. Large collective dwellings of a circula plan also exist, as among the Yanoama in Braz and the Hakka in China.

Generally speaking, plan types are constraine by construction systems, and especially by th dimensions and structural spanning capacitie of the materials. Circular buildings are mo commonly made of earth, small stone masonr branches or woven materials, although circula structures made of timber do occur. In som cases, as when sun-dried brick or wet earth wal are used, the circular plan may be essential the structural stability of the building. As th map of Africa exemplifies, a variety of build ing forms may be combined with circular plan including domes, cones and cylinders. In som cases, the circular plan exists alongside othe plan types such as the rectangle, the difference in plan relating to variations in the function, ag or status of the buildings.

The use of circular plans has been traced back t prehistoric times. Still, there are many example from the distant and recent past in which circu lar buildings have been replaced by rectangula or square plan types, either as part of a gradua process or in a relatively short period of time Though the reasons for these developments ar complex and will differ per individual case, i many cases the introduction of different mater als and technologies that encourage the use o rectangular or square plans seems important.

Kikuyu compound, Kenya. *Photograph: Paul Oliver*

World

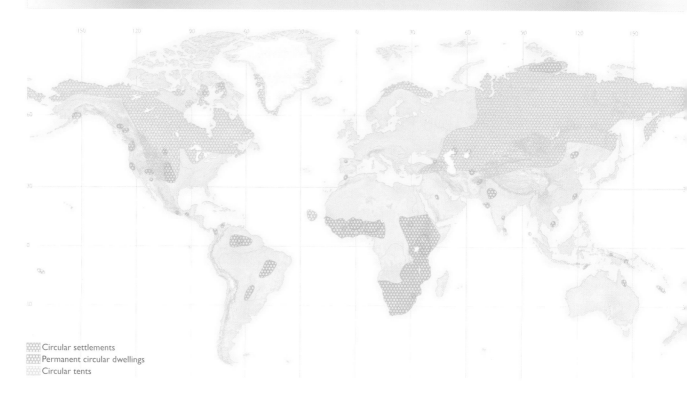

Circular settlements
Permanent circular dwellings
Circular tents

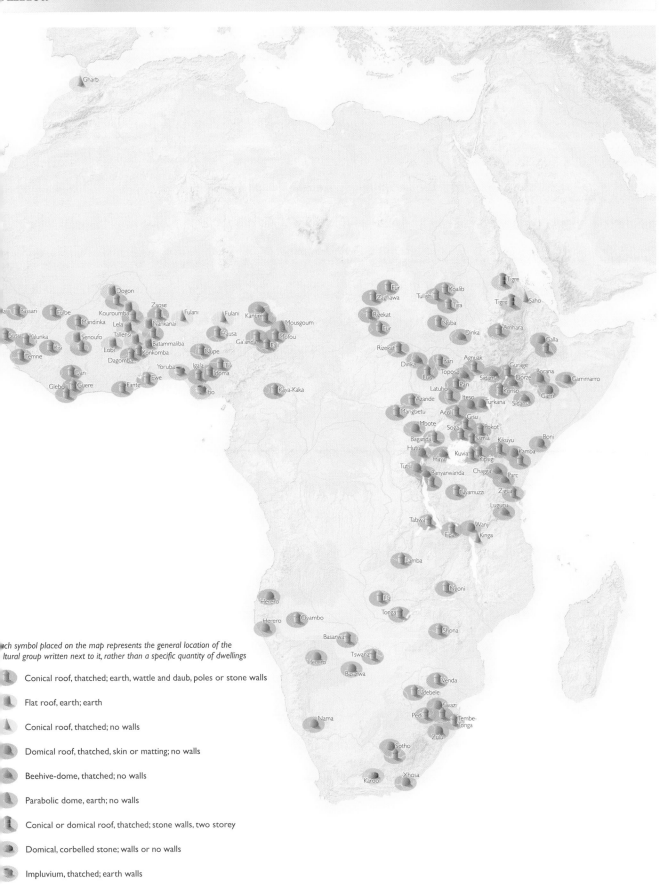

Each symbol placed on the map represents the general location of the cultural group written next to it, rather than a specific quantity of dwellings

Conical roof, thatched; earth, wattle and daub, poles or stone walls

Flat roof, earth; earth

Conical roof, thatched; no walls

Domical roof, thatched, skin or matting; no walls

Beehive-dome, thatched; no walls

Parabolic dome, earth; no walls

Conical or domical roof, thatched; stone walls, two storey

Domical, corbelled stone; walls or no walls

Impluvium, thatched; earth walls

Plans: courtyards

Though mainly associated with Islamic or Arab building traditions in North Africa and the Middle East, the courtyard has been a common building form in cultures and climates throughout the world, dating back to at least Roman times. Variations of the courtyard house are found in regions as diverse and wide apart as China, the Indian subcontinent, the Middle East, the Mediterranean and West Africa. Brought along by Spanish immigrants, it is also common in parts of urban Latin America.

A courtyard can be characterised as an outdoor space that is clearly bounded and defined by surrounding buildings, rooms or walls. Although there is a huge variation in terms of plan, size, decoration, closeness and permanence, a courtyard generically provides a secluded and private space, and often acts as a focal point in a building, accommodating important daily activities such as the preparation and consumption of food, the entertainment of guests or the performance of crafts.

In the hot and arid climates of the Middle East, the courtyard also acts as a passive cooling device. Found throughout the region (apart from some wet and cold mountainous areas), it traps cool night time air that replaces the existing hot air which accumulated during the day, and cools the surrounding rooms for much of the next day. It is particularly common in urban areas, where it is often built in clusters, the aggregation of houses providing shade and reducing the direct exposure of the walls to solar heat.

In China, the use of courtyards has a long history, dating back to at least the eleventh century BC. A variety of courtyard houses can be identified, the diversity revealing the versatility and flexibility of the form. The quintessential Chinese courtyard house (siheyuan) is found in northern China. Variations on its form are found in Shaanxi, where courtyards are elongated and narrow, and in Fujian and Guangdong, where they may be circular, octagonal or rectangular. In Henan and Shanxi, courtyards have been dug deep into the earth, whilst small and compact 'skywells' are common throughout southern China.

The widespread diffusion and formal diversity of the Chinese courtyard is related to the migration patterns of the Han, who adapted their courtyard buildings to the climatic and geographic conditions they encountered. As a result, the courtyards found in the cold and dry northern parts of China are generally large and open, whilst in the hot and humid south the smaller, compact skywells that restrict the infiltration of intense sun rays and induce ventilation prevail.

Today the courtyard remains a popular house form among Chinese living in rural and urban areas. Nonetheless, in recent decades the pressures of economic growth have led to the destruction of many historical courtyard houses, especially in major cities. Although preservation efforts have increased significantly in recent years, the protection of the historical character of China's built environment remains the focus of debate.

XINJIANG

World

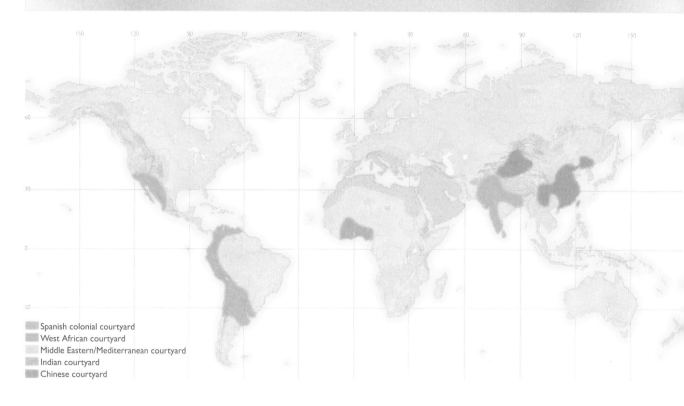

Spanish colonial courtyard
West African courtyard
Middle Eastern/Mediterranean courtyard
Indian courtyard
Chinese courtyard

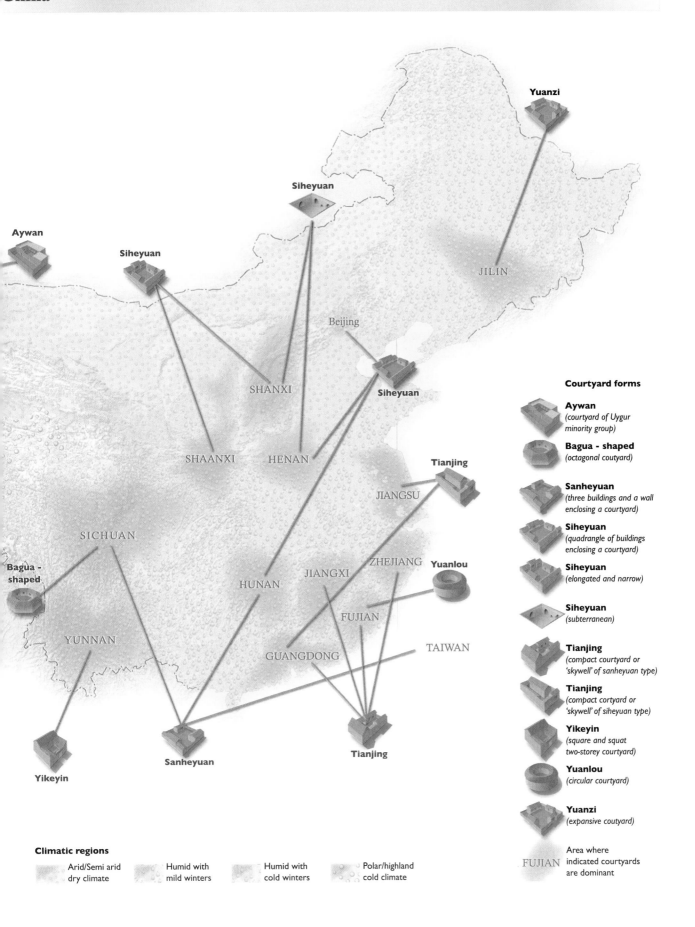

Yuanzi

Siheyuan

JILIN

Aywan

Siheyuan

Beijing

SHANXI

Siheyuan

SHAANXI

HENAN

Tianjing

JIANGSU

SICHUAN

Bagua - shaped

ZHEJIANG

Yuanlou

JIANGXI

HUNAN

YUNNAN

FUJIAN

TAIWAN

GUANGDONG

Tianjing

Sanheyuan

Yikeyin

Courtyard forms

Aywan
(courtyard of Uygur minority group)

Bagua - shaped
(octagonal coutyard)

Sanheyuan
(three buildings and a wall enclosing a courtyard)

Siheyuan
(quadrangle of buildings enclosing a courtyard)

Siheyuan
(elongated and narrow)

Siheyuan
(subterranean)

Tianjing
(compact courtyard or 'skywell' of sanheyuan type)

Tianjing
(compact cortyard or 'skywell' of siheyuan type)

Yikeyin
(square and squat two-storey courtyard)

Yuanlou
(circular courtyard)

Yuanzi
(expansive coutyard)

FUJIAN Area where indicated courtyards are dominant

Climatic regions

Arid/Semi arid dry climate

Humid with mild winters

Humid with cold winters

Polar/highland cold climate

Multi-storey buildings

Areas where multi-storey buildings are predominant

Areas where multi-storey buildings are found amongst single-storey buildings

In the increasingly globalised world of the twenty-first century, high rise buildings are becoming ever more widespread. Multi-storey housing blocks built to provide homes for the masses can be found in various parts of the world. At the same time, skyscrapers that house government departments or the headquarters of multinational corporations are built in major cities in all continents of the world, constituting a metaphor for modernity, economic development and political power.

In a vernacular context, however, the construction of multi-storey buildings is much less ubiquitous. The vast majority of vernacular architecture in the world is single storey, allowing activities to take place at one level, though often in complex spatial arrangements that may

include multiple rooms within one building or a variety of outbuildings constructed in close vicinity to one another. As such, movement within and about a building and the site it occupies can be easily facilitated. The multiplicity of storeys makes internal and external circulation more complex, necessitating different kinds of access as well as the use of staircases and corridors.

Nonetheless, significant traditions of vernacular high rise buildings do exist. In Yemen and neighbouring upland areas of the western Arabian peninsula, tower houses are built that sometimes rise to eight storeys, housing families, shops and stores. Throughout large parts of the Mediterranean, as well as in Nepal, Kash-

mir and other parts of the Himalayas, two and three storey dwellings are predominant. Besides, there are a number of areas where multi-storey buildings exist alongside single storey ones. This is mainly the case in the United States, as well as in parts of western and central Europe, the Middle East and the Caribbean. In Africa and Latin America, the distribution of multi-storey buildings shows a more restricted and scattered pattern.

The reasons for the predominance of multi-storey buildings in some parts of the world and their absence in others are complex and relate to aspects of geography, materials, technology and form. Stone and earth seem to be the most commonly used materials in vernacular high rise

construction, but multi-storey buildings made of timber do exist, as for example in Karelia in northern Russia. Similarly, many multi-storey traditions seem to be found in mountainous regions such as the Himalayas, the Alps and the Atlas, but again significant exceptions can be noted.

So far, research into the subject has been virtually non-existent. Still, given the complex way in which the multiplicity of storeys relates to issues of social structure, economy, status and environment, a better knowledge and understanding seems desirable, especially in the context of the rapidly increasing world population and the concomitant growth in housing demands, and shortage of land and resources that it entails.

Pile dwellings

Livingstone

Ciénaga
Grande

Delta Amacuro

Tonga

Chiloé

Chiloé Recorded location of one or more lacustrine dwellings

Ewe Recorded case of a cultural group using lacustrine dwellings

Distribution of pile dwellings

Areas affected by tropical climate

Among the most widely distributed forms of structural system in the world is the use of pile foundations. Pile dwellings, characterised by the use of timber posts and a raised floor that creates a void between the occupied structure and the ground, can be found throughout mainland and insular Southeast Asia, Melanesia, the Caribbean and coastal areas of the southern United States, parts of northern Latin America, and in isolated regions of Africa and inner Asia. In parts of China and Southeast Asia, the existence of pile dwellings has been traced back to Neolithic times.

Kanembou

Turkana

Luo

Chokwe

Bangkok

Bajau
Laut

Orang
Laut

Kampung
Air

Badjao

Motu

Port
Moresby

Pile dwellings are built in diverse locations, including open plains and forests, hilltops, slopes and valleys, by lakes and rivers, on coastal shorelines and also off-shore. Although also influenced by the availability of resources and defensive requirements, the contemporary distribution of pile dwellings mainly seems restricted to tropical areas. In hot and humid places, pile dwellings offer distinct advantages in terms of ventilation and cooling. Often used in combination with floors made of planks or bamboo slats, the pile foundations allow cool breezes to enter the house from below, simultaneously protecting the inhabitants against rodents, insects, snakes, wild animals and flooding.

In some places, pile dwellings are built over water. Often connected by jetties and walkways, such lacustrine dwellings, built over lakes, rivers or the sea-shore, may provide easier access to important resources such as water and fish, facilitate transportation between settlements and, in some cases, offer protection from enemies. Archaeological evidence supporting the existence of lacustrine dwellings in Neolithic times has been found throughout Europe.

Soil conditions influence the way in which the piles are placed. In many areas the posts are embedded in the ground, being inserted into post-holes that have been dug before. A common technique in insular Southeast Asia is to rest the piles on stones or, nowadays, concrete foundations. This makes the piles less vulnerable to rotting and helps to make it more resistant to earthquakes, which are very common in this part of the world. The height of the raised floor varies. Frequently the exposed length of the post is above head height, but lengths as low as 50 cm and as high as 10 m have been reported.

Community and multi-family houses

Multi-family houses
Community houses
Community houses (historical location)

World

In some societies, an entire village community may live in one or several houses only. In such cases, the house basically is the whole settlement, comprising both public and private space, and providing shelter to the members of a number of households. Each of these households, which may be nuclear or extended families, occupies a particular part of the building and will take part in its communal construction and maintenance. Though such community houses are becoming increasingly less common, they can today still be found in parts of Southeast Asia, Latin America and China.

Perhaps the most well-know example of a community house is the Southeast Asian longhouse. Found discontinuously throughout the region, in parts of Myanmar, Vietnam and Malaysia, it is especially widespread in Borneo. Typically the Bornean longhouse consists of a number of individually owned apartments, joined by a long gallery and sometimes a veranda. Believed to have originated because of defensive needs, various types of longhouse have been documented, indicating significant differences in details of form, structure and spatial layout.

Similar community houses combining private and public space in one building and housing the members of several families are found along the north coast of Latin America and in parts of the Amazonian basin. Other examples exist in isolated areas of New Guinea and, in former times, were found in both the northeast and northwest

of the United States. The Hakka in Fujian (China), the Pashtun in Pakistan and the Yanoama in Venezuela build large structures in which different dwellings form part of the same building, surrounding an open communal space.

Houses that provide shelter to various nuclear families, but that in contrast to community houses do not comprise a public space within them, also exist. Such multi-family houses are today mainly found in parts of mainland and insular Southeast Asia, especially Indonesia, as well as in parts of northeast, northwest and south India.

Community houses require a large investment in money, time and organisation to build. In recent decades their construction has become less common, with many peoples now opting for individual buildings that are often regarded as signs of wealth and modernity and allow for more privacy. Many of the community houses in New Guinea have disappeared. A great number of Bornean longhouses has undergone a similar fate, while many others have been modernised or divided into nuclear dwelling units. In contrast, new community houses are again being built among the Northwest Coast peoples in the United States, but these are mainly used for symbolic, ceremonial and functional purposes.

Bidayuh

Iban

Uut Danum

Borneo

Based on a map by Antonio Guerreiro and Léo Legendre

Western cultural zone

Central cultural zone

Highland cultural zone

Melanau cultural zone

Barito cultural zone

Murut (Sabah)

Kayang - Kajang

Melanau

Kelabit

Modang

Kenyah

Maloh (Taman)

Ngaju

Bungalow: diffusion

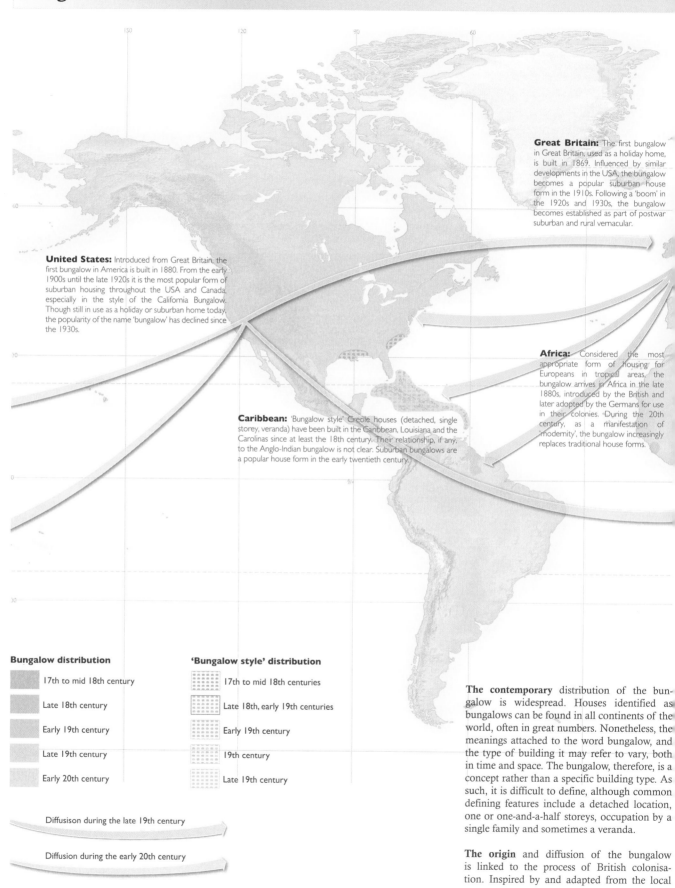

Great Britain: The first bungalow in Great Britain, used as a holiday home, is built in 1869. Influenced by similar developments in the USA, the bungalow becomes a popular suburban house form in the 1910s. Following a 'boom' in the 1920s and 1930s, the bungalow becomes established as part of postwar suburban and rural vernacular.

United States: Introduced from Great Britain, the first bungalow in America is built in 1880. From the early 1900s until the late 1920s it is the most popular form of suburban housing throughout the USA and Canada, especially in the style of the California Bungalow. Though still in use as a holiday or suburban home today, the popularity of the name 'bungalow' has declined since the 1930s.

Africa: Considered the most appropriate form of housing for Europeans in tropical areas, the bungalow arrives in Africa in the late 1880s, introduced by the British and later adopted by the Germans for use in their colonies. During the 20th century, as a manifestation of 'modernity', the bungalow increasingly replaces traditional house forms.

Caribbean: 'Bungalow style' Creole houses (detached, single storey, veranda) have been built in the Caribbean, Louisiana and the Carolinas since at least the 18th century. Their relationship, if any, to the Anglo-Indian bungalow is not clear. Suburban bungalows are a popular house form in the early twentieth century.

Bungalow distribution

- 17th to mid 18th century
- Late 18th century
- Early 19th century
- Late 19th century
- Early 20th century

'Bungalow style' distribution

- 17th to mid 18th centuries
- Late 18th, early 19th centuries
- Early 19th century
- 19th century
- Late 19th century

Diffusison during the late 19th century

Diffusion during the early 20th century

The contemporary distribution of the bungalow is widespread. Houses identified as bungalows can be found in all continents of the world, often in great numbers. Nonetheless, the meanings attached to the word bungalow, and the type of building it may refer to vary, both in time and space. The bungalow, therefore, is a concept rather than a specific building type. As such, it is difficult to define, although common defining features include a detached location, one or one-and-a-half storeys, occupation by a single family and sometimes a veranda.

The origin and diffusion of the bungalow is linked to the process of British colonisation. Inspired by and adapted from the local

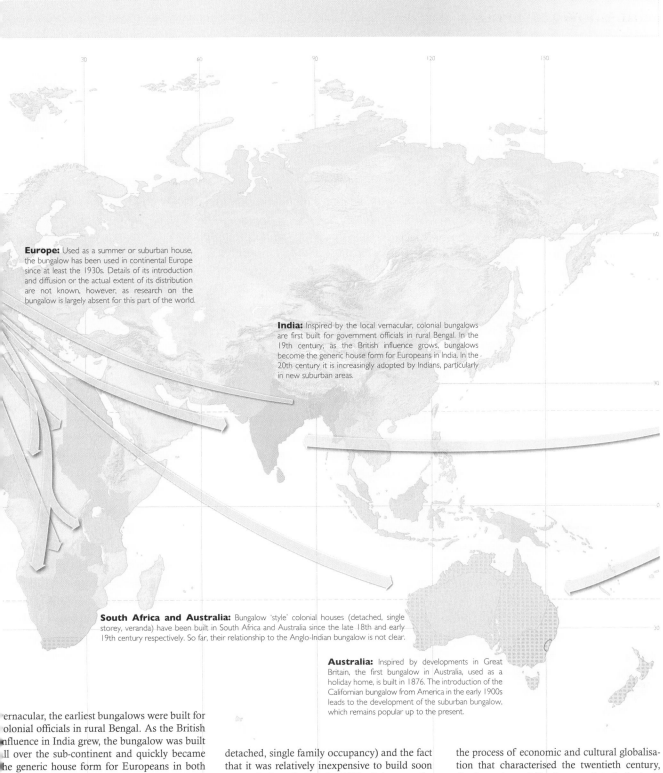

Europe: Used as a summer or suburban house, the bungalow has been used in continental Europe since at least the 1930s. Details of its introduction and diffusion or the actual extent of its distribution are not known, however, as research on the bungalow is largely absent for this part of the world.

India: Inspired by the local vernacular, colonial bungalows are first built for government officials in rural Bengal. In the 19th century, as the British influence grows, bungalows become the generic house form for Europeans in India. In the 20th century it is increasingly adopted by Indians, particularly in new suburban areas.

South Africa and Australia: Bungalow 'style' colonial houses (detached, single storey, veranda) have been built in South Africa and Australia since the late 18th and early 19th century respectively. So far, their relationship to the Anglo-Indian bungalow is not clear.

Australia: Inspired by developments in Great Britain, the first bungalow in Australia, used as a holiday home, is built in 1876. The introduction of the Californian bungalow from America in the early 1900s leads to the development of the suburban bungalow, which remains popular up to the present.

vernacular, the earliest bungalows were built for colonial officials in rural Bengal. As the British influence in India grew, the bungalow was built all over the sub-continent and quickly became the generic house form for Europeans in both urban and rural areas. In the late nineteenth century it was regarded as the most appropriate form of tropical housing and exported to other colonies in the Empire.

At around the same time, the bungalow was introduced from India to Britain, and from there to the United States and Australia. Initially used as a summer home because of its ideological associations with rusticity, space and nature, its physical and social characteristics (single storey, detached, single family occupancy) and the fact that it was relatively inexpensive to build soon saw to it that, during the 1920s, it became the most popular form of middle class home in a time of rapid suburbanisation.

Although bungalows have been built and used in Britain, the United States and Australia up to the present, its popularity in the last two of these countries declined from the 1930s, being overtaken by the larger ranch house. Since that time, however, the bungalow has been an increasingly dominant house form elsewhere. Facilitated by the process of economic and cultural globalisation that characterised the twentieth century, the bungalow, defined as a detached single storey house that generally accommodates one family, can nowadays be found in many parts of Europe, Africa and Southeast Asia, including India.

From its origins as an Anglo-Indian vernacular house type, the bungalow has thus developed into an international architectural concept, the diffusion of which represents the development of an increasingly global economy and culture.

Services & Functions

Dogon granaries, Mali. *Photograph: Paul Oliver*

Hygiene: sweat baths

Native American sweat lodges: Sweat bathing is a common tradition in many Native American cultures. Using either hot rocks and water or the direct heat of fire to create steam, various types of Native American sweat lodges can be found throughout North and Central America, including small temporary structures built of branches and skins, and large, permanent semi-underground lodges. The sweat lodge continues to play an important part in issues related to physical, mental and spiritual health.

Sauna: Finnish

Sweat lodge: Native American (hot rock type)

Sweat lodge: Native American (direct heat type)

Bania: Russian

Hammam: Islamic

Prescriptions and regulations about personal cleanliness and hygiene exist in all cultures. Often related to ideas about religion, health and fertility, as well as to climatic conditions and the availability of water, many distinct bathing traditions have developed throughout the world. Though it is universally recognised that hygiene, sanitation and health are interrelated, the frequency, regularity and thoroughness of these different ways of bathing is culturally determined

Finnish sauna: The sauna is an important part of everyday life in Finland. Commonly built of timber, it is found in a variety of sizes and types, and uses hot rocks and water to create steam. Though the main function of the sauna relates to bathing, it is also used for childbirth, healing and the smoking of meat. Its vernacular construction and related folklore and ritual are closely related to the Russian bath house (bania).

Russian bania can be found all over Russia and in those parts of Central and East Asia settled by Russians. Showing marked similarities to the Finnish sauna in terms of its construction and folklore, the bania is commonly used for bathing, healing and childbirth. In the late eighteenth century Russian colonists introduced the bania to North America, where it is believed to have influenced native Inuit groups in the Aleutians.

Islamic hammam: Communal sweat bathing has been common in the Middle East and Mediterranean since at least Greek and Roman times. The practice was incorporated into Islamic doctrine in the seventh century AD, leading to the development of public bath houses (hammam). Used for socialising, religious purification and healing, today hammam can still be found in Iran, Asia Minor and across North Africa from Egypt to Morocco.

Very much an individual experience in contemporary western society, in various cultures bathing is a communal affair, with people of different ages and sexes frequently bathing together. In many of these cases, dedicated buildings used to facilitate such communal bathing practices can be found. Although often in decline because of the individualising influences of urbanisation and modernisation, such communal bathing practices and the buildings that accommodate them remain important in many cultures today.

One of the most common forms of communal bathing is the sweat bath. Found throughout most parts of the colder regions of Northern America, Europe and Asia, as well as in large parts of the Middle East and Mediterranean, its best known example is probably the sauna. Closely related to this Finnish tradition is the Russian bath house (bania), which until the early twentieth century formed part of vernacular rural farmsteads throughout Russia and parts of Central and East Asia. Other widespread traditions are the Native American sweat lodge, found in large parts of North and Central America, and the Islamic hammam.

Throughout history, communal sweat baths often have been regarded as a threat to morality, health and hygiene. Thus in large parts of Europe, where the practice was once common, its use disappeared since the time of the Reformation. Elsewhere in the world, the Church and colonial governments have equally tried to abandon communal bathing practices, with varying success. Although the use of the bania and hammam has been in decline since the late nineteenth century, the Finnish sauna underwent a revival after World War II and is now in a modernised way used throughout the Western world. Among many contemporary Native American groups the sweat lodge to this day continues to be a vital social institution, playing an important part in purification and healing rituals.

Cooking and heating: open hearths, stoves and ovens

Recorded use (in the twentieth century) of:

Open hearths for cooking and heating

Enclosed stoves and ovens for cooking and heating

Hypocaust heating systems

The preparation and cooking of food are essential activities that, in all cultures, take place in, around or in the vicinity of the dwelling. Depending on the climate, the heating of indoor spaces may also be a recurring necessity. Both services are often closely related, as prevalent heating systems may be adapted to culinary pursuits or, in some cases, devices may have been explicitly designed for a dual purpose.

The most common vernacular cooking and heating device is the hearth or open fireplace. Regardless of climate or economy, the hearth is often central to the provision of heat and the cooking of food, and in many cultures is at the heart of hospitality and the constitution of social togetherness. Often it also serves as the primary night-time light source, making the husbandry of fire an extra essential part of the daily round.

Employed by humans since prehistoric times, the contemporary use of the hearth is widespread. Open fireplaces are used for cooking and heating purposes throughout most parts of Latin America, Asia, Southeast Asia and Africa, making their distribution near universal. During at least the first half of the twentieth century, their use has also been recorded in the United States, as well as in specific rural areas of Europe.

In various parts of the world, a desire for better controlled, longer burning, safer and less smoky cooking and heating devices led to the development of enclosed stoves and ovens. Throughout Europe, different kinds of brick, stone and tiled stoves and ovens have been in use since at least early medieval times, leading to the virtual extinction of open fireplaces. In

northern China and Korea, a unique hypocaust heating system developed, which utilises hot air that passes through a warren of flues embedded in brick structures.

From the sixteenth century onwards, the use of European enclosed stoves and ovens diffused to the United States and other colonies settled by Europeans, as well into the Caucasus and Central and Arctic Asia. In some of these areas, however, indigenous enclosed cooking and heating systems already existed. In many parts of the world, enclosed stoves or ovens of one kind or another are now used for cooking and heating, though often alongside open hearths.

Though essential in all cultures, vernacular cooking and heating systems have not received much attention in terms of research. In view of the safety issues related to the use of open fire, the implications of smoke and particulate matter in terms of health, and the predicted demise in fossil fuels, it nonetheless seems an important area for dedicated future study.

Smoke vents: chimneys and smoke holes

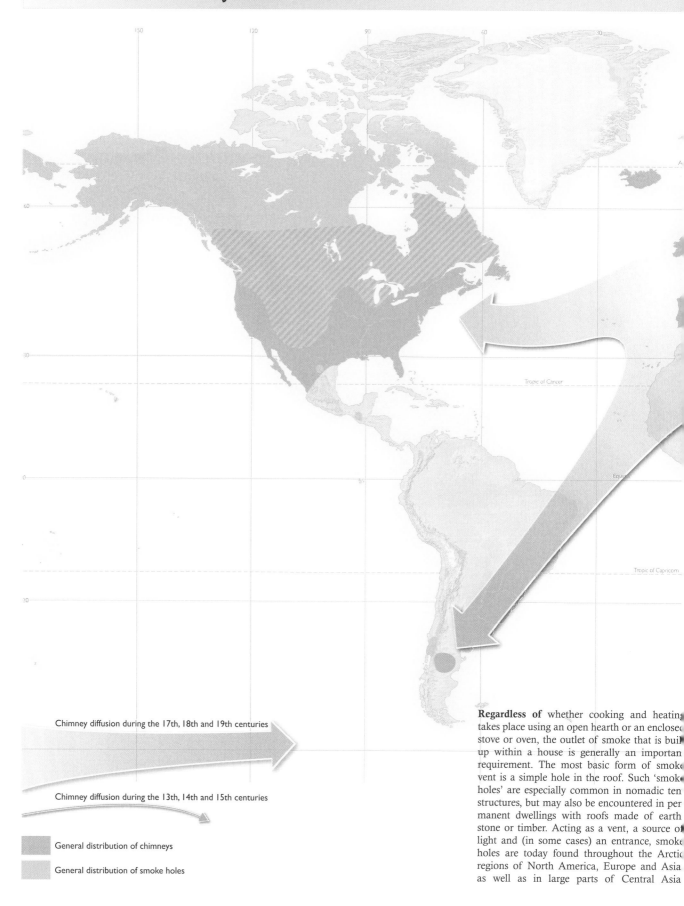

Chimney diffusion during the 17th, 18th and 19th centuries

Chimney diffusion during the 13th, 14th and 15th centuries

General distribution of chimneys

General distribution of smoke holes

Regardless of whether cooking and heating takes place using an open hearth or an enclosed stove or oven, the outlet of smoke that is built up within a house is generally an important requirement. The most basic form of smoke vent is a simple hole in the roof. Such 'smoke holes' are especially common in nomadic tent structures, but may also be encountered in permanent dwellings with roofs made of earth, stone or timber. Acting as a vent, a source of light and (in some cases) an entrance, smoke holes are today found throughout the Arctic regions of North America, Europe and Asia as well as in large parts of Central Asia

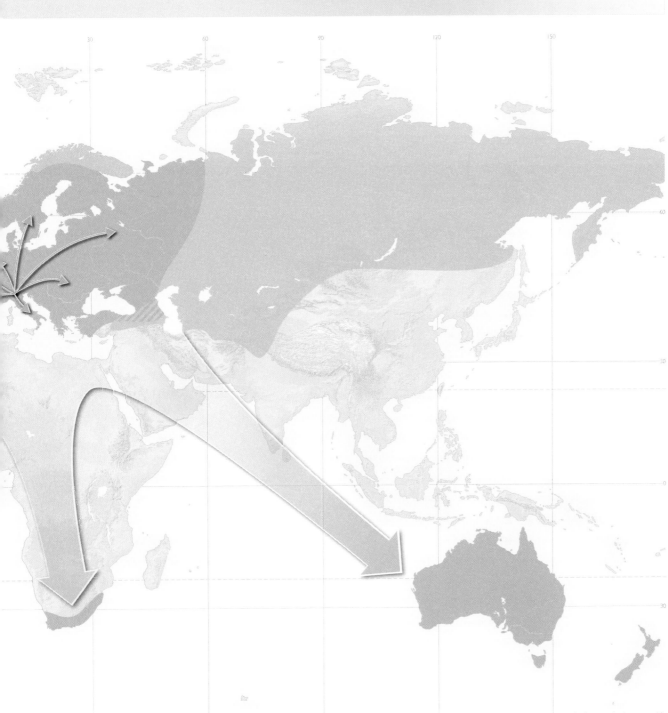

Up until medieval times, however, smoke holes were common throughout Europe. They co-existed with so-called 'hoods', conical structures made of wood or wattle and daub that fed smoke into a roof space, to escape through openings in the roof or gable. During the thirteenth century, both devices were superseded by the chimney, which was structurally connected to the heating source and as such represented a significant improvement in terms of the outlet of smoke. Initially introduced in northern Italy, the chimney quickly spread throughout Europe and, from there, to North America and parts of South Africa and Australia.

Today, a great variety of chimneys can be found in these parts of the world. As such, the distribution of smoke holes and chimneys is largely restricted to the northern hemisphere, both devices being virtually absent in Latin America, Africa and South and Southeast Asia. This absence is perhaps related to climate, seeing that warmer and tropical climates tend to dominate in the southern hemisphere. Smoke holes and chimneys are perhaps less needed in these areas because cooking often takes place outside or in separate structures, smoke has tended to function as an insect repellent and soot is sometimes valued as a fertiliser.

Still, much more research is needed to verify such hypothetical relationships, or indeed to come to a better understanding of the historical development of smoke holes and chimneys generally. As respiratory diseases, currently one of the main causes of infant mortality in developing countries, have been linked to poor indoor heating and regular exposure to particulate matter, research into the efficacy and performance of smoke holes and chimneys is also welcome. So far, despite the widespread distribution of both devices, such research has been extremely limited.

Ventilation and cooling: Middle East and Southwest Asia

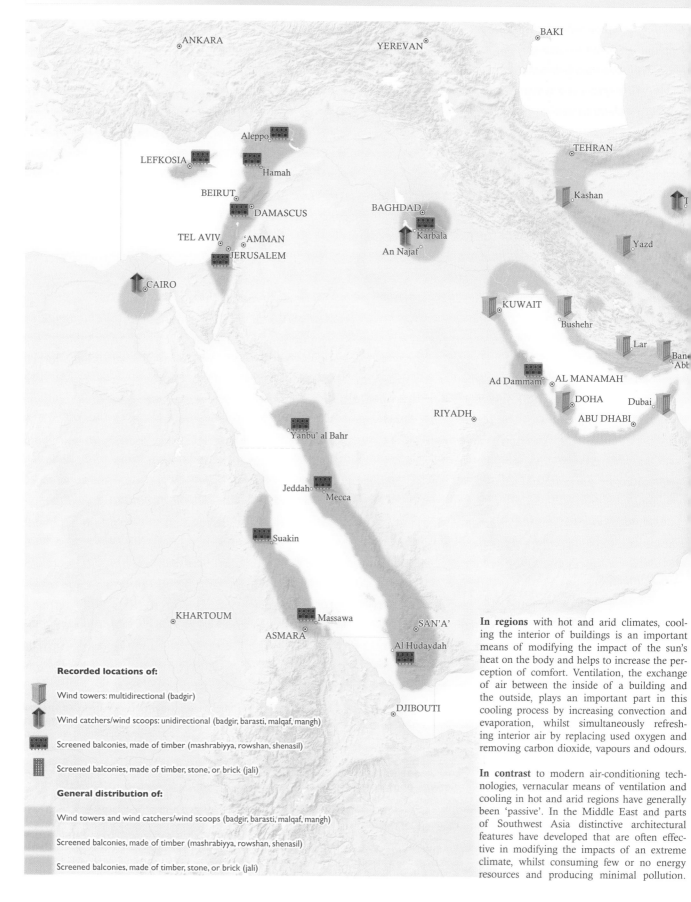

Recorded locations of:

Wind towers: multidirectional (badgir)

Wind catchers/wind scoops: unidirectional (badgir, barasti, malqaf, mangh)

Screened balconies, made of timber (mashrabiyya, rowshan, shenasil)

Screened balconies, made of timber, stone, or brick (jali)

General distribution of:

Wind towers and wind catchers/wind scoops (badgir, barasti, malqaf, mangh)

Screened balconies, made of timber (mashrabiyya, rowshan, shenasil)

Screened balconies, made of timber, stone, or brick (jali)

In regions with hot and arid climates, cooling the interior of buildings is an important means of modifying the impact of the sun's heat on the body and helps to increase the perception of comfort. Ventilation, the exchange of air between the inside of a building and the outside, plays an important part in this cooling process by increasing convection and evaporation, whilst simultaneously refreshing interior air by replacing used oxygen and removing carbon dioxide, vapours and odours.

In contrast to modern air-conditioning technologies, vernacular means of ventilation and cooling in hot and arid regions have generally been 'passive'. In the Middle East and parts of Southwest Asia distinctive architectural features have developed that are often effective in modifying the impacts of an extreme climate, whilst consuming few or no energy resources and producing minimal pollution.

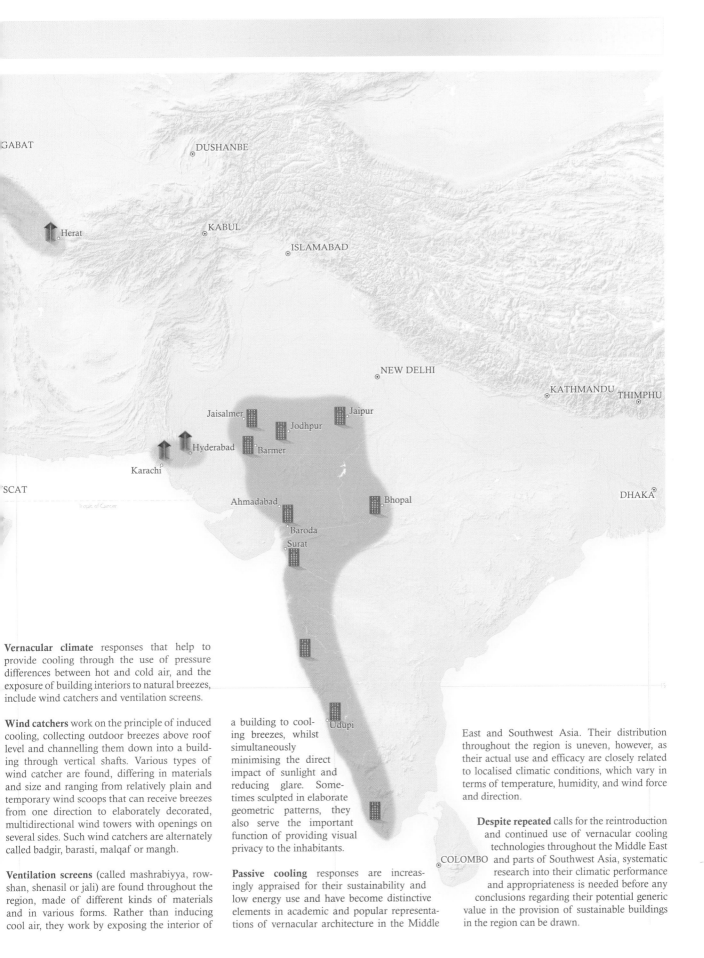

GABAT

DUSHANBE

Herat

KABUL

ISLAMABAD

NEW DELHI

KATHMANDU THIMPHU

Jaisalmer Jaipur

Jodhpur

Hyderabad

Barmer

Karachi

SCAT

Tropic of Cancer

Ahmadabad

Baroda

Surat

DHAKA

Bhopal

Udupi

COLOMBO

Vernacular climate responses that help to provide cooling through the use of pressure differences between hot and cold air, and the exposure of building interiors to natural breezes, include wind catchers and ventilation screens.

Wind catchers work on the principle of induced cooling, collecting outdoor breezes above roof level and channelling them down into a building through vertical shafts. Various types of wind catcher are found, differing in materials and size and ranging from relatively plain and temporary wind scoops that can receive breezes from one direction to elaborately decorated, multidirectional wind towers with openings on several sides. Such wind catchers are alternately called badgir, barasti, malqaf or mangh.

Ventilation screens (called mashrabiyya, rowshan, shenasil or jali) are found throughout the region, made of different kinds of materials and in various forms. Rather than inducing cool air, they work by exposing the interior of

a building to cooling breezes, whilst simultaneously minimising the direct impact of sunlight and reducing glare. Sometimes sculpted in elaborate geometric patterns, they also serve the important function of providing visual privacy to the inhabitants.

Passive cooling responses are increasingly appraised for their sustainability and low energy use and have become distinctive elements in academic and popular representations of vernacular architecture in the Middle

East and Southwest Asia. Their distribution throughout the region is uneven, however, as their actual use and efficacy are closely related to localised climatic conditions, which vary in terms of temperature, humidity, and wind force and direction.

Despite repeated calls for the reintroduction and continued use of vernacular cooling technologies throughout the Middle East and parts of Southwest Asia, systematic research into their climatic performance and appropriateness is needed before any conclusions regarding their potential generic value in the provision of sustainable buildings in the region can be drawn.

Ventilation and cooling: veranda

North America Introduced during the second half of the seventeenth century, the veranda is one of the most widely shared features of North American architecture. Nonetheless, the development of the 'porch' (as the veranda is here commonly referred to) remains a matter of debate, with several cultural origins and patterns of diffusion having been suggested.

Latin America and Caribbean The veranda has been in use in parts of Latin America and the Caribbean since the end of the seventeenth century, when it was introduced by the Portuguese and Spanish. Diffused throughout those parts of the continent that were settled by colonists, it is still a common feature of many vernacular traditions in the region.

The veranda, an open or partially walled, roofed and often slightly raised living area on the ground floor, is a feature of vernacular traditions in many parts of the world. Alternatively or simultaneously used for socialising, working, storage or sleeping purposes, it is generally found throughout North America, the Caribbean, Australia, China and India, as well as in large parts of Latin America, Africa and the Middle East. Though less common, verandas can also be found in isolated parts of Europe and insular Southeast Asia.

Distribution of the veranda

East and South Asia: Throughout large parts of East, South and Southeast Asia, houses are provided with verandas. As elsewhere, they serve a climatic function, providing access to or shelter from the sun, whilst also serving as spaces for socialising and storage. Though its origin may in some regions be related to European colonialism, in others the veranda seems to be an indigenous architectural feature.

Africa: Because of its climatic advantages, the veranda became a popular feature of African colonial architecture during the nineteenth century, quickly spreading through those areas of the continent that were settled by Europeans. The use of verandas on indigenous West African building types may be the result of colonial influences, but may also represent an independent architectural development.

Australia: The first veranda in Australia was built in 1793, shortly after the first colonial settlements were established. During the nineteenth century, it quickly became a common feature of Australian architecture, both in the town and country. Today the Australian veranda comes in various forms, materials and sizes, and is represented in a diverse range of building types.

The use of the veranda clearly relates to climate, although its actual function in modifying climatic influences may differ per region. In hot and humid areas it serves as a dry and shaded space where breezes can be obtained; cooling the house whilst at the same time protecting the walls, windows and inhabitants from the heat of the sun and torrential rains. In places with more temperate climates, it may instead be used to buffer the impact of the wind and provide access to or trap the sun's heat. In any case, in social terms, the veranda facilitates circulation between the outside and inside of a building, serving communication, hospitality and work purposes according to need.

Though common functions can be identified, the distribution of the veranda is characterised by an enormous variety in form, construction, location, enclosure and size. For example, a veranda may be integral to a building, forming part of the construction; or it may be built in addition to it. Similarly, it may be found on the back, front or side of a building only, or be multi-sided or even encircling. A lot of variety and confusion also exists with regard to nomenclature, with terms like porch, balcony or gallery alternatively being used as synonyms for veranda, or instead to identify a related yet different (e.g. upper storey) building element.

Although the word veranda has been found in use in Portuguese and Spanish as early as the late fifteenth century, the origins of the veranda as a building element are unclear and probably multi-cultural. The contemporary widespread distribution of the veranda is undoubtedly related to European colonialism, which facilitated its diffusion throughout America, Asia, Africa and Australia during the seventeenth, eighteenth and nineteenth centuries, in response to the climatic challenges presented by the tropics. Nonetheless, in China, New Guinea, and parts of Southeast Asia and Africa, the veranda seems to have been an indigenous building element that developed independent from colonial influences.

Outbuildings: granaries

Rectangular, earth or stone, not raised

Rectangular, timber, raised

Rectangular, earth or stone, raised

Circular, earth, raised

Circular, earth, unknown if raised

Circular, earth, not raised

Areas where maize, millet, rice or wheat are grown

In agricultural societies, dwellings are generally supported by other units. When such units are detached from the main dwelling, they are commonly referred to as 'outbuildings'. Outbuildings may be used for a variety of purposes, including the storage of crops, the housing of livestock and the processing of farm products. The type of outbuildings used by a culture and the actual form they assume depends on various factors, including economy and climate. Some types of outbuilding, like the granary and barn, are nonetheless widespread throughout the world.

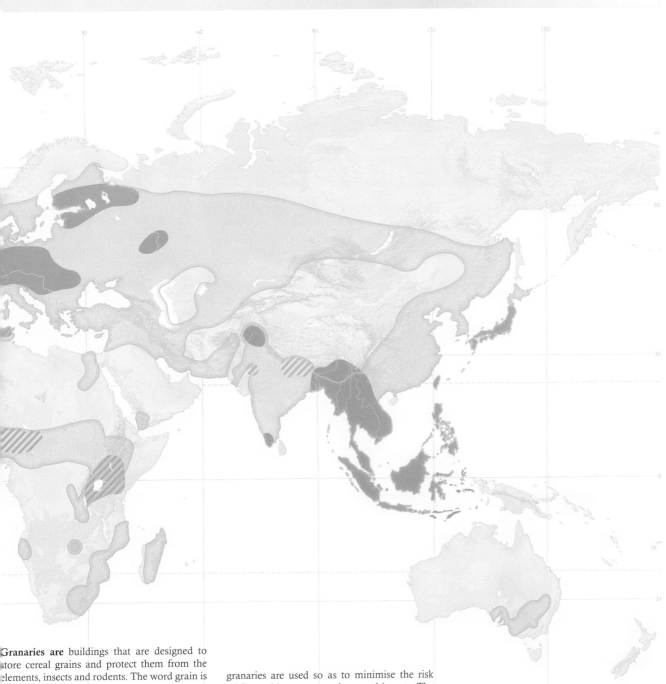

Granaries are buildings that are designed to store cereal grains and protect them from the elements, insects and rodents. The word grain is commonly used as an overarching term to identify a variety of crops including wheat, maize, oats, barley, rice, millet and sorghum. In large parts of the world, especially Asia, Africa and Latin America, cereal grains form an essential part of human diets. In Europe and North America the human consumption of grains is more moderate, though still substantial. Some grains, especially maize, sorghum and oats, are also important as animal fodder.

As seasonal crops, cereal grains need to be stored in dry conditions to allow for consumption the whole year round. In some cultures, this storage takes place in house lofts. More commonly, however, dedicated and detached granaries are used so as to minimise the risk of fire and keep away rodents and insects. The use of separate granaries has been recorded throughout Southeast Asia, Africa and Mexico, as well as, until well into the twentieth century, in parts of Europe and North America.

As a result of differences in climate, cereal type and harvesting methods, the variety in granaries in terms of their form, material, size and location is large. Circular plan earth granaries, used to store millet and sorghum, are common in large parts of Africa and are also found in Mexico, where they are used to protect maize. Timber granaries of rectangular or square plan are found throughout Southeast Asia and, again, Mexico, and used to be common throughout

North America and Europe. Stone granaries are still in use in Portugal and parts of Spain. In many cases, the granaries have been raised to minimise damp and deter insect and rodents.

In North America and Europe, changes in technology and transportation have meant that granaries are hardly used nowadays. Nonetheless, they are still essential to the storage of grains in large parts of Asia and Africa. More research is needed to document the distribution of the granary in relation to the cultivation of grains, as well as to understand its complex relationship to climate, materials and types of cereal.

Outbuildings: barns

The types of outbuildings that a community utilises depend on the kind of economy that it follows. In peasant or market economies, where crops are grown for domestic consumption as well as the market, the storage and processing of surplus agricultural products sometimes took place in barns. Frequently used to house farm equipment or animals as well, barns are mainly found in Europe and North America, as well as in some parts of the world settled by European immigrants. Because they house surplus crops, farm machinery and livestock, barns have often been regarded as embodiments of economic wealth and as such they may have a symbolic significance that goes beyond their utilitarian value.

Because of differences in climate, site, economy and function, a large variety of barn types can be identified. This variety relates to size, form, location, structural system, materials and the relationship of the barn to other buildings in the farmstead. In Europe, where many medieval examples today remain, barns were mainly used for the storage and processing of grains. Generally speaking they were detached from the dwellings in order to reduce the risk of fire, although in the Lowlands and parts of Germany houses and barns frequently formed part of one building. The barns were made of timber, stone or brick and were mostly equipped with large doors to allow for the easy access of wagons and carts.

Many European settlers in North America brought their barn traditions with them and adapted them to the local climate and environment. This process resulted in a great variety of American barn types, especially in the East, many of which are distinguished on the basis of their forms, structural systems, plans and ethnic origins. In contrast to their European counterparts, North American barns were generally used to house livestock as well as store and process grains. Commonly built of timber, they were most often detached from the farm dwellings to reduce the fire hazard. In the West in particular, where settlement took place later, barns sometimes assumed enormous proportions so as to be able to serve large herds of livestock.

function of vernacular barns changed duri the late nineteenth and early twentieth centur Improvements in transportation, the introdu tion of new storage technologies (refrigerato chemical preservatives) and the rapid expa sion of urban populations led to the emergen of mechanised ways of farming in whic industrially manufactured barns and sil replaced vernacular barns. Many barns ha had to make way for new developments, or hav been converted into houses, offices or touri accommodation. As a result, efforts to conser vernacular barns have increased significantly recent decades.

World

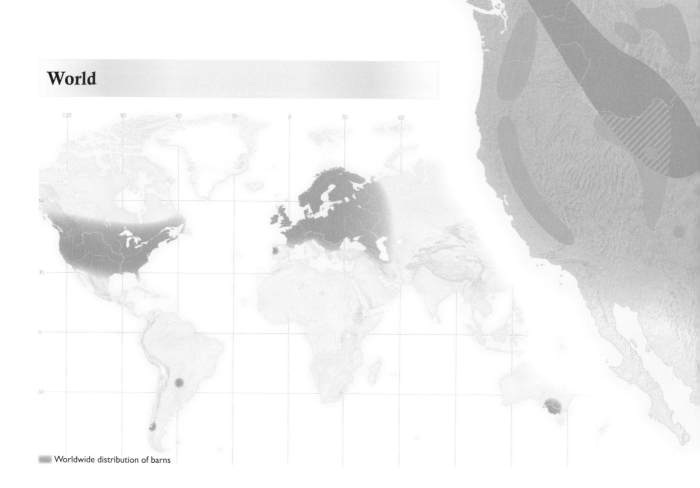

Worldwide distribution of barns

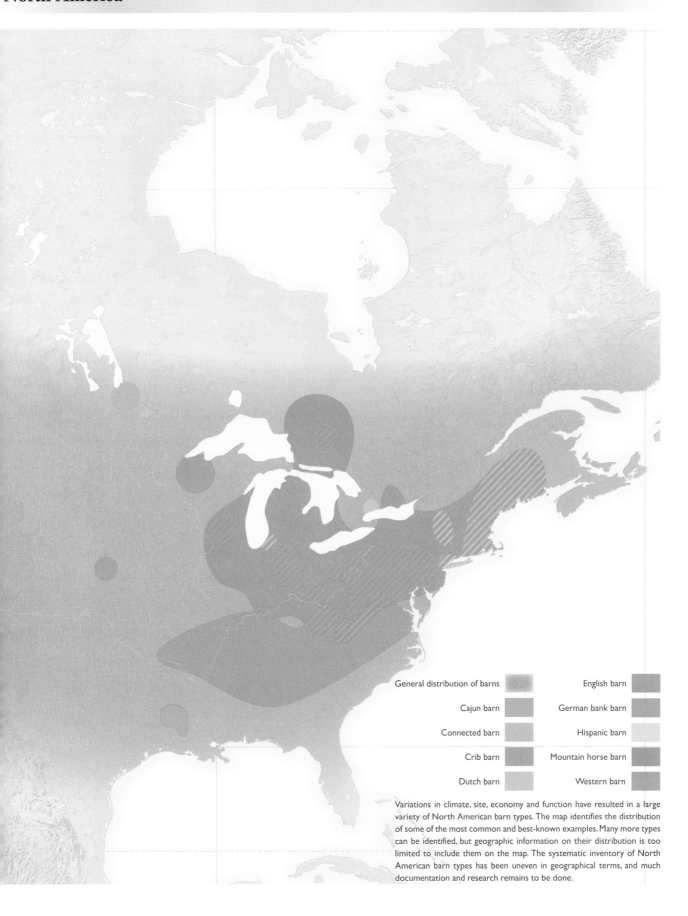

General distribution of barns		English barn	
Cajun barn		German bank barn	
Connected barn		Hispanic barn	
Crib barn		Mountain horse barn	
Dutch barn		Western barn	

Variations in climate, site, economy and function have resulted in a large variety of North American barn types. The map identifies the distribution of some of the most common and best-known examples. Many more types can be identified, but geographic information on their distribution is too limited to include them on the map. The systematic inventory of North American barn types has been uneven in geographical terms, and much documentation and research remains to be done.

Outbuildings: mills

The harnessing of water and wind power to drive millstones, grinders and pumps was one of the most significant technological advances in history, resulting in significant increases in productivity. The use of the watermill, first recorded around the beginning of the Christian era, developed from the animal powered noria system that has been used in the Middle East since at least 300 BC. The windmill was invented some 1000-1200 years later, in northwestern Europe and the Middle East. Today both water- and windmills can be found in large areas of Europe, the Middle East and the eastern United States, as well as in isolated parts of South Africa.

Various forms of water- and windmills exist, which mainly have been used for grinding grain, as well as irrigation, sawing or pumping. The earliest form of watermill is the horizontal mill, consisting of blades that are struck in a horizontal plane. Though once widespread, it has mainly been replaced by vertical watermills consisting of wheels that rotate around a horizontal axis. Horizontal windmills exist as well, in Iran, Afghanistan and China. Though such mills are also known to have been built in Europe and the United States, the vertical windmill is much more common here. Various types of vertical windmill can be distinguished, including the tower mill, the post mill and the smock mill.

The occurrence of water- and windmills relate to geography and climate. Watermills are usuall more powerful than windmills, but depend on strong water flow. As such, their use is mainl restricted to hilly regions with steep streams o rivers. In areas lacking such conditions, lik the Netherlands, East Anglia in Britain or th plains of northern Europe, windmills are mor effective. The use of different kinds of wind mill also depends on geographical and climati factors. For example, the wooden post mill i more common in forested parts of norther Europe than in the deforested Mediterranean European kinds of windmill are absent in th west of the United States because of light win speeds. Instead, annular and multi-bladed 'win engines' are common, as is also the case in par of South Africa, Latin America and Australia.

Having reached a peak from the seventeent century onwards, the importance of wate and windmills began to wane in the lat nineteenth century with the invention of steam engines. Although some mills in Europe an the United States are still active, most stan idle, whilst many have been demolished Nonetheless, preservation efforts in variou parts of the world have been successful i safekeeping many historical mills. Beside modern wind turbines used to generate clea electricity are increasingly popular, exemplify ing that the technology may still have much t contribute to the provision of sustainable futur built environments.

Smock mills, Kinderdijk, The Netherlands. *Photograph: Marcel Vellinga*

Watermills

Recorded use of horizontal and vertical watermills since:
- 300 BC to present day
- 100 BC to present day
- 500 AD to present day
- 1700 AD to present day

Windmills

Wind engines

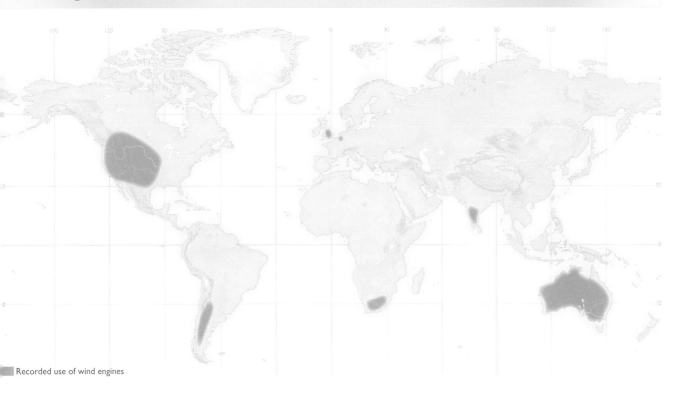

Recorded use of wind engines

Symbolism & Decoration

Wood Carving, Bernese Alps, Switzerland. *Photograph: Alex Bridge*

Colour decoration: exterior mural painting

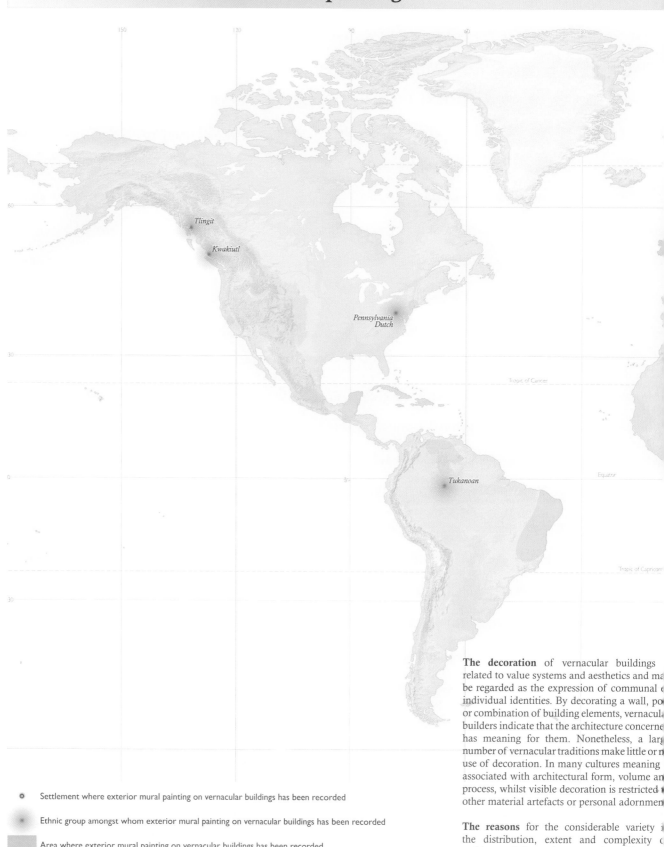

Tlingit

Kwakiutl

Pennsylvania
Dutch

Tukanoan

○ Settlement where exterior mural painting on vernacular buildings has been recorded

Ethnic group amongst whom exterior mural painting on vernacular buildings has been recorded

Area where exterior mural painting on vernacular buildings has been recorded

Area where colour-washing of vernacular buildings has been recorded

The decoration of vernacular buildings
related to value systems and aesthetics and ma
be regarded as the expression of communal o
individual identities. By decorating a wall, po
or combination of building elements, vernacula
builders indicate that the architecture concerne
has meaning for them. Nonetheless, a larg
number of vernacular traditions make little or n
use of decoration. In many cultures meaning
associated with architectural form, volume an
process, whilst visible decoration is restricted t
other material artefacts or personal adornmen

The reasons for the considerable variety i
the distribution, extent and complexity c
architectural decoration are various. The stru
tural limitations of resources appear to play
part, as some materials lend themselves mor

Lowicz
Tyrolean
EGYPT
Cooli
Rajasthan
Orissa
Nubian
Hausa
Lafofo
Igbo
Mangbetu
Karo Batak
Toba Batak
Minangkabau
Kenyah
Sa'dan
Toraja
Abelam
Trobriand
Islands
Tswana
Ndebele
/Pedi
Southern
Sotho

readily to decoration than others. At the same time, wealth and the nature of economies also play a part. Nomadic people who built temporary buildings are generally disinclined to embellish them. Overall, decoration is a feature of sedentary societies, whose members may have the wealth and time to concern themselves with architectural ornamentation.

The means by which buildings may be embellished vary and include carving, moulding, incision and painting. One conspicuous form of vernacular decoration is exterior mural painting. Although it is less common than the washing of external walls in uniform colours (common in parts of Latin America and Europe), distinctive traditions in which walls and facades are

painted on the outside using colourful motifs, patterns and designs are found in southern Africa, the American northwest coast, northern India, Indonesia, Ethiopia and Latin America.

In most of these cases specific building elements are painted (mainly walls and facades), and not the structure as a whole. The extent of decoration depends on form, materials, visibility and function. Even in the case of wall decorations it is unusual to find all walls of a building painted. As with other forms of vernacular ornamentation, the painted designs and motifs, which may include human, animal, floral and geometric forms, are commonly applied using rule systems or schemata. Random decoration is rare, if it is ever applied at all.

The decoration of vernacular architecture and the aesthetics related to it have generally not been subject to extensive research. Many questions regarding the distribution, application, transmission and recognition of painted ornamentations therefore remain unanswered. In-depth studies of local traditions and comparative analyses of their diversity, richness and meanings are needed to come to a better understanding of this important aspect of the vernacular.

Symbolism: motifs

Generically motifs are defined as identifiable indices or icons that are represented on buildings in two- or three-dimensional visual form. In vernacular architecture, they are commonly incised or painted and frequently appear in positions that emphasise their importance or singularity. Often used in decorative schemes, motifs may act as signs, symbols or both. They always have meaning and are rarely used for solely ornamental purposes. Their meaning, however, is multi-layered and dynamic: meanings depend on social and historic contexts and as such can be varied, lost or newly acquired. They may also remain undisclosed to outsiders.

The variety of motifs used in vernacular architecture is large. Nevertheless, many motifs are expressions of universal symbols that emanate from the shared human experience of natural phenomena. Concepts surrounding life, fertility and birth are important in all societies and are often represented through solar motifs. The sun is often depicted in relation to the moon, sometimes in binary opposition. Cloud and stellar motifs may also be used in association with the sun and moon, representing rain or life-giving water and the cycle of life respectively.

Associations with fertility and the rhythm of life are also common in the case of the spiral. Used in various parts of the world since Palaeolithic times, it may have many different meanings, according to where, how and by whom it is applied. Other motifs inspired by the natural world are vegetal, including leaves, flowers and the widespread 'tree of life'. In Islamic areas, the Koranic injunction to abstain from figurative representation has been a special incentive to the development of vegetal motifs, though in many cases the motifs have a much longer history.

Although the term does not define any particular shape, many vernacular motifs may be described as geometric. Geometric designs are drawn with straight or curved lines, either from one point to another or to enclose a graphic field. Subdivisions by diagonals or the joining of points can produce shapes that are echoed in many societies, often by the placing of linear intersections within square or circular fields. Widespread and common geometric motifs include the square, triangle, diamond and cross.

Many of the motifs used in vernacular architecture have ancient origins. This raises questions about the extent to which a compatibility of motifs indicates similar sources of inspiration, or relations through diffusion. Motifs and their meanings may migrate and be adopted, or change. The sources and diffusion of decorative motifs involves many factors. Like the study of vernacular aesthetics and decoration generally, research into the issue so far has been limited.

Vegetal motif, West Sumatra, Indonesia. Photograph: Marcel Vellinga

Geometric

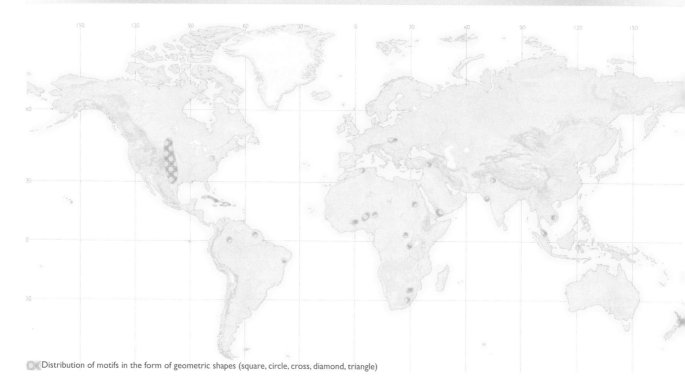

Distribution of motifs in the form of geometric shapes (square, circle, cross, diamond, triangle)

Natural

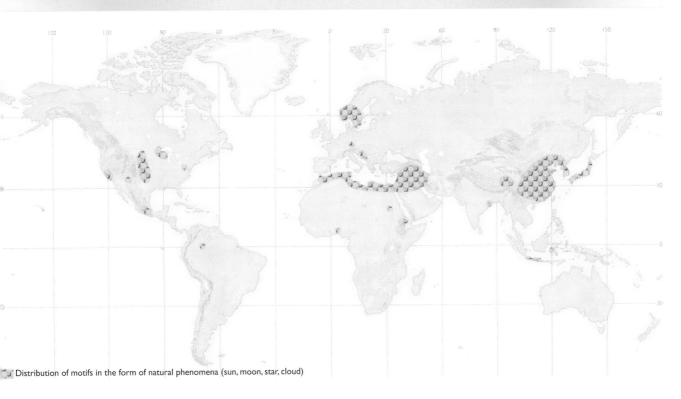

Distribution of motifs in the form of natural phenomena (sun, moon, star, cloud)

Vegetal

Distribution of motifs in the form of vegetation (spiral, flowers, leaves, 'tree of life,)

Decorated elements: roof finials

Wooden crossed horns, sometimes decorated

Wooden column, sometimes decorated

Woven thatch

Upturned pottery

Ostrich eggs

When a vernacular building has been decorated, the ornamentation is generally restricted
to specific elements rather than applied to the
structure as a whole. The selection of elements
is frequently an indication of the relative importance given to specific parts of a building or their
function, although factors like viewability and
accessibility also play a part. In many cultures
posts, bargeboards, doorways and structurally
important elements like brackets and tenons
are selected for decorative embellishment.

One distinctive form of ornamentation is the
roof finial, a decorative detail used to crown
a gable or, in the case of conical roof forms,
a peak. Decorative roof finials are found in
parts of Africa, Southeast Asia and Europe.
Although their variety in terms of form and

material is large, finials are generally employed for a combination of architectural, aesthetic and religious reasons, protecting the roof from leakage whilst simultaneously communicating status and warding off misfortune.

A widespread form of finial in Europe is a wooden column, decorated or otherwise, placed at the top of a front gable, sometimes above a wooden bonnet. Such gable finials also can be found in other parts of the world, for instance in east Africa, New Caledonia and New Zealand. Another common finial in Europe, dating back to medieval times, is formed by crossed beams covering the heads of roof laths. The ends of these crossed beams may have been carved in the shape of birds' or horses' heads.

Decorative gable finials in the form of crossed horns also recur repeatedly in large parts of mainland and insular Southeast Asia. Sometimes they consist of simple extensions of the rafters, but in other cases they may have been elaborately carved and shaped like birds', snakes' or buffalo heads. Often likened in local idiom to the horns of the water buffalo, they appear to serve a symbolically protective function and may act as an indicator of rank and status. Also found in parts of New Guinea, Madagascar and Japan, the relationship of the Southeast Asian crossed finials to their European counterparts is as yet unclear.

In Africa roof finials are generally attached to the peak of the widespread cylinder-cone houses. Made of various materials, including straw, wood, ostrich egg and horns, they function to hold the roof together and prevent the rain from entering at this point of high structural stress. In some cases, such as among the Kanuri or Nupe, upturned pots have been used for this purpose, a practice that has also been recorded in parts of Indonesia and Mexico.

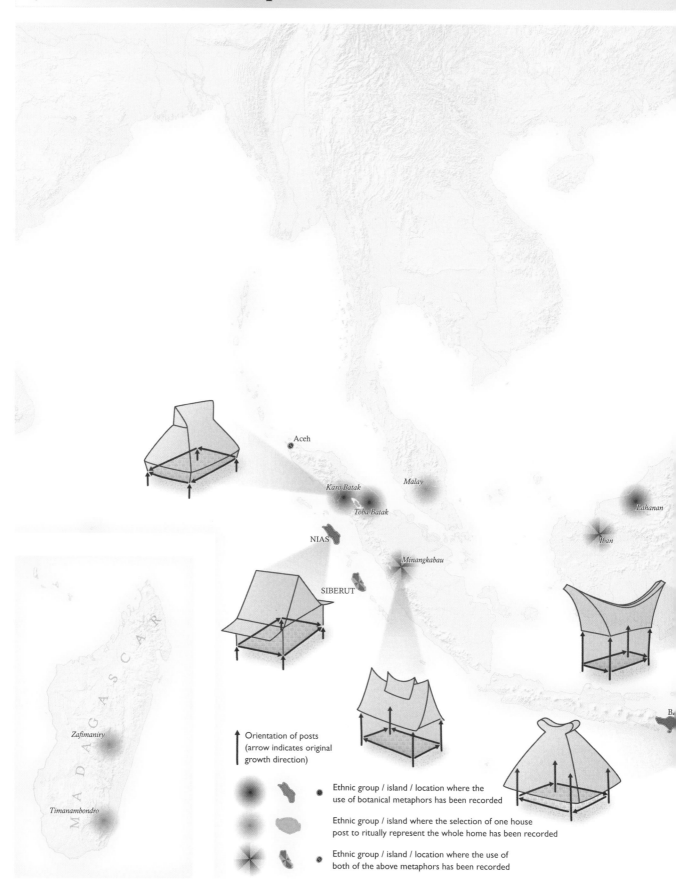

Aceh

Karo Batak

Malay

Toba Batak

Lahanan

NIAS

Iban

SIBERUT

Minangkabau

MADAGASCAR

Zafimaniry

B.

Timanambondro

Orientation of posts
(arrow indicates original
growth direction)

Ethnic group / island / location where the
use of botanical metaphors has been recorded

Ethnic group / island where the selection of one house
post to ritually represent the whole home has been recorded

Ethnic group / island / location where the use of
both of the above metaphors has been recorded

Throughout large parts of insular Southeast Asia, vernacular houses are commonly regarded as animate structures. The house, as a place for dwelling, celebration and the storage of ancestral property, is seen as a living entity that possesses a vitality of its own. The coming into being of this vitality (which is often referred to by the term semangat or one of its cognates) is elusive, but seems to take place through the process of construction, the rituals performed during this process and the animate qualities inherent in the timbers used for building. The intimate relationship between the house and the group of people associated with it also plays an important part.

The animate nature of the Southeast Asian house is symbolically expressed in the construction of the house, the naming of its parts and the social use of space. One pervasive notion is that the timbers to build the house need to be used according to their natural orientation. Hence, though examples of inversions exist, house posts generally need to be placed with their natural base side down, whilst in various parts of the region prescriptions exist regarding the proper use of timber in a horizontal plane. This botanical imagery, which refers to notions of origin, natural growth and precedence, is important in terms of the construction of the house and is related to the spatial use and movement within the houses. It is also expressed through the widespread practice to select one house post to ritually represent the house as a whole.

Though the use of house posts as 'ritual attractors' has been recorded since at least the nineteenth century, for a long time the prevalence of botanical symbolism went unrecognised by scholars studying Southeast Asian vernacular architecture. Since the 1970s, however, its application to the orientation of timber and use of space has increasingly been recorded throughout the region, especially in Indonesia. In recent years the hypothesis has been put forward that the use of botanical metaphors forms part of a cultural heritage that is shared by peoples whose language belongs to the Austronesian family. To verify this hypothesis, much more research would seem necessary to document its actual distribution throughout the Austronesian speaking world, outside of Indonesia.

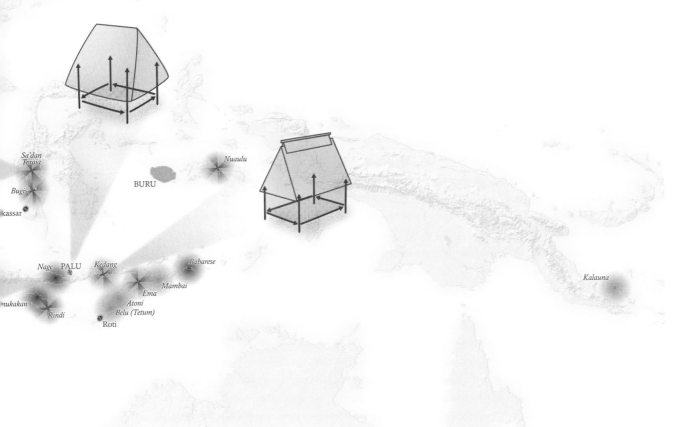

Development & Sustainability

Open air museum, Seurasaari, Finland. *Photograph: Paul Oliver*

Population growth

Percentage of population change 2000 to 2005

- 3.51% to 7.50%
- 1.51% to 3.50%
- 0.51% to 1.50%
- 0.01% to 0.50%
- 0.00% to -0.49%
- -0.50% to -1.49%

(Source: United Nations (2005): World Population Prospects:
The 2004 Revision, New York: UN Department of Economic and Social Affairs)

In 2005 the world population had risen to 6.5 billion. The vast majority of people, 5.3 billion (or 81 per cent), lived in what the United Nations defines as the 'less developed' or 'developing' regions, a category that comprises all countries in Africa, Asia (excluding Japan) and Latin America, as well as Melanesia, Micronesia and Polynesia. Almost half of this number (2.4 billion) was found in China and India alone. With 1.2 billion inhabitants, the 'more developed' regions including Europe, Australia and New Zealand, North America and Japan, accounted for the remaining 19 per cent of the world population.

Having steadily risen since the early twentieth century, the most recent predictions made by the Department of Economic and Social Affairs of the United Nations state that the global

population will continue to grow in the foreseeable future. In the medium variant, which assumes that fertility will decline from 2.6 children per woman to just over two, the world population will have reached 9.1 billion by 2050; an increase of 34 million a year. If fertility will not decline but remain constant, it will go up to 11.7 billion; if it were to decline more than expected, it may only go up to 7.7 billion. In any case, a significant increase in world population is likely to take place over the next fifty years or so.

Dependent on factors such as fertility, mortality and the HIV/AIDS epidemic, the demographic dynamics are nonetheless very varied. The vast majority of the population increase (95 per cent)

will be absorbed by the less developed countries, some of which will have seen their population doubled or even tripled by 2050. Even in the low variant, population growth in the developing world is likely to be robust. In contrast, the population of the developed countries as a whole is expected to remain virtually unchanged at about 1.2 billion. In fact, some developed countries will experience a decline in population or only see it remain constant because of immigration from developing countries.

The consequences of population growth for architecture are evident. The billions of people inhabiting the earth in the twenty-first century will all require housing, as well as essential

services like cooling, heating, ventilation, lighting and waste disposal. This demand for housing and servicing, which is unprecedented in history, has not yet attracted the amount of publicity paid to issues of health, food, poverty, climate change or the depletion of bio-diversity. It is nonetheless of similar importance and requires urgent attention. Given the fact that the vast majority of population growth will take place in those regions where vernacular traditions are still dominant, it would seem that the conservation, regeneration and development of vernacular traditions is essential to meet the future challenge of housing the world.

Urbanisation

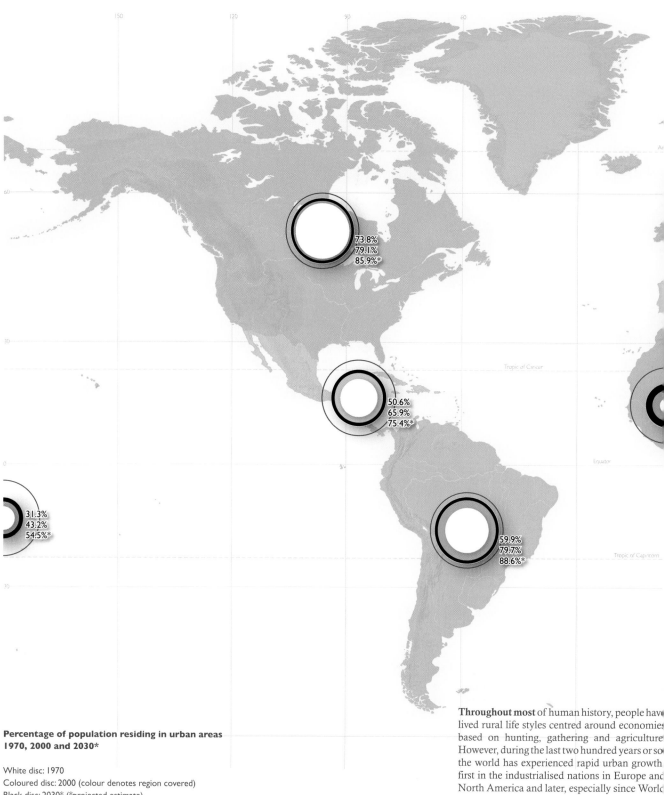

**Percentage of population residing in urban areas
1970, 2000 and 2030***

White disc: 1970
Coloured disc: 2000 (colour denotes region covered)
Black disc: 2030* (*projected estimate)
Adjacent figures give exact percentages in chronological order
The outer ring represents the entire (100%) population of the region

*(Source: United Nations (2004): World Urbanization Prospects: The 2003 Revision, New York:
UN Department of Economic and Social Affairs/Population Division)*

Throughout most of human history, people have
lived rural life styles centred around economies
based on hunting, gathering and agriculture.
However, during the last two hundred years or so
the world has experienced rapid urban growth,
first in the industrialised nations in Europe and
North America and later, especially since World
War II, in the developing countries in Africa,
Asia and Latin America. This unprecedented
process of urbanization is expected to continue
well into the twenty-first century. Virtually all
estimated growth of the world's population until
2030 is expected to take place in urban areas

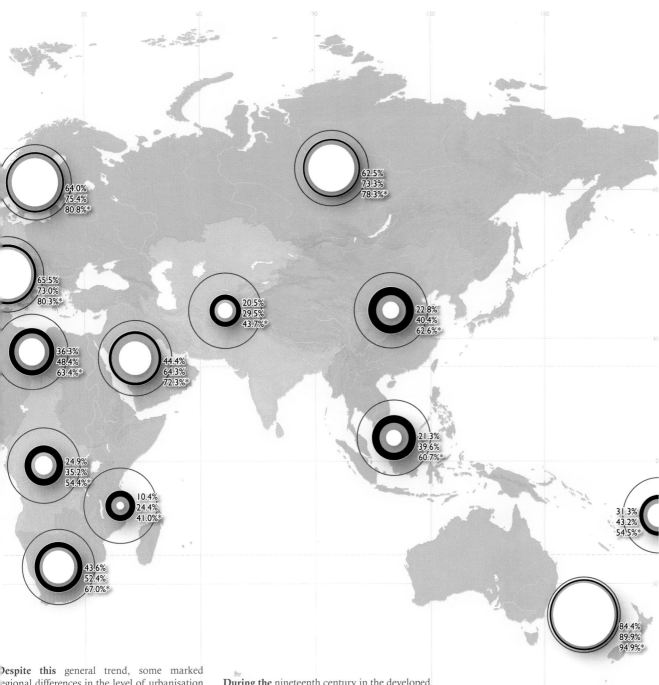

64.0%
75.4%
80.8%*

62.5%
73.3%
78.3%*

65.5%
73.0%
80.3%*

20.5%
29.5%
43.7%*

22.8%
40.4%
62.6%*

36.3%
48.4%
63.4%*

44.4%
64.3%
72.3%*

21.3%
39.6%
60.7%*

24.9%
35.2%
54.4%*

10.4%
24.4%
41.0%*

31.3%
43.2%
54.5%*

43.6%
52.4%
67.0%*

84.4%
89.9%
94.9%*

Despite this general trend, some marked regional differences in the level of urbanisation can be identified. Most significantly, the majority of the estimated population increase will be absorbed by the urban areas of the developing world; the urban population of the more developed world is expected to increase only slowly. At the same time variations can be seen between countries in the developing world. The level of urbanisation in Latin America, for example, is much higher that that in Africa (75 versus 38 per cent). Also, in many countries in Africa, the majority of urban citizens live in small cities of fewer than 10,000 inhabitants, whilst in Argentina 38 per cent of the urban population lives in the mega city of Buenos Aires alone.

During the nineteenth century in the developed world, the main cause of urbanisation was migration in response to employment opportunities created by rapid industrialisation. Today, in most developing countries, the vast majority of growth is attributable to high levels of natural increase within cities. In combination with migration from rural hinterlands (still a significant factor in many areas) and the increased popularity of international styles of building, this natural growth in many cases has contributed to the replacement of historical urban environments, acute shortages of housing, poor sanitation and the emergence of rapidly expanding informal settlements.

Nevertheless, urbanisation does not necessarily lead to the wholesale destruction of vernacular building traditions. Formal housing policies are often determined by local circumstances and may as such contribute to the continuation of distinctive architectural forms. Furthermore, in many countries, migrants retain strong roots with their rural homelands. Frequently these ties find expression in the persistence of ethnic or village identities, resulting in marked spatial patterns and divisions within urban areas and an interspersing of rural and modern building types that in turn may result in the emergence of new urban vernaculars.

Squatter settlements

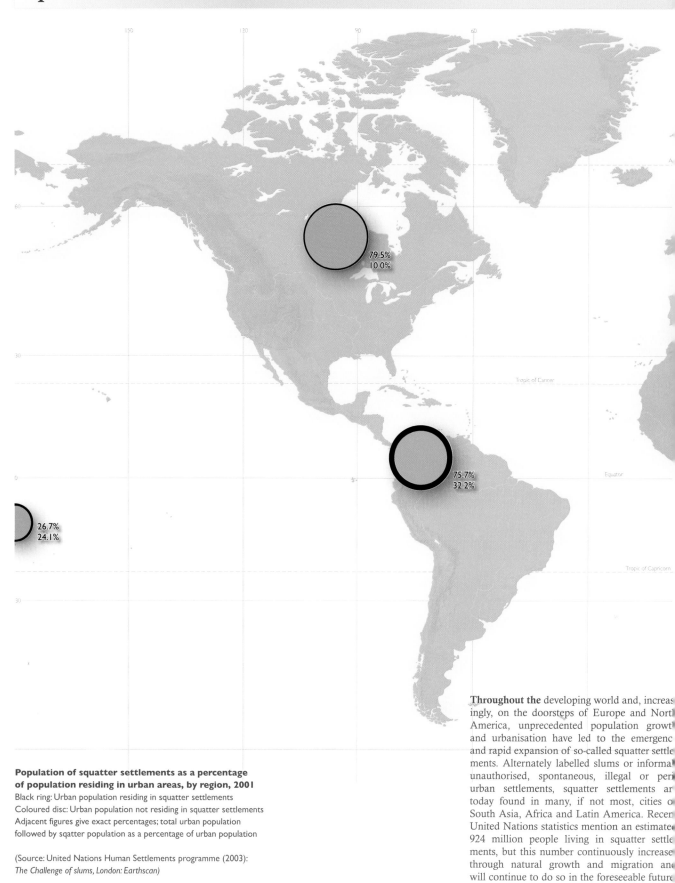

79.5%
10.0%

75.7%
32.2%

26.7%
24.1%

**Population of squatter settlements as a percentage
of population residing in urban areas, by region, 2001**
Black ring: Urban population residing in squatter settlements
Coloured disc: Urban population not residing in squatter settlements
Adjacent figures give exact percentages; total urban population
followed by sqatter population as a percentage of urban population

(Source: United Nations Human Settlements programme (2003):
The Challenge of slums, London: Earthscan)

Throughout the developing world and, increasingly, on the doorsteps of Europe and North
America, unprecedented population growth
and urbanisation have led to the emergence
and rapid expansion of so-called squatter settlements. Alternately labelled slums or informal,
unauthorised, spontaneous, illegal or peri-
urban settlements, squatter settlements are
today found in many, if not most, cities of
South Asia, Africa and Latin America. Recent
United Nations statistics mention an estimated
924 million people living in squatter settlements, but this number continuously increases
through natural growth and migration and
will continue to do so in the foreseeable future.

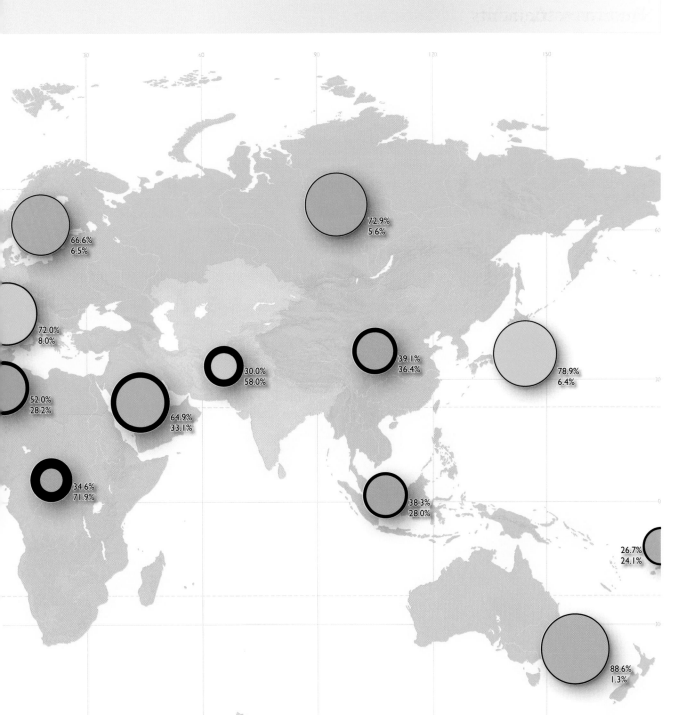

66.6%
6.5%

72.9%
5.6%

72.0%
8.0%

52.0%
28.2%

64.9%
33.1%

30.0%
58.0%

39.1%
36.4%

78.9%
6.4%

34.6%
71.9%

38.3%
28.0%

26.7%
24.1%

88.6%
1.3%

Definitions of squatter settlements vary and regional differences in patterns and developments make it difficult to define universally applicable criteria. Nonetheless, some common attributes can be indicated, such as a lack of basic services, a high population density, high levels of poverty and social exclusion, and insecure land tenure. Substandard and illegal housing is another common characteristic, most squatter construction being peripheral, makeshift, self-built from urban waste and perpetually threatened with demolition. In combination, these attributes have made the problem of squatter settlements one of the biggest challenges faced by the global community today.

Because of the informal nature of squatter settlements, accurate statistics on their distribution, density and characteristics are not available. Estimates nonetheless have been undertaken by the United Nations Human Settlements Programme, based on available census and household survey data. These estimates indicate that in 2001 about 32 per cent of the urban population of the world lived in squatter settlements. Most of these squatter settlements (sixty per cent) were found in cities in south and eastern Asia. Africa and Latin America accounted for twenty and fourteen per cent respectively, but the number of squatters in these continents is growing rapidly.

Governmental responses to the challenge of squatter settlements have ranged from bulldozing to the implementing upgrading programmes. In the case of the latter, many successful projects have been run in various parts of the world, even though debates about whether upgrading programmes consolidate or even exploit the problem continue. The accumulated vernacular knowledge and experience of the inhabitants of the settlements may play an important part in these upgrading programmes, alongside modern technologies, servicing and infrastructure. More research is needed, however, to establish the utility of vernacular traditions in relation to solving the problem of squatter settlements.

Resources depletion: deforestation

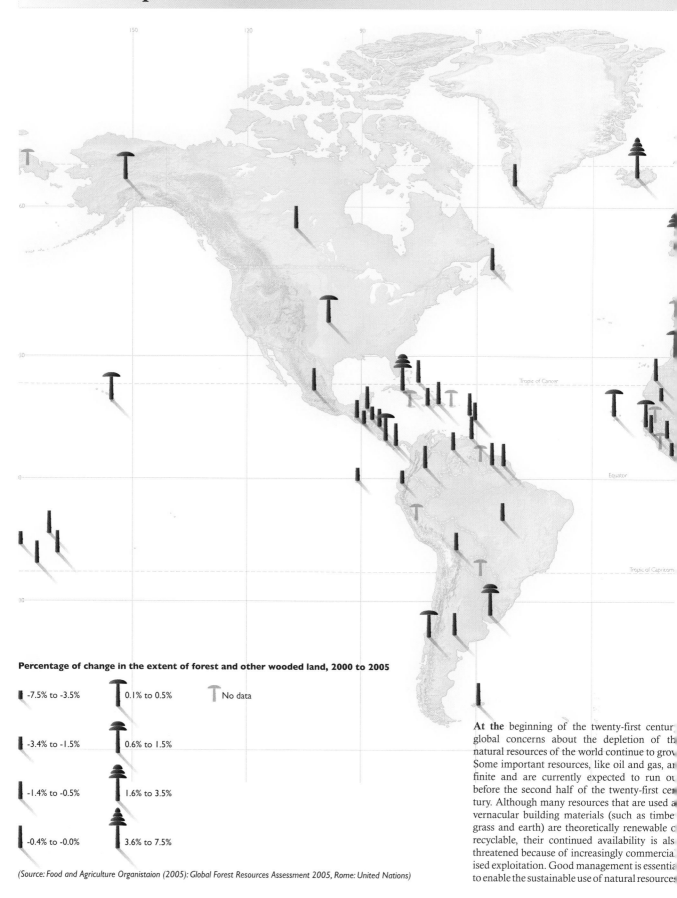

Percentage of change in the extent of forest and other wooded land, 2000 to 2005

-7.5% to -3.5%   0.1% to 0.5%   No data

-3.4% to -1.5%   0.6% to 1.5%

-1.4% to -0.5%   1.6% to 3.5%

-0.4% to -0.0%   3.6% to 7.5%

(Source: Food and Agriculture Organistaion (2005): Global Forest Resources Assessment 2005, Rome: United Nations)

At the beginning of the twenty-first centur
global concerns about the depletion of th
natural resources of the world continue to grov
Some important resources, like oil and gas, ar
finite and are currently expected to run ou
before the second half of the twenty-first cen
tury. Although many resources that are used a
vernacular building materials (such as timbe
grass and earth) are theoretically renewable c
recyclable, their continued availability is als
threatened because of increasingly commercia
ised exploitation. Good management is essentia
to enable the sustainable use of natural resources

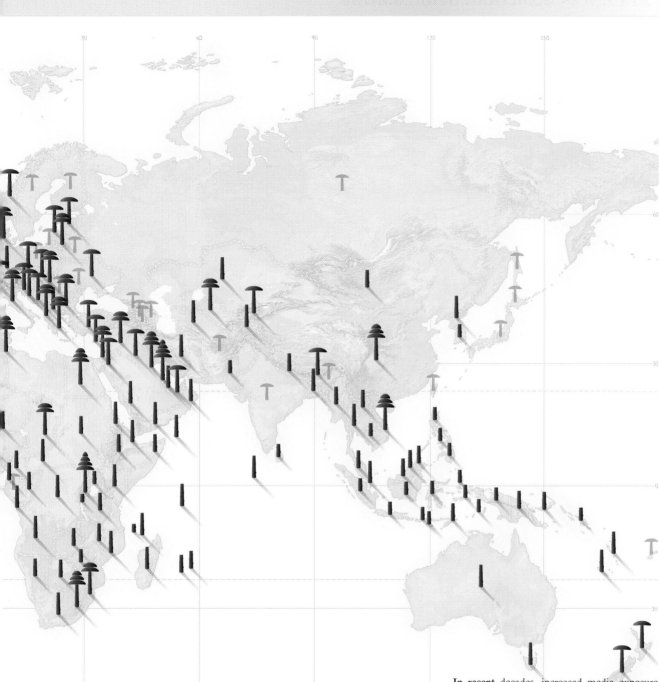

ne of the most common and durable vernacu-
r building materials is timber. Its importance
flects the widespread distribution of forests,
hich today still cover thirty per cent of the
tal land area of the world. Nonetheless, the
tal forest area has been decreasing at an alarm-
gly high rate in recent decades. Although
gional variations are large, on average about
3 million hectares of forest were lost per year
uring the period 2000-2005. Most of this
eforestation takes place in tropical areas and
the result of the conversion of forests to
gricultural land. The demand for wood as
uilding material and as source of fuel plays an
nportant part as well.

The ecological impacts of deforestation include
a loss of bio-diversity and the erosion of soils,
which in turn has increased the occurrence
of floods, landslides and avalanches. In social
terms, it threatens the cultural survival of indigenous peoples whose economy depends on the
exploitation of forest resources. All of these
impacts relate to the development and sustainability of vernacular traditions. The loss of
durable timber in many regions has meant that
traditional materials can no longer be used and
alternative technologies have to be employed.
On the other hand, the commercialisation of
the timber trade has meant that many species
of timber have become more widely available as
building material.

In recent decades, increased media exposure
and focused research efforts have led to a greater
awareness and understanding of the problem of
deforestation. As a result, national and local
governments, international organizations and
citizen groups have initiated many conservation
and reforestation projects. These have resulted
in a slowing down of the rate of net loss, though
not necessarily in an increase in bio-diversity.
Important work has also been done to help
vernacular builders adapt to situations in which
timber is no longer available as a building material. However, much more research still needs to
be done to help support the sustainable management and exploitation of timber and to assess
the role that vernacular knowledge and skills
may play in it.

Natural disasters: earthquakes

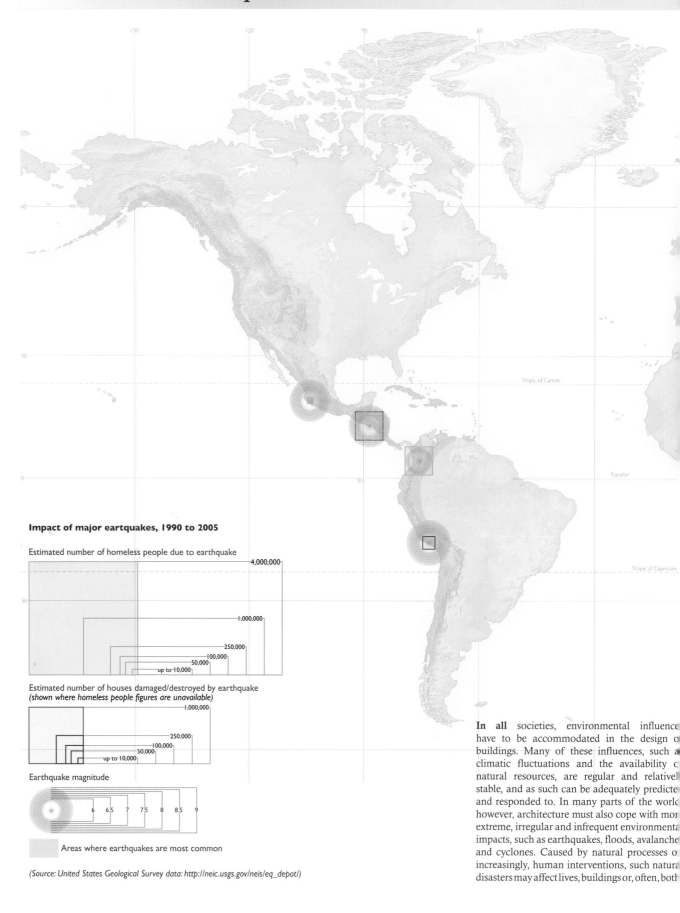

Impact of major eartquakes, 1990 to 2005

Estimated number of homeless people due to earthquake

4,000,000

1,000,000

250,000

100,000

50,000

up to 10,000

Estimated number of houses damaged/destroyed by earthquake
(shown where homeless people figures are unavailable)

1,000,000

250,000

100,000

50,000

up to 10,000

Earthquake magnitude

6   6,5   7   7,5   8   8,5   9

Areas where earthquakes are most common

(Source: United States Geological Survey data: http://neic.usgs.gov/neis/eq_depot/)

In all societies, environmental influence have to be accommodated in the design o buildings. Many of these influences, such a climatic fluctuations and the availability o natural resources, are regular and relativel stable, and as such can be adequately predicte and responded to. In many parts of the worl however, architecture must also cope with mor extreme, irregular and infrequent environmenta impacts, such as earthquakes, floods, avalanche and cyclones. Caused by natural processes o increasingly, human interventions, such natura disasters may affect lives, buildings or, often, bot

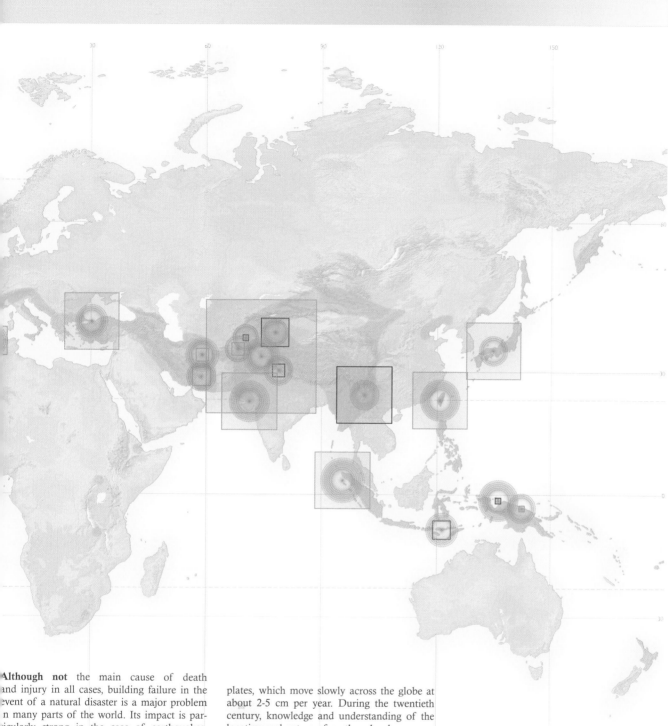

Although not the main cause of death and injury in all cases, building failure in the event of a natural disaster is a major problem in many parts of the world. Its impact is particularly strong in the case of earthquakes, which result from the release of tectonic energy through volcanic activity or shifts in the earth's crust. Involving the fracturing and shaking of ground surfaces and, sometimes, the transformation of stable soils into a muddy liquid state, earthquakes frequently cause unresistant buildings to collapse or sink. Secondary hazards caused by earthquakes include fire, avalanches, floods and tsunamis.

Varying in terms of their magnitude and impact, earthquakes mainly take place along the boundaries of the earth's continental plates, which move slowly across the globe at about 2-5 cm per year. During the twentieth century, knowledge and understanding of the location and nature of earthquakes has grown rapidly, resulting in sophisticated seismic reading and warning systems. Nonetheless, it is still impossible to accurately predict the time, place or severity of earthquakes and as such, their destructive impacts remain significant. Every year tens of thousands of people lose their lives in an earthquake, whilst hundreds of thousands are left homeless because their houses have been damaged or destroyed.

In many parts of the world, vernacular builders have developed strategies and technologies to prepare for the impacts of earthquakes.

These include the selection of resistant building materials, the avoidance of unsafe sites and the modification of structural systems. The importance of this vernacular knowledge is increasingly recognised by international donors. In a time when the combined effects of climate change, urbanisation and rapid population growth continue to increase the destructive impacts of natural disasters, more research is needed into the way in which this knowledge may be put to good use in the reconstruction of towns and villages, and in the design and development of new buildings.

Conservation: open air museums

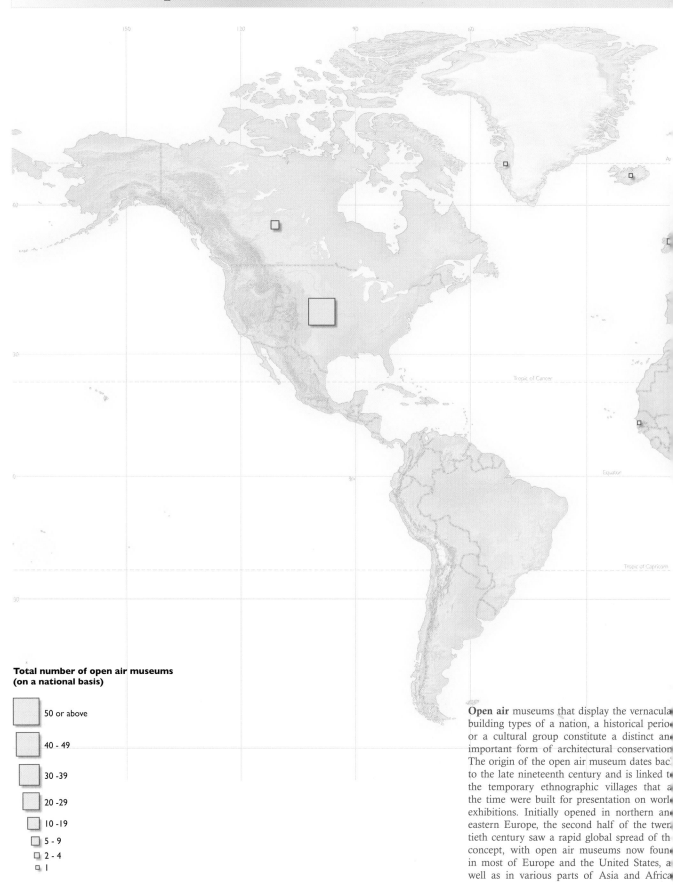

**Total number of open air museums
(on a national basis)**

- 50 or above
- 40 - 49
- 30 -39
- 20 -29
- 10 -19
- 5 - 9
- 2 - 4
- 1

Open air museums that display the vernacula
building types of a nation, a historical perio
or a cultural group constitute a distinct an
important form of architectural conservation
The origin of the open air museum dates bac
to the late nineteenth century and is linked t
the temporary ethnographic villages that a
the time were built for presentation on worl
exhibitions. Initially opened in northern an
eastern Europe, the second half of the twer
tieth century saw a rapid global spread of th
concept, with open air museums now foun
in most of Europe and the United States, a
well as in various parts of Asia and Africa

The development and diffusion of the open air museum concept reflects a growing interest in the conservation of building traditions that since the late nineteenth century have been increasingly threatened by the impacts of modernisation and globalisation. Housing buildings that have been relocated to avoid deterioration or destruction, the open air museum plays an important part in the preservation of vernacular architecture. Exhibiting the vernacular buildings of a particular region or nation (or replicas of them) in a park or recreated village setting, it helps to complement the conservation of building traditions in situ and raises the awareness and understanding of their significance and value.

At the same time, the worldwide popularity of the open air museum can be explained by its ideological entanglement. Although some museums exhibit building traditions from all over the world, most display buildings associated with particular regions, periods, countries or cultures. In many of these cases, the vernacular traditions are used to demonstrate collective relatedness and solidarity, the museum and the buildings in it becoming symbols of the nation, culture, ethnic group or religious community. This ideological component is still very strong in some of the Asian and African examples, and played an important part in the development of the concept in nineteenth century Europe.

Despite its important role in terms of conservation and education, the open air museum concept has been subject to much criticism. Consisting of buildings that have been removed from their original location, or comprising houses that have been newly built for the purpose of exhibition, the authenticity of the representation of vernacular architecture has been questioned. Open air museums have been accused of presenting artificial, sanitised and misleading images of vernacular traditions. In recent years, in response to this criticism, the concept of the ecomuseum in which buildings are left in situ and are conserved within their natural and social context, has been developed.

Conservation: world heritage sites

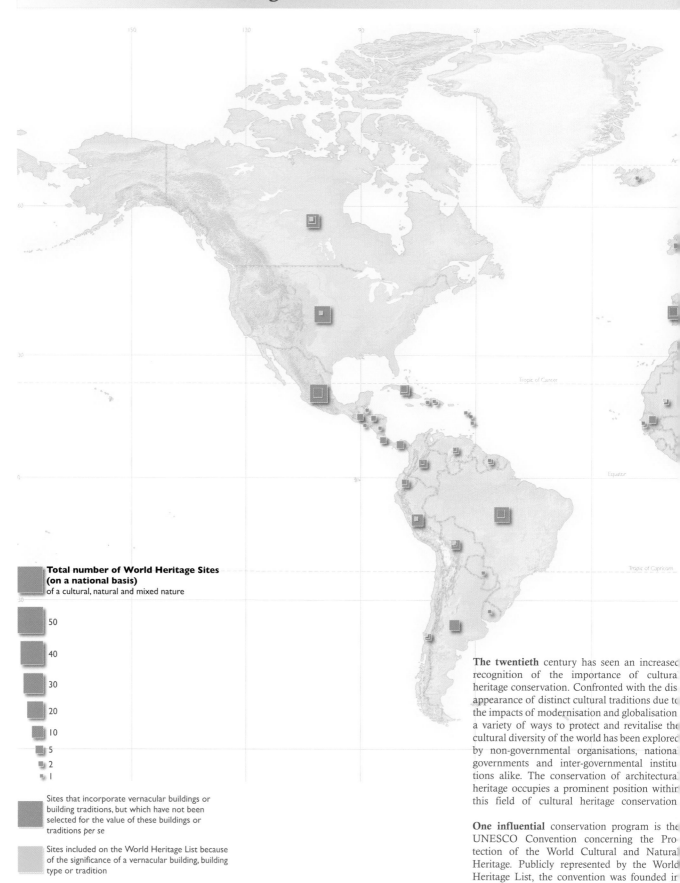

Total number of World Heritage Sites (on a national basis)
of a cultural, natural and mixed nature

50

40

30

20

10

5

2

1

Sites that incorporate vernacular buildings or building traditions, but which have not been selected for the value of these buildings or traditions *per se*

Sites included on the World Heritage List because of the significance of a vernacular building, building type or tradition

The twentieth century has seen an increased recognition of the importance of cultural heritage conservation. Confronted with the disappearance of distinct cultural traditions due to the impacts of modernisation and globalisation, a variety of ways to protect and revitalise the cultural diversity of the world has been explored by non-governmental organisations, national governments and inter-governmental institutions alike. The conservation of architectural heritage occupies a prominent position within this field of cultural heritage conservation.

One influential conservation program is the UNESCO Convention concerning the Protection of the World Cultural and Natural Heritage. Publicly represented by the World Heritage List, the convention was founded in

972 by UNESCO, with the aim of identifying, safeguarding and transmitting, through international co-operation and supervision, the most outstanding natural and cultural heritage of the world. Respecting national sovereignty, the convention lacks real executive power and mainly acts as a catalyst to raise awareness about the importance of heritage conservation.

To date, the World Heritage Convention has been signed by 178 nations or State Parties. Each nation has prepared a list of sites which it can nominate for inscription on the World Heritage List. After it has received evaluations and recommendations from its advisory bodies (ICOMOS, IUCN and ICCROM), the World Heritage Committee decides if it will inscribe

a nominated site on the World Heritage List. As from July 2004, there were 788 sites on the World Heritage List, 611 of which were cultural, 154 natural and 23 mixed.

Providing evaluations and recommendations to the World Heritage Committee, the advisory bodies exert a major influence on the inscription of sites. However, because a site will have to have been nominated by a State Party before it can be inscribed, the selection of World Heritage Sites ultimately reflects the attitudes and interests of the nations that adhere to the World Heritage Convention, revealing which parts of their national heritage they regard as being of outstanding universal value and worthy of extra protection.

In view of its numerical prominence and threatened status in many parts of the world, vernacular architecture seems underrepresented on the List. This is particularly clear when compared to the inscription of archaeological sites or works of monumental architecture and reveals the ambiguous status of vernacular architecture in many parts of the world. In 1994, recognising the thematic and regional biases inherent in the World Heritage Convention, the World Heritage Committee adopted a Global Strategy for a Representative World Heritage List to encourage the nomination of sites in underrepresented categories and parts of the world.

Hay-drying frame (kozalec), Slovenia. *Photograph: Paul Oliver*

Afterword

Although this is an afterword to the *Atlas of Vernacular Architecture of the World* (AVAW) it is not a conclusion. Many issues arise from the study and research that has been undertaken, which relate to the content of the maps, their application and the fields where, with further research, new maps can, and should, be created. The question as to who will be interested in the maps, and who will find the maps useful, is clearly one that may have many answers. Those who study vernacular traditions regionally may be surprised by the cross-cultural nature of some architectural features, as well as the more specialised focus of others. For example, the use of posts, piers and stilts to support houses and granaries is very widespread across three continental regions, but the reasons may be varied, being a matter of traditional associations of height with status, or a means of defence and protection. Alternatively, it may be one of cooling in increased shade, of safeguard against the risk of flooding, the avoidance of mosquitoes or the repelling of rodents.

When speaking of vernacular architecture we are mainly referring to built structures, even if these may be temporarily erected or raised by nomads for dismantling the following day. As dwellings or other accommodations they assume geometrical forms and these have been discussed and mapped. It is noteworthy that cylindrical, conical or pitched roof forms may be evident in both permanent buildings and in tents, which draws attention to the issue of the structural systems employed in the building of the roofs. These may vary considerably, from the familiar variants of the truss to the Chinese *tailiang* system. Related to the roofs in many traditions where cylindrical, octagonal or otherwise encircling walls are used, central posts may provide the main support for the radial roofs. Extended upwards from the living space and pointing skywards, in some cultures such posts are regarded as the *axis mundi*, or axis of the world, although it is as yet uncertain how extensive this symbolic connotation of the structural element may be. Roofs are also supplemented with ceilings, sometimes supported by beams to which they are fixed, or in many cultures, suspended from above so as to present an uninterrupted plane, made more evident by thin plaster.

By means of the principle of geographic visualisation, the data collected and brought together in the maps often reveals curious or unexpected information. For instance, the mapping of bamboo, which was undertaken at an early stage, reveals that its many species are grown in immense regions across the world, but the mapping of the use of bamboo in building does not correspond directly with this. For example, bamboo grows extensively in the Sub-Saharan Africa region, but very little information has been gathered on its employment there. To an extent, this may be due to descriptions of the buildings which have not paid any attention to the materials, or which have assumed a general understanding about their nature. Yet, on the evidence collected and presented on the map, the lack of a close correspondence between buildings and bamboo suggests that the valuable, fast-growing and flexible natural material could well contribute substantially to meeting the housing needs of much of the continent.

Bamboo is an example that illustrates one of the many aspects of the mapping of vernacular architecture that may have direct application to housing conservation, construction or, most importantly, to meeting the growing demand for housing that will practically and economically accommodate the world's rapidly expanding population. Comparison of the mapped data can give important insights not only into the problems of access to materials such as timber, but also into those brought about by thoughtless deforestation. Indications on maps of the prevalence of certain architectural characteristics in form and detail, may aid the introduction of compatible and acceptable building developments that conform, rather than compete, with traditions in specific cultural areas. This requires an in-depth understanding of the vernacular tradition, including the functions of the structures that are built. These may be small in size, but significant in use, such as the *espigueiros*, or *horreos*, the millet stores of Northern Portugal and Galicia, Spain. Other functional buildings may also be locally used, like the *kozalec*, the hay-drying frames of Slovenia, or the woolsheds for sheep-shearing in Australia. Such examples underline the necessity for more regional studies of specific traditions which may be shared by cultures in a specific cultural area, or which could be the subject of regional maps covering two or three cultural areas in which diffusion can be demonstrated as having taken place.

These are structural and functional features, but many social characteristics are evident in the cross-cultural mapping, like the great collective community longhouses which are each a virtual village under one roof. The map on *Community and multi-family houses* reveals the prevalence of such houses in Southeast Asia, both mainland and insular, but it also indicates a similar concentration of families clustered in singular longhouses in western Amazonia. There is little likelihood that they are connected historically but, rather, that they reflect certain common elements in social organisation. Nonetheless, inter-cultural connections are significant, as the presence in Madagascar of Southeast Asian cultural elements, including certain aspects of music and traditional architecture, demonstrates. This example is not explicitly mapped in AVAW (although it is referred to in the map *Symbolism: Botanical metaphor*) but, coupled with other instances of trans-oceanic influences, could well be the subject of future mapping.

Those who are interested in taking the mapping of vernacular architecture further, need not feel bereft of subjects for study and cartographically recording. In fact, a number of instances have been cited in the texts that accompany the maps of further research that needs to be undertaken. These include, among others: ventilation and cooling methods; cooking and heating, including open hearths; triple-storey and higher buildings; outbuildings; resources depletion, and anthropomorphic symbolism. But there is much more to be done: on openings, for instance, such as, doorways. Although they may seem similar, their presence is sometimes surprising, such as the doorway and door frame that is found in the yurt, the armature and mat tent of Asian nomads, which is the first element to be raised on arrival at a site. The prevalence of certain types of closure, whether in boards or woven panels, is yet to be mapped, let alone the use of 'harr-hung' (pivoted) doors and the employment of different kinds of hinges. Related to these are the windows and window openings, which are prevalent in the buildings of most European cultures, but which are largely absent in the traditional dwellings of Africa. Tracing the number and dimensions of window openings for light and for ventilation is necessary, but it is extended by the need to record the use of translucent materials such as mica, shell and thin alabaster for illumination, and the origins of the use and distribution of window glazing in Asia. There are numerous extensions of this, from the introduction of dormer windows, of fanlights and casements, to the use of oriel and bay windows to accept more light. The use of leaded lights and of multiple panes may be recorded and mapped, including the sources of production of these component elements. Openings, whether doorways or windows, are examples of the kinds of related subject which may arise from any identified architectural features. Space does not permit more than this single example, but it indicates the research that can and should be done. In so doing, cultural preferences as well as environmental and climatic modifications can be demonstrated on cross-cultural maps.

What applies to types of a basic detail or feature may also apply to types of building related to a particular kind of economy. This might encompass the wine 'cellar' or hut-and-cellar, a tradition that is to be found in Austria and other eastern European countries, or it can apply to the rice barns, tobacco sheds or other produce stores which are built in considerable numbers in central and Southeast Asia. Although fishing communities are to be found in all Mediterranean countries, in much of north-western Europe, in the Caribbean and Oceanic islands, and in numerous coastal strips elsewhere, their vernacular traditions have received remarkably little attention. Yet the boat sheds and quays, the fish stores and markets, the harbour buildings and boat-building yards, when compared across the continents have much in common, as well as many features that differ in function and scale. This particularly applies to the variety of harbour types and forms, frequently conditioned by the depth of water, the configuration of coast and river, the size of the boats in harbour and the communication routes both to the interior land and across the sea.

Fishing and other coastal functions of these kinds and locations, emphasise another aspect of the vernacular which requires more research, namely settlement patterns. The factors that may determine the form of settlements vary considerably, in some instances reflecting the importance of the economy. In others, they may act as a mirror to the social organisation of particular kinds of community, whether, for instance, as complementary moieties, or as phratries of related clans. Such social structures which may determine village layouts are to be found in most continents. Settlements may also be classified by their form, many that are close to rivers or roads, or other communication routes, being linear in plan. Others, benefiting from a specific resource, or limited by the topography of the land, may be clustered, perhaps with an open space or a place of worship at the focal point. While some settlements may be nodal, with a market centre served by routes from the adjacent country, others may be dispersed in a cultivated landscape. The latter particularly applies where mountains have been terraced for generations, in some of which cases the buildings may be 'banked', or set against the hill-slope with piles supporting the fore-edge of the structure. All such instances merit study and documentation, but they occur sufficiently and over such distances that they also invite mapping.

These instances relate directly to the mapping of building features and settlement types, but environmental issues are of considerable importance, especially where they threaten the survival of the former. Earthquake areas have been the subject of one of the maps in AVAW, but maps of other hazards in relation to the vernacular are also vitally necessary. Among these are the floods, which in Bangladesh are already of immense scale and annual occurrence. But the changing climate and the anticipated global warming will result in flooding on a scale which will lead to the destruction of vast numbers of settlements and buildings, if no attempts are made to secure their safety. Mapping of the flood threat should be augmented by maps of the hurricane, typhoon and cyclone belts, such that the communities in their paths are better forewarned and informed measures may be taken for their protection. Not all these subjects need to be mapped solely on a global scale; many need more concentrated emphasis on cultural regions, singularly or in related groups.

What these and other potential maps exemplify, whether they are completed or need to be researched, is the relevance of such cartographic evidence to the work of non-governmental organisations (NGOs), as well as to that of multi-national commissions and housing associations. The mapping of communities, their buildings and their settlements, of the resources that are available and others that are in decline, the impact of environmental and climate change, the sustainability of many traditions and the possibilities of their development in the anticipation of massive population growth – all this and much more is of immediate relevance to conservationists, architects and planners, and should be to politicians, although few have shown interest. Perhaps the greatest cartographic task, but one that is essential in view of the neglect so far, is the global mapping of vernacular traditions. But these maps must be related to numerous contextual phenomena, and the identification of many material resources; they would reflect population growth and the economies that support it, and will have to do so increasingly in the future. At the household plane, they will embrace the pragmatic details of structures and services on the one hand, and the abstractions of the symbolic associations of their houses to the people of numerous societies on the other.

It may seem that the potential for mapping aspects of the vernacular architecture of cultures throughout the world is without limits, and readers may well question the basis on which the selection of appropriate maps has been made. Where, one may ask, can the information be found that provides the basis for such cartographic analysis and synthesis? As has been noted in the Introduction and has been evident in the organisation of AVAW and the references cited with each map, AVAW is complementary to the *Encyclopedia of Vernacular Architecture of the World* (EVAW). It is in the nature of an encyclopedia that it is compiled of a large number of separate entries which can be read individually as sources of information. In EVAW, basic bibliographies of key works and cross-references to other entries have been made in the margins, but customarily the entries 'stand alone', their order often subordinated only to the sequence of the alphabet. In the planning of entries in EVAW every effort was made to relate each entry to others within the same Section, so that these could be read in their entirety if this was desired. However, the problem remained insofar that the Sections and their entries could not be cross-referential and comparable on a truly global basis.

It was from the work on this problem that AVAW was created, in that it could demonstrate the comparability and sometimes the contrasts in the consideration of specific subjects on a worldwide basis. As this involved much further research as well as cartography, it was clearly not possible to map every subject. Instead, significant and, in many cases, widely dispersed examples have been used which complemented the majority of the major Sections in Volume One of EVAW, *Theories and Principles*, and used, where their application was appropriate, many of the *Cultures and Habitats* included in Volumes Two and Three.

With respect to the Introductory Section of EVAW, AVAW is especially representative of the Anthropological, Architectural, Conservationist, Developmental, Geographical and Spatial 'Approaches and Concepts'. Under the general title of *Contexts*, maps have been devised which express the global implications of the 'Culture Traits and Attributes' category in EVAW, together with maps that detail the 'Environment' category with the fundamental, naturally-occurring aspects, on which all cultures depend. Materials and resources are represented by the maps under that title, considering availability and use, diffusion and certain technologies. Maps of technologies and of different structural systems used across the world, relate to the EVAW Section entitled 'Production'. The necessary 'Services', and the 'Uses and Functions' categories in EVAW are encompassed in the *Services and Functions* maps, while the 'Typologies' are mapped under *Forms, Plans and Types*. *Symbolism and Decoration* is the title employed for this subject in both works, but AVAW concludes with a new and important category, *Development and Sustainability*, which addresses some of the major issues highlighted in the twenty-first century.

The sixty-nine maps in AVAW illustrate all Sections of Volume One of EVAW, representing approximately ten per cent of the entries in that volume. The examples demonstrate their relevance to virtually all the Cultural Areas of the world, as and where they are applicable. The cross-cultural and inter-cultural, multi-national implications of every subject mapped reveals much that is new, and indeed was new to the authors as research developed. It is in order to indicate these possibilities and to take the initial steps on this great path, that this *Atlas of Vernacular Architecture of the World* has been compiled.

References

Introduction

AlSayyad, N. (2001); AlSayyad, N. (2004); Andrews, P.A. (1997); Asquith, L. and Vellinga, M. (2006); Bagenal, P. and Meades, J. (1980); Beazley, M. (1984); Bertin, J. et al (1971); Brunskill, R.W. (1981); Brunskill, R.W. (1985); Brunskill, R.W. (1997); Clarke, R. (2004); Cornell, T. and Matthews, J. (1982); Cruickshank, D. (1996); Davies, D.H. (1971); Denyer, S. (1978); Dorling, D. and Fairbairn, D. (1997); Drew, P. (1979); Driver, H.E. (1961); Faegre, T. (1979); Ford, M., El Kadi, H. and Watson, L. (1999); Freeman, W.H. and Bracegirdle, B. (1963); Glassie, H. (1975); Hallet, S.I. and Samizay, R. (1980); Harley, J.B. (1988); Harley, J.B. (1989); Harvey, M.E. (1966); Henderson-Sellers, A. and Hansen, A-M. (1995); Houben, H. and Guillaud, H. (1994); Knapp, R.G. (1997); Knapp, R.G. (2000); Knapp, R.G. (2003); Knapp, R.G. and Lo, K-Y, (2005); Kniffen, F.B. (1986); Kniffen, F.B. and Glassie, H. (1986); Kostof, S. (1985); MacEachren, A.M. and Monmonier, M. (1992); McGuire, B. et al. (2004); Moffett, M. (2003); Monmonier, M. (1991); Neal, J. (2000); Noble, A.G. (1984a); Noble, A.G. (1984a); Oliver, P. (1969); Oliver, P. (1997); Oliver, P. (2003); Oliver, P. (2004); Pattison, I.R., Pattison, D.S. and Alcock, N.W. (1992); Phaidon (2004); Prizeman, J. (1975); Rapoport, A. (1969); Rapoport, A. (2006); Slocum, T.A. (1999); Smith, J.T. (1975); Szabo, A. and Barfield, T.J. (1991); Tunnard, C. and Reed, H.H. (1956); Upton, D. and Vlach, J.M (1986); Waterson, R. (1990); West, R.C. (1974); Wurm, S.A. (1996).

Part 1: Contexts

Nations

EVAW references: 1.III.6 (f).
Smith, A.D. (1995).

Topography

EVAW references: 1.III.2; 1.III.5; 1.III.6.
Allen, E. (1969); Hudson, J.C. (1969); Oliver, P. (2003).

Water

EVAW references: 1.III.2 (b, f, h, i); 1.III.3 (c).
Clapham, W.B. (1973); Food and Agriculture Organisation (2003); Tvedt, T. (2006).

Climate

EVAW references: 1.III.1; 1.III.3 (a, c, e, f).
Akin, W.E. (1991); Aronin, J.E. (1953); Clapham, W.B. (1973); Evans, M. (1980); Gaisford, J. (1983); Oliver, P. (2003).

Vegetation

EVAW references: 1.III.2 (d, e); 1.IV.3; 1.IV.5.
Akin, W.E. (1991); Clapham, W.B. (1973); Gaisford, J. (1983); Oliver, P. (2003); Spence, R.J. and Cook, D.J. (1988); Westoby, J. (1989).

Soils

EVAW references: 1.IV.2.
Agarwal, A. (1981); Akin, W.E. (1991); Bridges, E.M. (1997); Clapham, W.B. (1973); Gaisford, J. (1983); Houben, H. and Guillaud, H. (1994); Oliver, P. (1983); Oliver, P. (2003); Spence, R.J.S. and Cook, D.J. (1988).

Economy

EVAW references: 1.II.2.
Broek, J.O.M. and Webb, J.W. (1978); Carter, G.F. (1964); Clarke, L. (1982); Dumont, R. (1970); Forde, C.D. (1950); Gaisford, J. (1983); Grigg, D.B. (1980); Herskovits, M. (1952); Johnson, A.N. and Easle, T. (1987); Lee, R.B. and Daly, R. (1999); Oliver, P. (2003); Plattner, S. (1980); Shanin, T. (1971).

Population

EVAW references: 1.III.4.
Broek, J.O.M. and Webb, J.W. (1978); Beaujeu-Garnier, J. (1966); Carr-Saunders, A.M. (1922); Carter, G.F. (1964); Clarke, J.I. (1972); Clarke, L.

(1982); Gaisford, J. (1983); Grigg, D.B. (1980); Hall, R. (1989); Jones, H. (1990); Oliver, P. (2003); Parnwell, M. (1993).

Language

EVAW references: 1.II.8.
Broek, J.O.M. and Webb, J.W. (1978); Carter, G.F. (1964); Clarke, L. (1982); Grimes, B.F. (1992); Gaisford, J. (1983); Katzner, K. (2002); Moseley, C. and Asher, R.E. (1994).

Religion

EVAW references: 1.II.13.
Broek, J.O.M. and Webb, J.W. (1978); Carter, G.F. (1964); Clarke, L. (1982); Deffontaines, P. (1948); Oliver, P. (2003); Gaisford, J. (1983); Radin, P. (1957); Rapoport, A. (1969); Sopher, D.E. (1967).

Cultural areas

EVAW references: Introduction.
Broek, J.O.M. and Webb, J.W. (1978); Murdock, G.P. (1967); Price, D.H. (1989).

Part 2: Cultural and material aspects

Materials and resources

Earth: technologies

EVAW references: 1.IV.2 (c, d, e, f, j); 1.IV.5 (i); 1.V.2 (g); 1.V.6 (k); 1.VIII.5 (d).
Agrawal, A. (1981); Beazley, E. and Harverson, M. (1982); Denyer, S. (1978); Dethier, J. (1981); Fernandes, M. and Correia, M. (2005); Houben, H. and Guillaud, H. (1994); International Conference on the Study and Conservation of Earthen Architecture (2000); MacDougall, B.G. (2003); McHenry, P.G. (1984); Norton, J. (1996); Oliver, P. (1983); Oliver, P. (2003); Paul, B.K. (2003); Spence, R.J.S. and Cook, D.J. (1988); Wojciechowska, P. (2001); Yampolsky, M. (1993).

Sun-dried brick: diffusion

EVAW references: 1.IV.2 (a, e, i, i-i); 1.V.1 (c, h, i); 1.V.6 (k); 1.VIII.5 (d).
Agrawal, A. (1981); Beazley, E. and Harverson, M. (1982); Bourgeois, J-L. (1989); Damluji, S. (1992); Denyer, S. (1978); Dethier, J. (1981); Houben, H. and Guillaud, H. (1994); Knapp, R.G. (2000); Lee, S-h. (2003); McHenry, P.G. (1984); McHenry, P.G. (1999); McHenry, P.G. (2000); Noble, A.G. (2003); Norton, J. (1996); Oliver, P. (1983); Oliver, P. (2003); Pieper, R. (1999); Prussin, L. (1976); Samizay, R. (2003); Sobti,

M.P. (2003); Spence, R.J.S. and Cook, D.J. (1988); Szabo, A. and Barfield, T.J. (1991); Taylor, M.R. (1999); Woodforde, J. (1976); Yampolsky, M. (1993); Zurick, D. and Shrestha, N. (2003).

Palm: availability and use

EVAW references: 1.IV.3 (c, c-i, c-ii, f, g, g-i, g-ii, g-iii, h); 1.V.2 (i, p-ii).
Cole, S. and Kulatea, V. (1996); Davey, N. (1961); Denyer, S. (1978); Hockings, E.J. (1989); Kahlenberg, M. H. and Schwartz, M. (1983); Koch, G. (1965); Kovoor, A. (1983); McCoy, R.E. (1988); Oliver, P. (2003); Spence, R.J.S. and Cook, D.J. (1988); Uhl, N.W. (1987); Yampolsky, M. (1993).

Timber: technologies

EVAW references: 1.IV.5 (b, c, d, e, f, g, h); 1.V.1 (d); 1.V.2. (c, m, m-i); 1.V.6 (a, a-i, a-ii, i,); I.VIII.5 (a, b, e).
Bootle, K.R. (1988); Denyer, S. (1978); Hansen, H.J. (1971); Jayanetti, L. (1990); Jordan, T.G. (1985); Knapp, R.G. (2000); Lee, S-h. (2003); Noble, A.G. (1984a); Noble, A.G. (2003); Oliver, P. (2003); Opolovnikov, A.V. and Opolovnikov, Y.A. (1989); Paul, B.K. (2003); Spence, R.J.S. and Cook, D.J. (1988); Weslager, C.A. (1969); Yampolsky, M. (1993); Zurick, D. and Shrestha, N. (2003).

Bamboo: availability and use

EVAW references: 1.IV.3 (a, a-i).
Dunkelberg, K. (1985); Farrelly, D. (1984); Hidalgo, O. (1974); Janssen, J.J.A. (1988); Knapp, R.G. (1986); Marden, L. (1980); McClure, F.A. (1953); McClure, F.A. (1966); Parsons, J.J. (1991): Piper, J. (1992); United Nations Secretariat (1972).

Reed: technologies

EVAW references: 1.IV.3 (j, m); 1.V.2 (f, p, p-i); 1.VIII.5 (c, h); 2.I.2 (i-i).
Davey, N. (1961); Denyer, S. (1978); Hall, N. (1988); Knapp, R.G. (2000); Maxwell, G. (1957); Nabokov, P. and Easton, R. (1989); Oliver, P. (2003); Spence, R.J.S. and Cook, D.J. (1988); Thesiger, W. (1964); United Nations Secretariat (1972).

Used and manufactured: fired brick

EVAW references: 1.IV.2 (b); 1.V.5 (b); 1.V.6 (j); 1.V.7 (a); 1.IX.7 (a).
Brunskill, R.W. and Clifton-Taylor, A. (1977); Campbell, J.W.P. (2003); Davey, N. (1961); Denyer, S. (1978); Knapp, R.G. (2000); Noble, A.G. (1984a); Noble, A.G. (2003); Oliver, P. (2003); Parry, J.P.M.

(1979); Szabo, A. and Barfield, T.J. (1991); Spence, R.J.S. and Cook, D.J. (1988); Woodforde, J. (1976); Yampolsky, M. (1993).

Used and manufactured: corrugated iron

EVAW references: 1.IV.6 (f, f-i); 1.V.2 (d).
Bell, P. (1984); Cooper, I. and Dawson, B. (1998); Denyer, S. (1978); Drew, P. (1985); Herbert, G. (1978); Jowitt, G. and Shaw, P. (1999); Knapp, R.G. (2003); Oliver, P. (1975); Oliver, P. (2003); Spence, R.J.S. and Cook, D.J. (1983); Vegas, F. (1985), Warren, K. (1990); Yampolsky, M. (1993).

Structural systems and technologies

Tents: membraneous and armature

EVAW references: 1.V.5 (B); 1.VIII.2 (e); 1.IX.8 (a, a-i, b, c, c-i, f, h, p, t, u, x); 2.I.1 (e-i); 3.VI.5 (l).
Andrews, P.A. (1997); Drew, P. (1979); Driver, H.E. (1961); Faegre, T. (1979); Kronenburg, R. (1995); Laubin, R. and Laubin, G. (1957); Nabokov, P. and Easton, R. (1989); Nicolaisen, J. (1963); Prussin, L. (1995); Szabo, A. and Barfield, T.J. (1991).

Underground architecture: cave, pit and semi-subterranean

EVAW references: 1.III.2 (a); 1.IV.4. (b, b-i, j, n); 1.V.1 (b); 2.I.1 (j-i); 2.III.4 (r-i); 2.IV.5 (b-i); 3.VI.5 (r); 3.VII.3 (n-i).
Buttler, W. (1936); Denyer, S. (1978); Golany, G.S. (1992); Kempe, D. (1988); Mulligan, H. and Forster, P.; Mulligan, H. and Forster, P.; Norris, H.T. (1953); Oliver, P. (2003); Solecki, R.S. (1978); Steen, A., Steen, B. and Komatsu, E. (2003); Szabo, A. and Barfield, T.J. (1991).

Horizontal log construction: diffusion

EVAW references: 1.III.4 (d); 1.IV.5 (c); 1.V.1 (h); 1.V.6 (l); 1.VIII.5 (d); 2.III.2 (h-i); 3.VI.3 (a-i); 3.VI.7 (c-i).
Attebery, J.E. (1998); Freeland, J. and Cox, P. (1969); Freeman, P. (1980); Hansen H.J. (1971); Jordan, T.G. (1985); Kalman, H. (1994); Kniffen, F.B. and Glassie, H. (1986); Lehr, J. (1980); Opolovnikov, A.V. and Opolovnikov, Y.A. (1989); Phleps, H. (1942); Shurtleff, H.R. (1939); Weslager, C.A. (1969); Winberry, J.J. (1974); Wonders, W.C. (1979).

Stone construction: wet and dry

EVAW references: 1.IV.4 (f); 1.V.6 (m, m-i, m-ii, m-iii).
Allen, E. (1969); Kahn, L.l. (2004); Oliver, P. (2003); Shadmon, A. (1996); Spence, R.J.S. and Cook, D.J. (1988); Tufnell, R. (1982); Tufnell, R. (1991).

Walling: timber-framed

EVAW references: 1.V.1 (d, e); 1.VIII.5 (a, b, c); 2.III.6 (j-i).
Alcock, N.W. (1981); Brunskill, R.W. (1971); Brunskill, R.W. (1985); Carver, N.F. (1981); Feduchi, L. (1977); Fréal, J. (1979); Hansen, H.J. (1971); Laws, B. (1991); Meirion-Jones, G.I. (1982); Noble, A.G. (1984a); Oliver, P. (2003); Smith, J.T. (1975).

Curtain walling: woven matting

EVAW references: 1.IV.3 (a, d, f, g, h, j, l); 1.V.2 (f); 1.VIII.5 (c, h).
Andersen, K.B. (1978); Cole, S. and Kulatea, V. (1996); Davey, N. (1961); Denyer, S. (1978); Knuffel, W.E. (1973); Maxwell, G. (1957); Nabokov, P. and Easton, R. (1989); Oliver, P. (2003); Rapoport, A. (1969); Thesiger, W. (1964); Waterson, R. (1990).

Finishes: mud plaster and limewash

EVAW references: 1.V.2 (e, g, j, j-i, l).
Agrawal, A. (1981); Atroshenko, V.I. (1991); Davey, N. (1961); Denyer, S. (1978); Dethier, J. (1981); Goldfinger, M. (1993); House, S. and House, C. (2004); Knapp, R.G. (2000); Lee, S-h. (2003); Noble, A.G. (2003); Norton, J. (1996); Paul, B.K. (2003); Samizay, R. (2003); Spence, R.J.S. and Cook, D.J. (1988); Szabo, A. and Barfield, T.J. (1991); Yampolsky, M. (1993).

Roof cladding: clay tiles, shingles and slate

EVAW references: 1.IV.3 (c-ii, m-i, m-ii); 1.IV.4 (m); 1.IV.5 (b); 1.V.2 (b, m, m-i, n, n-i, o, p, p-i, p-ii, p-iii, q).
Askew, M. (2003); Atroshenko, V.I. (1991); Balderstone, S. and Logan, W. (2003); Cooper, I. and Dawson, B. (1998); Goldfinger, M. (1993); House, S. and House, C. (2004); Kawashima, C. (1986); Knapp, R.G. (2000); Lee, S-h. (2003); Noble, A.G. (1984a); Noble, A.G. (2003); Oliver, P. (2003); Spence, R.J.S. and Cook, D.J. (1983); Woodforde, J. (1976); Wright, A. (1991); Yampolsky, M. (1993); Zurick, D. and Shrestha, N. (2003).

Roofing: thatch

EVAW references: 1.IV.3 (c-i, c-ii, d, f, g, g-i, g-ii, g-iii, h, j, l, m, m-i, m-ii); 1.V.2 (i); 1.V.2 (p, p-i, p-ii, p-iii).
Davey, N. (1961); Hall, N. (1981); Hall, N. (1988); Knapp, R.G. (1990); Knapp, R.G. (2000); Spence, R.J.S. and Cook, D.J. (1988).

Forms, plans and types

Roof forms: pitched, hipped and vaulted

EVAW references: 1.V.5 (A, f, g, m-i, m-ii, m-iii, m-iv).
Cooper, I. and Dawson, B. (1998); Denyer, S. (1978); Knapp, R.G. (2000); Nabokov, P. and Easton, R. (1989); Noble, A.G. (1984a); Noble, A.G. (2003); Oliver, P. (2003); Samizay, R. (2003); Szabo, A. and Barfield, T.J. (1991); Yampolsky, M. (1993).

Roof forms: flat

EVAW references: 1.V.5 (A, c, e).
Atroshenko, V.I. (1991); Beazley, E. and Harverson, M. (1982); Cooper, I. and Dawson, B. (1998); Denyer, S. (1978); Goldfinger, M. (1993); House, S. and House, C. (2004); Knapp, R.G. (2000); Nabokov, P. and Easton, R. (1989); Noble, A.G. (2003); Oliver, P. (2003); Rooney, J.F., Zelinsky, W. and Louder, D.R. (1982); Samizay, R. (2003); Szabo, A. and Barfield, T.J. (1991); Yampolsky, M. (1993).

Plans: Circular

EVAW references: 1.VII.3 (c).
Andersen, K.B. (1977); Blier, S.P. (1987); Bourdier, J-P. and Minh-ha Trinh, T. (1996); Denyer, S. (1978); Knapp, R.G. (2000); Noble, A.G. (2003); Oliver, P. (1971); Oliver, P. (2003); Yampolsky, M. (1993).

Plans: courtyards

EVAW references: 1.VI.4 (c, c-i); 1.VIII.3 (b, d); 2.IV.4 (n).
Blaser, W. (1979); Blaser, W. (1985); Cooper, I. and Dawson, B. (1998); Edwards, B., Sibley, M., Hakmi, M. and Land, P. (2006); Ho, P-P. (2003); Knapp, R.G. (1986); Knapp, R.G. (2000); Knapp, R.G. and Lo, K-Y. (2005); Lee, S-h. (2003); Lo, K-Y. and Ho, P-P. (1999); Noble, A. (2003); Oliver, P. (2003); Petherbridge, G.T. (1978); Prasad, S. (1988); Sinha, S. (1994).

Multi-storey buildings

Albini, M. (1990); Atroshenko, V.I. (1991); Denyer, S. (1978); House, S. and House, C. (2004); King, A.D. (2004); Knapp, R.G. (2000); Marchand, T.H.J. (2001); Nabokov, P. and Easton, R. (1989); Noble, A.G. (1984a); Talib, K. (1984); Zurick, D. and Shrestha, N. (2003).

Pile dwellings

EVAW references: 1.III.2 (f); 1.IV.5 (d); 1.V.6 (i).
Clément, P. and Charpentier, S. (1974); Cranstone, B.A.L. (1972); Jayanetti, L. (1990); Knapp, R.G. (2000);
Nguyen Van Huyen (1934); Sunley, J. and Bedding, B. (1985); Waterson, R. (1990); Xing, R. (2003).

Community and multi-family houses

Alexander, J. (1993); Freeman, D. (1960); Guerreiro, A.J. (2003); Hauser-Schäublin, B. (1985); Hugh-Jones, C. (1979); Hugh-Jones, S. (1985); Knapp, R.G. (2000); Loeb, E.M. and Broek, J.O.M. (1947); Nabokov, P. and Easton, R. (1989); Oliver, P. (2003); Sather, C. (1993); Szabo, A. and Barfield, T.J. (1991); Waterson, R. (1990); Winzeler, R.L. (1998).

Bungalow: diffusion

Betting, W. and Vriend, J.J. (1958); Edwards, J.D. (2001); Kalman, H. (1994); King, A.D. (1982); King, A.D. (1995); Kipling, J.L. (1911); Maddex, D. (2003); Pigou-Dennis, E. (2002); Srivastava, Y. (2003); Sumner, R. (1978).

Services and functions

Hygiene: sweat baths

EVAW references: 1.VI.3 (a, c, n, n-i, o).
Aaland, M. (1978); Alba, H.R. (2005); Bruchac, J. (1993); Krickeberg, W. (1939); Nabokov, P. and Easton, R. (1989); Waldman, C. (1985).

Cooking and heating: open hearths, stoves and ovens

EVAW references: 1.VI.2 (b, b-i, b-ii, c, e, e-i, f, f-i, h, h-i, i, j, l, l-i, l-ii, l-iii, l-iv, l-v, m, m-i, m-ii); 3.VI.8 (g-ii).
Cooper, I. and Dawson, B. (1998); Denyer, S. (1978); Gebhart, T. (1980); Knapp, R.G. (2000); Knapp, R.G. (2003); Oliver, P. (2003); Waterson, R. (1990); Yampolsky, M. (1993).

Smoke vents: chimneys and smoke holes

EVAW references: 1.V.4 (k, k-i); 1.VI.2 (d, d-i, d-ii, e, e-i).
Denyer, S. (1978); Knapp, R.G. (2003); Meir, I.A. and Roaf, S.C. (2006); Noble, A.G. (1984a); Yampolsky, M. (1993).

Ventilation and cooling: Middle East and Southwest Asia

EVAW references: 1.III.1 (c); 1.VI.4 (A, B, g, i, i-i, m, m-i, m-ii); 2.I.6 (q-i).
Beazley, E. and Harverson, M. (1982); Bonine, M.E. (1980); Cain, A., Afshar, F. and Norton, J. (1975); Cooper, I. and Dawson, B. (1998); Edwards, B., Sibley, M., Hakmi, M. and Land, P. (2006); Elawa, S. (1981); Lari, Y. (1989); Lewcock, R. (1978); Petherbridge, G.T. (1978); Roaf, S. (1990); Roaf, S. (1991).

Ventilation and cooling: veranda

EVAW references: 1.VI.1 (m, m-i, m-ii).
Askew, M. (2003); Crouch, D.P. and Johnson, J.G. (2001); Denyer, S. (1978); Drew, P. (1992); Edwards, J.D. (1989); Paul, B.K. (2003); Knapp, R.G. (2000); Lee, S-h. (2003); Long, C. (2003); Naonori, M. (2003); Noble, A.G. (1984a); Noble, A.G. (2003); Oliver, P. (2003); Szabo, A. and Barfield, T.J. (1991); Yampolsky, M. (1993); Yin, L.H. (2003); Zurick, D. and Shrestha, N. (2003).

Outbuildings: granaries

EVAW references: 1.IX.2 (j, k, k-i,); 1.IX.3 (A, f, l, l-i, l-ii, m, q).
Bertin, J. et al. (1971); Brunskill, R.W. (1982); Cooper, I. and Dawson, B. (1998); Denyer, S. (1978); Knapp, R.G. (2003); Larkin, D. (1995); Loftas, T. (1972); Noble, A.G. (1984b); Noble, A.G. and Wilhelm, H.G.H. (1995); Oliver, P. (2003); Prussin, L. (1972); Steen, A., Steen, B. and Komatsu, E. (2003); Waterson, R. (1990); Yampolsky, M. (1993).

Outbuildings: barns

EVAW references: 1.IX.3 (A, B, a, a-i, a-ii).
Anonymous (2006); Arthur, E. and Witney, D. (1972); Brunskill, R.W. (1982); Endersby, E. Greenwood, A. and Larkin, D. (1992); Ensminger, R. (1992); Harris, B. (1991); Hubka, T.C. (1984); Hughes, G. (1985); Jordan, T.G.; Kilpinen, J.T. and Gritzner, C.F. (1997); Kirk, M. (1994); Larkin, D. (1995); Noble, A.G. (1984b); Noble, A.G. and Cleek, R.K. (1995); Noble, A.G. and Wilhelm, H.G.H. (1995); Oliver, P. (2003); Rooney, J.F. Zelinsky, W. and Louder, D.R. (1982).

Outbuildings: mills

EVAW references: 1.VI.5 (d, e, e-i, l); 1.IX.7 (C, b, b-i, d, d-i, d-ii, e, e-i, e-ii, e-iii, g, h, i, i-i, i-ii, i-iii, j, j-i, j-ii, j-iii, j-iv, j-v).
Baker, T.L. (1985); Beedell, S. (1979); Brangwyn, F. and Preston, H. (1975); Brown, J.E and Ensign, A. (1977); Brown, R.J. (1976); De Little, R.J. (1972); Hills, R.L. (1994); Notebaart, J.C. (1972); Reynolds, J. (1970); Syson, L. (1965); Tyrwhitt, J. (1976); Walton, J. (1974).

Symbolism and decoration

Colour decoration: exterior mural painting

EVAW references: 1.VII.1 (A, m, m-i, m-ii); 1.VII.5 (A, b-i, e, e-i, e-ii, f-ii, g-i).
Becom, J. and Aberg, S.J. (1997); Cooper, I. and Dawson, B. (1998); Denyer, S. (1978); Duly, C. (1979);

Lenclos, J-P. and Lenclos, D. (1999); Matthews, T. and Changuion, A. (1989); Oliver, P. (1975); Oliver, P. (2003); Parker, A. and Neal, A. (1995); Steen, A., Steen, B. and Komatsu, E. (2003); Vegas, F. (1985); Waterson, R. (1990); Wyk, G.N. van (1998); Yampolsky, M. (1993).

Symbolism: motifs

EVAW references: 1.VII.3 (c, f, i, j, k, m, n, q, r, r-i, s, t, v, w).
Cooper, I. and Dawson, B. (1998); Cooper, J.C. (1978); Denyer, S. (1978); Duly, C. (1979); Faik-Nzuji, C.M. (1992); Matthews, T. and Changuion, A. (1989); Moon, B. (1991); Oliver, P. (1975); Oliver, P. (2003); Petrie, F. (1990); Steen, A., Steen, B. and Komatsu, E. (2003); Waterson, R. (1990); Wittkower, R. (1977); Wyk, G.N. van (1998); Yampolsky, M. (1993).

Decorated elements: roof finials

EVAW references: 1.VII.1 (A, f, f-i).
Bourdier, J-P. and Minh-ha Trinh, T. (1996); Denyer, S. (1978); Duly, C. (1979); Kirk, M. (1994); Oliver, P. (1971); Oliver, P. (2003); Steen, A., Steen, B. and Komatsu, E. (2003); Waterson, R. (1990); Winzeler, R.L. (1998) Yampolsky, M. (1993).

Symbolism: botanical metaphor

Barnes, R.H. (1974); Beatty, A. (1992); Domenig, G. (2003); Forth, G. (1981); Forth, G. (2003); Fox, J.J. (1993); Reuter, T.A. (2002); Sather, C. (1993); Schefold, R. (2003); Singarimbun, M. (1975); Vellinga, M. (2004); Vischer, M. (2003); Volkman, T. (1985); Waterson, R. (1990); Waterson, R. (1993).

Development and sustainability

Population growth

EVAW references: 1.III.4 (b, c).
United Nations (2005).

Urbanisation

EVAW references: 1.III.4 (e).
United Nations (2004).

Squatter settlements

Aldrich, B.C. and Sandhu, R.S. (1995); Cairncross, S.; Hardoy, J.E. and Satterthwaite, D. (1990); Neuwirth, R. (2005); United Nations Centre for Human Settlements (1982); United Nations Human Settlements Programme (2003).

Resources depletion: deforestation

Food and Agriculture Organization (2005); United Nations Statistic Division (2005).

Natural disasters: earthquakes

EVAW references: 1.III.3; 1.III.3 (b).
Davis, I. (1978); Davis, I. (1981); Davis, I. (1985); United Nations Disaster Relief Organisation (1982); United States Geological Survey Earthquake Hazards Program (2006).

Conservation: open air museums

EVAW references: 1.I.16.
Association for Living History, Farm and Agricultural Museums (2005); Jong, A. de and Skougard, M. (1992); Langer, J. (2005); Nowacki, H. (1981); Oliver, P. (2003); Uldall, K. (1957); Zippelius, A. (1974); Zook, N. (1971).

Conservation: World Heritage Sites

EVAW references: 1.I.7.
Pressouyre, L. (1996); UNESCO (2004).

Bibliography

Aaland, M. (1978) *Sweat: The Illustrated History and Description of the Finnish Sauna, Russian Bania, Islamic Hammam, Japanese Mushi-Buro, Mexican Temescal, and American Indian and Eskimo Sweat Lodge*, Santa Barbara: Capra Press.

Agrawal, A. (1981) *Mud, Mud: The Potential of Earth-Based Materials for Third World Housing*, London: Earthscan.

Akin, W.E. (1991) *Global Patterns: Climate, Vegetation and Soils*, London: University of Oklahoma Press.

Alba, H.R. (2005) *Temazcal: The Traditional Mexican Sweat Bath*. Online. Available http://www.oaxacainfo.com/oaxaca/temazcal.htm (accessed 12 November 2005).

Albini, M. (1990) *Traditional Architecture in Saudi Arabia: The Central Region*, Riyadh: Department of Antiquities and Museums.

Alcock, N.W. (1981) *Cruck Construction: An Introduction and Catalogue*, London: The Council for British Archaeology (Research Report No. 42).

Aldrich, B.C. and Sandhu, R.S. (eds)(1995) *Housing the Urban Poor: Policy and Practice in Developing Countries*, London: Zed.

Alexander, J. (1993) 'The Lahanan longhouse', in J.J. Fox (ed.) *Inside Austronesian Houses: Perspectives on Domestic Designs for Living*, Canberra: Research School for Pacific and Asian Studies.

Allen, E. (1969) *Stone Shelters*, Cambridge, Mass. and London: MIT Press.

AlSayyad, N. (ed.)(2001) *Consuming Tradition, Manufacturing Heritage*, London: Routledge.

AlSayyad, N. (ed.)(2004) *The End of Tradition?* London: Routledge.

Andersen, K.B. (1977) *African Traditional Architecture: A Study of the Housing and Settlement Patterns of Rural Kenya*, Nairobi: Oxford University Press.

Andrews, P.A. (1990) *The Middle East: Nomad Tent Types*, Wiesbaden: Ludwig Reichert Verlag.

Andrews, P.A. (1997) *Nomad Tent Types in the Middle East, Part 1: Framed Tents*, Wiesbaden: Ludwig Reichert Verlag.

Anonymous (2006) *The Old House Web*. Online. Available http://www.oldhouseweb.com/stories/Detailed/235a.shtml (accessed 23 January 2006).

Aronin, J.E. (1953) *Climate and Architecture*, New York: Reinhold Publishing Corporation.

Arthur, E. and Witney, D. (1972) *The Barn: A Vanishing Landmark in North America*, Toronto: Feheley Arts.

Askew, M. (2003) '"Ban Thai": House and culture in a transforming society', in R.G. Knapp (ed.) *Asia's Old Dwellings: Tradition, Resilience and Change*, New York: Oxford University Press.

Asquith, L. and Vellinga, M. (eds)(2006) *Vernacular Architecture in the Twenty-First Century: Theory, Education and Practice*, London: Taylor & Francis.

Association for Living History, Farm and Agricultural Museums (2005) *Living History Links*. Online. Available http://www.alhfam.org/alhfam.links.html (accessed 12 December 2005).

Attebery, J.E. (1998) *Building with Logs: Western Log Construction in Context*, Moscow: University of Idaho Press.

Atroshenko, V.I. (1991) *Mediterranean Vernacular: A Vanishing Architectural Tradition*, London: Anness.

Bagenal, P. and Meades, J. (1980) *The Illustrated Atlas of the World's Great Buildings*, London: Bedford Editions.

Baker, T.L. (1985) *A Field Guide to American Windmills*, Norman: University of Oklahoma Press.

Balderstone, S. and Logan, W. (2003) 'Vietnamese dwellings: Traditions, resilience and change', in R.G. Knapp (ed.) *Asia's Old Dwellings: Tradition, Resilience and Change*, New York: Oxford University Press.

Barnes, R.H. (1974) *Kédang: A Study of the Collective Thought of an Eastern Indonesian People*, Oxford: Clarendon.

Beaujeu-Garnier, J. (1966) *Geography of Population*, London: Longman.

Beatty, A. (1992) *Society and Exchange in Nias*, Oxford: Clarendon Press.

Beazley, M. (ed.)(1984) *The World Atlas of Architecture*, London: Mitchell Beazley Publications.

Beazley, E. and Harverson, M. (1982) *Living with the Desert: Working Buildings of the Iranian Plateau*, Warminster: Aris & Phillips.

Becom, J. and Aberg, S.J. (1997) *Maya Color: The Painted Villages of Mesoamerica*, New York: Abbeville Press.

Beedell, S. (1979) *Windmills*, New York: Scribner's.

Bell, P. (1984) *Timber and Iron*, St Lucia: Queensland University Press.

Bertin, J. et al. (1971) *Atlas of Food Crops*, Paris: Ecole Pratiques des Hautes Etudes et Mouton.

Betting, W. and Vriend, J.J. (1958) *Bungalows: Deutschland, England, Italien, Holland, Belgien, Dänemark*, Darmstadt: Die Planung Verlag, H. Müller-Wellborn.

Blaser, W. (1979) *Courtyard House in China: Tradition and Present*, Basel: Birkhäuser Verlag.

Blaser, W. (1985) *Atrium: Five Thousand Years of Open Courtyards*, Basel/New York: Wepf and Co.

Blier, S.P. (1987) *The Anatomy of Architecture: Ontology and Metaphor in Batammaliba Architectural Expression*, Cambridge: Cambridge University Press.

Bonine, M.E. (1980) 'Aridity and structure: Adaptations of indigenous housing in central Iran', in K.N. Clark and P. Paylore (eds) *Desert Housing: Balancing Experience and Technology for Dwelling in Hot Arid Zones*, Tucson: University of Arizona Office of Arid Lands Studies.

Bootle, K.R. (1988) *Wood in Australia: Type, Properties and Uses*, McGraw: H.M. Book Company.

Bourdier, J-P. and Minh-ha Trinh, T. (1996) *Drawn from African Dwellings*, Indiana: Indiana University Press.

Bourgeois, J-L. (1989) *Spectacular Vernacular: The Adobe Tradition*, New York: Aperture.

Brangwyn, F. and Preston, H. (1975) *Windmills*, Detroit: Gale.

Bridges, E.M. (1997) *World Soils*, Cambridge: Cambridge University Press.

Broek, J.O.M. and Webb, J.W. (1978) *A Geography of Mankind*, London: McGraw-Hill.

Brown, J.E. and Ensign, A. (1977) *Harness the Wind: The Story of Windmills*, New York: Dodd.

Brown, R.J. (1976) *Windmills of England*, London: Robert Hale.

Bruchac, J. (1993) *The Native American Sweatlodge: History and Legends*, Freedom, California: The Crossing Press.

Brunskill, R.W. (1971) *Illustrated Handbook of Vernacular Architecture*, London: Faber and Faber.

Brunskill, R.W. (1981) *Traditional Buildings of Britain: An Introduction to Vernacular Architecture*, London: Gollancz/Crawley.

Brunskill, R.W. (1982) *Traditional Farm Buildings of Britain*, London: Gollancz/Crawley.

Brunskill, R.W. (1985) *Timber Building in Britain*, London: Gollancz/Crawley.

Brunskill, R.W. (1997) *Houses and Cottages of Britain*, London: Gollancz/Crawley.

Brunskill, R.W. and Clifton-Taylor, A. (1977) *English Brickwork*, London: Ward Lock.

Buttler, W. (1936) 'Pit and pit-dwellings in southeast Europe', *Antiquity*, 10 (37): 25–36.

Cain, A., Afshar, F. and Norton, J. (1975) 'Indigenous building and the Third World', *Architectural Design*, 45 (4): 207–224.

Cairncross, S., Hardoy, J.E. and Satterthwaite, D. (eds)(1990) *The Poor Die Young: Housing and Health in Third World Cities*, London: Earthscan.

Campbell, J.W.P. (2003) *Brick: A World History*, London: Thames and Hudson.

Carr-Saunders, A.M. (1922) *The Population Problem: A Study in Human Evolution*, Oxford: Oxford University Press.

Carter, G.F. (1964) *Man and the Land: A Cultural Geography*, New York: Holt Rinehart and Winston.

Carver, N.F. (1981) *Iberian Villages: Portugal and Spain*, Kalamazoo, MI: Documan Press.

Clapham, W.B. (1973) *Natural Ecosystems*, New York: Macmillan.

Clarke, J.I. (1972) *Population Geography*, Oxford: Pergamon Press.

Clarke, L. (ed.)(1982) *The Atlas of Mankind*, London: Mitchell Beazley.

Clarke, R. (2004) *The Atlas of Water: Mapping the World's Most Critical Resource*, London: Earthscan.

Clément, P. and Charpentier, S. (1974) 'Notes sur l'habitation sur pilotis en Asie du Sud-Est', *Asie du Sud-est et Monde Insulindien*, 5(2): 13–24.

Cole, S. and Kulatea, V. (1996) *Cultural Crafts of Niue: Pandanus Weaving*, Suva, Fiji: Institute of Pacific Studies.

Cooper, I. and Dawson, B. (1998) *Traditional Buildings of India*, London: Thames and Hudson.

Cooper, J.C. (1978) *An Illustrated Encyclopaedia of Traditional Symbols*, London: Thames and Hudson.

Cornell, T. and Matthews, J. (1982) *Atlas of the Roman World*, Oxford: Equinox.

Cranstone, B.A.L. (1972) 'Environment and choice in dwelling and settlement: An ethnographic survey', in P. Ucko, R. Tringham and G.W. Dimbleby (eds) *Man, Settlement and Urbanism*, Cambridge, Mass.: Schenken.

Crouch, D.P. and Johnson, J.G. (2001) *Traditions in Architecture: Africa, America, Asia and Oceania*, New York: Oxford University Press.

Cruickshank, D. (ed.)(1996) *Sir Banister Fletcher's A History of Architecture*, Oxford: Architectural Press.

Damluji, S. (1992) *The Valley of Mud Brick Architecture*, Reading: Garnet.

Davey, N. (1961) *A History of Building Materials*, London: Phoenix House.

Davies, D.H. (1971) *Zambia in Maps*, London: University of London Press.

Davis, I. (1978) *Shelter after Disaster*, Oxford: Oxford Polytechnic Press.

Davis, I. (ed.)(1981) *Disasters and the Small Dwelling*, Oxford: Pergamon Press.

Davis, I. (1985) *Shelter after Earthquakes*, unpublished thesis, University College London.

De Clercq, H. (2002) 'Corrugated iron: The ultimate sustainable building material?', paper presented at Built Environment Professions Convention, Johannesburg, 1–3 May 2002.

Deffontaines, P. (1948) *Géographie et Religions*, Paris: Librairie Gallimard.

De Little, R.J. (1972) *The Windmill: Yesterday and Today*, London: John Baker.

Denyer, S. (1978) *African Traditional Architecture: An Historical and Geographical Perspective*, London: Heinemann.

Dethier, J. (1981) *Down to Earth: Mud Architecture, an Old Idea, a New Future*, London: Thames and Hudson.

Domenig, G. (2003) 'Inverted posts for the granary: Opposition and reversal in Toba Batak architecture', in S. Sparkes and S. Howell (eds) *The House in Southeast Asia: A Changing Social, Economic and Political Domain*, London: Routledge/Curzon.

Dorling, D. and Fairbairn, D. (1997) *Mapping: Ways of Representing the World*, Harlow: Longman.

Drew, P. (1979) *Tensile Architecture*, London: Granada.

Drew, P. (1985) *Leaves of Iron*, Sydney: Law Book.

Drew, P. (1992) *Veranda: Embracing Place*, Sydney: Angus and Robertson.

Driver, H.E. (1961) *Indians of North America*, Chicago: University of Chicago Press.

Duly, C. (1979) *The Houses of Mankind*, London: Thames and Hudson.

Dumont, R. (1970) *Types of Rural Economy: Studies in World Agriculture*, London: Methuen.

Dunkelberg, K. (1985) *Bamboo as a Building Material*, Stuttgart: Institut fur Leichte Fachentragwerke.

Edwards, B., Sibley, M., Hakmi, M. and Land, P. (2006) *Courtyard Housing: Past, Present and Future*, London: Taylor & Francis.

Edwards, J.D. (1989) 'The complex origins of the American domestic piazza-veranda-gallery', *Material Culture*, 21 (2): 3–58.

Edwards, J.D. (2001) 'Architectural creolization: The importance of colonial architecture', in M-J. Amerlinck (ed.) *Architectural Anthropology*, Westport: Bergin and Garvey.

Elawa, S. (1981) 'Impact of the environmental climate on elements of the house', in S. Elawa (ed.) *Housing Design in Extreme Hot Arid Zones*, Lund: University of Lund.

Endersby, E., Greenwood, A. and Larkin, D. (1992) *Barn: The Art of a Working Building*, Boston: Houghton Mifflin.

Ensminger, R. (1992; 2nd edn 2003) *The Pennsylvania Barn: Its Origin, Evolution, and Distribution in North America*, Baltimore: John Hopkins University.

Evans, M. (1980) *Housing, Climate and Comfort*, London: Architectural Press.

Faegre, T. (1979) *Tents: Architecture of the Nomads*, London: John Murray.

Faik-Nzuji, C.M. (1992) *Symboles Graphiques en Afrique Noire*. Paris: Louvain-La-Neuve, Editions Karthala et Ciltade.

Farrelly, D. (1984) *The Book of Bamboo: A Comprehensive Guide to this Remarkable Plant, its Uses, and its History*, London: Thames and Hudson.

Feduchi, L. (1977) *Spanish Folk Architecture: The Northern Plateau*, Barcelona: Editorial Blume.

Fernandes, M. and Correia, M. (2005) *Earth Architecture in Portugal*, Lisboa: Argumentum.

Food and Agriculture Organisation (2003) *Review of World Water Resources by Country*, Rome: United Nations.

Food and Agriculture Organization (2005) *Global Forest Resources Assessment 2005*, Rome: United Nations.

Ford, M., El Kadi, H. and Watson, L. (1999) 'The relevance of GIS in the evaluation of vernacular architecture', *Journal of Architectural Conservation*, 3: 64–75.

Forde, C.D. (1950) *Habitat, Economy and Society: A Geographical Introduction to Ethnology*, London: Methuen.

Forth, G. (1981) *Rindi: An Ethnographic Study of a Traditional Domain in Eastern Sumba*, The Hague: Nijhoff.

Forth, G. (2003) 'Change and continuity in Nage house form', in R. Schefold, P.J.M. Nas and G. Domenig (eds) *Indonesian Houses: Tradition and Transformation in Vernacular Architecture*, Leiden: KITLV Press.

Fox, J.J. (1993) 'Introduction', in J.J. Fox (ed.) *Inside Austronesian Houses: Perspectives on Domestic Designs for Living*, Canberra: Research School of Pacific and Asian studies.

Fréal, J. (1979) *L'architecture Paysanne en France: La Maison*, Paris: Berger-Levrault.

Freeman, D. (1960) *Report on the Iban*, London: London School of Economics.

Freeland, J. and Cox, P. (1969) *Rude Timber Buildings in Australia*, London: Thames and Hudson.

Freeman, P. (1980) *The Woolshed: A Riverina Anthology*, Melbourne: Oxford University Press.

Freeman, W.H. and Bracegirdle, B. (1963) *An Atlas of Embryology*, London: Heinemann.

Gaisford, J. (ed.)(1983) *Atlas of Man*, London: Marshall Cavendish.

Gebhart, T. (1980) *Kachelofen: Mittelpunkt Hauslichen Lebens, Entwicklung, Form, Technik*, Munich: Callwey.

Glassie, H. (1975) *Folk Housing in Middle Virginia: A Structural Analysis of Historic Artifacts*, Knoxville: University of Tennessee Press.

Golany, G.S. (1992) *Chinese Earth-Sheltered Dwellings: Indigenous Lessons for Modern Urban Design*, Honolulu: University of Hawaii.

Goldfinger, M. (1993) *Villages in the Sun: Mediterranean Community Architecture*, New York: Rizzoli.

Grigg, D.B. (1980) *Population Growth and Agrarian Change: An Historical Perspective*, Cambridge: Cambridge University Press.

Grimes, B.F. (ed.)(1992) *Ethnologue: Languages of the World*, Dallas: Summer Institute of Linguistics.

Guerreiro, A.J. (2003) 'The Bornean longhouse in historical perspective, 1850–1990: Social processes and adaptation to changes', in R. Schefold, P.J.M. Nas and G. Domenig (eds) *Indonesian Houses: Tradition and Transformation in Vernacular Architecture*, Leiden: KITLV Press.

Hall, N. (1981) 'Has thatch a future?', *Appropriate Technology*, 8 (3): 7–9.

Hall, N. (1988) *Thatching: A Handbook*, London: Intermediate Technology Publications.

Hall, R. (1989) *World Population Trends*, Cambridge: Cambridge University Press.

Hallet, S.I. and Samizay, R. (1980) *Traditional Architecture of Afghanistan*, New York: Garland Press.

Hansen, H.J. (1971) *Architecture in Wood: A History of Wood Building and its Techniques in Europe and North America*, London: Faber and Faber.

Harley, J.B. (1988) 'Maps, knowledge, and power', in D. Cosgrove and S. Daniels (eds) *The Iconography of Landscape: Essays on the Symbolic Representation, Design and Use of Past Environments*, Cambridge: Cambridge University Press.

Harley, J.B. (1989) 'Deconstructing the map', *Cartographica*, 26 (2): 1–20.

Harris, B. (1991) *Barns of America*, New York: Crescent Books.

Harvey, M.E. (1966; 2nd edn 1969) 'Rural house types', in J.I. Clarke (ed.) *Sierra Leone in Maps*, London: Hodder and Stoughton.

Hauser-Schäublin, B. (1985) *Kulthäuser in Nordneuguinea*, Berlin: Akademie-Verlag.

Henderson-Sellers, A. and Hansen, A-M. (1995) *Climate Change Atlas: Greenhouse Simulations from the Model Evaluation Consortium for Climate Assessment*, London: Kluwer Academic.

Herbert, G. (1978) *Pioneers of Prefabrication: The British Contribution in the Nineteenth Century*, Baltimore and London: John Hopkins University Press.

Herskovits, M. (1952) *Economic Anthropology: A Study in Comparative Economics*, New York: Alfred Knopf.

Hidalgo, O. (1974) *Bambu: Su Cultivo y Aplicaciones en Fabricacion de Papel, Construccion, Arquitecture, Ingeniera, Artesania*, Bogota: Estudios Tecnicos Colombianos.

Hills, R.L. (1994) *Power from Wind: A History of Windmill Technology*, Cambridge: Cambridge University Press.

Ho, P-P. (2003) 'China's vernacular architecture', in R.G. Knapp (ed.) *Asia's Old Dwellings: Tradition, Resilience and Change*, New York: Oxford University Press.

Hockings, E.J. (1989) *Traditional Architecture in the Gilbert Islands*, Brisbane: University of Queensland.

Houben, H. and Guillaud, H. (1994) *Earth Construction: A Comprehensive Guide*, Villefontaine Cedex: Intermediate Technology Centre.

House, S. and House, C. (2004) *Mediterranean Villages: An Architectural Journey*, Mulgrave: Images.

Hubka, T.C. (1984) *Big House, Little House, Back House, Barn: The Connected Farm Buildings of New England*, Hanover and London: University Press of New England.

Hudson, J.C. (1969) *A Geography of Settlements*, London: Macdonald and Evans.

Hugh-Jones, C. (1979) *From the Milk River: Spatial and Temporal Processes in North-West Amazonia*, Cambridge: Cambridge University Press.

Hugh-Jones, S. (1985) 'The Maloca: A world in a house', in E. Carmichael et al. (eds) *The Hidden Peoples of the Amazon*, London: British Museum Publications.

Hughes, G. (1985) *Barns of Rural Britain*, London: The Herbert Press.

International Conference on the Study and Conservation of Earthen Architecture (2000) *Terra 2000: 8th International Conference on the Study and Conservation of Earthen Architecture*, London: James and James.

Janssen, J.J.A. (1988) *Building with Bamboo: A Handbook*, London: Intermediate Technology Publications.

Jayanetti, L. (1990) *Timber Pole Construction*, London: Intermediate Technology Publications.

Johnson, A.N. and Easle, T. (1987) *The Evolution of Human Societies from Foraging Group to Agrarian State*, Stanford, Stanford University Press.

Jones, H. (1990) *Population Geography*, London: Chapman.

Jong, A. de and Skougard, M. (1992) 'Early open-air museums: Traditions of museums about traditions', *Museum*, 175 (3): 151–157.

Jordan, T.G. (1985) *American Log Buildings: An Old World Heritage*, Chapel Hill and London: The University of North Carolina Press.

Jordan, T.G., Kilpinen, J.T. and Gritzner, C.F. (1997) *The Mountain West: Interpreting the Folk Landscape*, Baltimore and London: The Johns Hopkins University Press.

Jowitt, G. and Shaw, P. (1999) *Pacific Island Style*, London: Thames and Hudson.

Kahlenberg, M.H. and Schwartz, M. (1983) *A Book about Grass*, New York: Dutton.

Kahn, L.I. (2004) *Home Work: Handbuilt Shelter*, Bolinas: Shelter Publications.

Kalman, H. (1994) *A History of Canadian Architecture*, Toronto: Oxford University Press.

Katzner, K. (2002) *The Languages of the World*, London: Routledge.

Kawashima, C. (1986) *Japan's Folk Architecture: Traditional Thatched Farmhouses*, Tokyo: Kodansha.

Kempe, D. (1988) *Living Underground: A History of Cave and Cliff Dwelling*, London: Herbert.

King, A.D. (1982) 'The bungalow: An Indian contribution to the West', *History Today*, 32: 38–45.

King, A.D. (1995) *The Bungalow: The Production of a Global Culture*, New York and Oxford: Oxford University Press.

King, A.D. (2004) *Spaces of Global Cultures: Architecture, Urbanism, Identity*, London: Routledge.

Kipling, J.L. (1911) 'The origin of the bungalow', *Country Life in America*, 19 (8): 308–310.

Kirk, M. (1994) *Silent Spaces: The Last of the Great Aisled Barns*, Boston: Bulfinch Press.

Knapp, R.G. (1986) *China's Traditional Rural Architecture: A Cultural Geography of the Common House*, Honolulu: University of Hawaii Press.

Knapp, R.G. (1990) *The Chinese House*, Hong Kong: Oxford University Press.

Knapp, R.G. (1997) 'Geographical', in P. Oliver (ed.) *Encyclopedia of Vernacular Architecture of the World*, Cambridge: Cambridge University Press.

Knapp, R.G. (2000) *China's Old Dwellings*, Honolulu: University of Hawaii Press.

Knapp, R.G. (ed.)(2003) *Asia's Old Dwellings: Tradition, Resilience and Change*, New York: Oxford University Press.

Knapp, R.G. and Lo, K-Y. (eds)(2005) *House, Home, Family: Living and Being Chinese*, Honolulu: University of Hawaii Press.

Kniffen, F.B. (1986) 'Folk housing: Key to diffusion', in D. Upton and J.M. Vlach (eds) *Common Places: Readings in American Vernacular Architecture*, Athens and London: University of Georgia Press. Originally published in the *Annals of the Association of American Geographers*, 55 (4): 549–577 (1965).

Kniffen, F.B. and Glassie, H. (1986) 'Building in wood in the eastern United States: A time-place perspective', in D. Upton and J.M. Vlach (eds) *Common Places: Readings in American Vernacular Architecture*, Athens and London: University of Georgia Press. Originally published in *Geographical Review*, 56 (1): 40–66 (1966).

Knuffel, W.E. (1973) *The Construction of the Bantu Grass Hut*, Graz: Akademische Druck-und-Verlagsanstalt.

Koch, G. (1965) *The Material Culture of Kiribati*, Suva, Fiji: Institute of Pacific Studies.

Kostof, S. (1985; 2nd edn 1995) *History of Architecture: Settings and Rituals*, Oxford: Oxford University Press.

Kovoor, A. (1983) *The Palmyrah Palm: Potential and Perspectives*, Rome: United Nations.

Krickeberg, W. (1939) 'The Indian sweat bath', *Ciba Symposia*, 1 (1): 19–25.

Kronenburg, R. (1995; 2nd edn 2002) *Houses in Motion: The Genesis, History and Development of the Portable Building*, Chichester: Wiley-Academy.

Langer, J. (2005) *Atlas Památek Evropská Muzea v Přírodě*, Prague: Baset.

Lari, Y. (1989) *Traditional Architecture of Thatta*, Karachi: The Heritage Foundation.

Larkin, D. (1995) *Farm: The Vernacular Tradition of Working Buildings*, New York: Monacelli Press.

Laubin, R. and Laubin, G. (1957) *The Indian Tipi*, New York: Ballantine Books.

Laws, B. (1991) *Traditional Houses of Rural France*, London: Collins and Brown.

Lee, R.B. and Daly, R. (eds)(1999) *The Cambridge Encyclopedia of Hunters and Gatherers*, Cambridge: Cambridge University Press.

Lee, S-h. (2003) 'Traditional Korean settlements and dwellings', in R.G. Knapp (ed.) *Asia's Old Dwellings: Tradition, Resilience and Change*, New York: Oxford University Press.

Lehr, J. (1980) 'The log buildings of Ukrainian settlers in western Canada', *Prairie Forum*, 2: 183–196.

Lenclos, J-P. and Lenclos, D. (1999) *Colors of the World: The Geography of Color*, New York and London: W.W. Norton & Company.

Lewcock, R. (1978) *Traditional Architecture in Kuwait and the Northern Gulf*, London: United Bank of Kuwait.

Lo, K-Y. and Ho, P-P. (eds)(1999) *Living Heritage: Vernacular Environment in China*, Hong Kong: Yungmingtang.

Loeb, E.M. and Broek, J.O.M. (1947) 'Social organisation and the long house in Southeast Asia', *American Anthropologist*, 49: 414–425.

Loftas, T. (ed.)(1972) *Atlas of the Earth*, London: George Philip and Son.

Long, C. (2003) 'The persistence of tradition in Laos', in R.G. Knapp (ed.) *Asia's Old Dwellings: Tradition, Resilience and Change*, New York: Oxford University Press.

McClure, F.A. (1953) *Bamboo as a Building Material*, Washington: US Department of Agriculture.

McClure, F.A. (1966; 2nd edn 1993) *The Bamboos*, Washington and London: Smithsonian Institution Press.

McCoy, R.E. (1988) 'What's killing the palm trees?', *National Geographic Magazine*, 174 (1): 120–130.

MacDougall, B.G. (2003) 'The Sinhala house: Landscape experience and domestic order in Kandyan Sri Lanka', in R.G. Knapp (ed.) *Asia's Old Dwellings: Tradition, Resilience and Change*, New York: Oxford University Press.

MacEachren, A.M. and Monmonier, M. (eds)(1992) 'Geographic visualisation', special issue of *Cartography and Geographic Information Systems*, 19 (4).

McGuire, B. et al. (2004) *World Atlas of Natural Hazards*, London: Arnold.

McHenry, P.G. (1984) *Adobe and Rammed Earth Buildings: Design and Construction*, New York and Chichester: John Wiley and Sons.

McHenry, P.G. (1999): 'Adobe today'. *Cultural Resource Management*, vol. 22 (6): 5–6.

McHenry, P.G. (2000) *The Adobe Story: A Global Treasure*. Albuquerque: University of New Mexico Press.

Maddex, D. (2003) *Bungalow Nation*, New York: Abrams.

Marchand, T.H.J. (2001) *Minaret Building and Apprenticeship in Yemen*, Richmond: Curzon.

Marden, L. (1980) 'Bamboo: The giant grass', *National Geographic Magazine*, 158 (4): 502–529.

Matthews, T. and Changuion, A. (1989) *The African Mural*, London: New Holland.

Maxwell, G. (1957) *A Reed Shaken by the Wind*, London: Longman.

Meir, I.A. and Roaf, S.C. (2006) 'The future of the vernacular: Towards new methodologies for the understanding and optimisation of the performance of vernacular buildings', in L. Asquith and M. Vellinga (eds) *Vernacular Architecture in the Twenty-First Century: Theory, Education and Practice*, London: Taylor & Francis.

Meirion-Jones, G.I. (1982) *The Vernacular Architecture of Brittany: An Essay in Historical Geography*, Edinburgh: Donald.

Moffett, M. (2003) *A World History of Architecture*, London: Laurence King.

Monmonier, M. (1991) *How to Lie with Maps*, Chicago and London: University of Chicago Press.

Moon, B. (1991) *An Encyclopedia of Archetypal Symbolism*. Boston and London: Shambhala for The Archive for Research in Archetypal Symbolism.

Moseley, C. and Asher, R.E. (1994) *Atlas of the World's Languages*, London: Routledge.

Mulligan, H. and Forster, P. *Troglodytes; Spain*. Unpublished manuscript.

Mulligan, H. and Forster, P. *Troglodytes: Tunisia*. Unpublished manuscript.

Murdock, G.P. (1967) *Ethnographic Atlas*, Pittsburgh: University of Pittsburgh Press.

Nabokov, P. and Easton, R. (1989) *Native American Architecture*, Oxford: Oxford University Press.

Naonori, M. (2003) 'Japan's traditional houses: The significance of spatial conceptions', in R.G. Knapp (ed.) *Asia's Old Dwellings: Tradition, Resilience and Change*, New York: Oxford University Press.

Neal, J. (2000) *Architecture: A Visual History*, London: Parkgate.

Neuwirth, R. (2005) *Shadow Cities: A Billion Squatters, a New Urban World*, London: Routledge.

Nguyen Van Huyen (1934) *Introduction a L'Etude De L'Habitation Sur Pilotis Dans L'Asie Du Sud-Est*. Paris: Librairie Orientaliste Paul Geuthner.

Nicolaisen, J. (1963) *Ecology and Culture of the Pastoral Tuareg*, Copenhagen: Nationalmuseets Skrifter Etnografisk Raekke IX.

Noble, A.G. (1984a) *Wood, Brick and Stone: The North American Settlement Landscape, vol. 1: Houses*, Amherst: The University of Massachusetts Press.

Noble, A.G. (1984b) *Wood, Brick and Stone: The North American Settlement Landscape, vol. 2: Barns and Farm Structures*, Amherst: The University of Massachusetts Press.

Noble, A.G. (2003) 'Patterns and relationships of Indian houses', in R.G. Knapp (ed.) *Asia's Old Dwellings: Tradition, Resilience and Change*, New York: Oxford University Press.

Noble, A.G. and Cleek, R.K. (1995) *The Old Barn Book: A Field Guide to North American Barns and other Farm Structures*, New Brunswick, N.J.: Rutgers University Press.

Noble, A.G. and Wilhelm, H.G.H. (eds)(1995) *Barns of the Midwest*, Athens: Ohio University Press.

Norris, H.T. (1953) 'Cave habitations and granaries in Tripolitania and Tunisia', *Man*, 53: 82–85.

Norton, J. (1996) *Building with Earth: A Handbook*, London: Intermediate Technology Publications.

Notebaart, J.C. (1972) *Windmühlen: Der Stand der Forschung über das Vorkommen und der Ursprung*, The Hague: Mouton.

Nowacki, H. (ed.)(1981) *Open-Air Museums in Poland*, Poznań: Państwowe Wydawnictwo Rolnicze i Leśne.

Oliver, P. (ed.)(1969) *Shelter and Society*, London: Barrie and Cresset.

Oliver, P. (ed.)(1971) *Shelter in Africa*, London: Barrie and Jenkins.

Oliver, P. (ed.)(1975) *Shelter, Sign and Symbol*, London: Barrie and Jenkins.

Oliver, P. (1983) 'Earth as a building material today', *Oxford Art Journal*, 5(2): 31–38; reprinted in Oliver, P. (2006) *Built to Meet Needs: Cultural Issues in Vernacular Architecture*, Oxford: Architectural Press.

Oliver, P. (ed.)(1997) *Encyclopedia of Vernacular Architecture of the World*, Cambridge: Cambridge University Press.

Oliver, P. (2003) *Dwellings: The Vernacular House World Wide*, London: Phaidon.

Oliver, P. (2004) 'Vernacular architecture', in R.S. Sennott (ed.) *Encyclopedia of 20ᵗʰ-Century Architecture*, New York and London: Fitzroy Dearborn.

Opolovnikov, A.V. and Opolovnikov, Y.A. (1989) *The Wooden Architecture of Russia: Houses, Fortifications, Churches*, London: Thames and Hudson.

Parker, A. and Neal, A. (1995) *Hajj Paintings: Folk Art of the Great Pilgrimage*, Washington: Smithsonian Institution Press.

Parnwell, M. (1993) *Population Movements and the Third World*, London: Routledge.

Parry, J.P.M. (1979) *Brickmaking in Developing Countries*, Watford: Building Research Establishment.

Parsons, J.J. (1991) 'Giant bamboo in the vernacular architecture of Colombia and Ecuador', *The Geographical Review*, 81 (2): 129–152.

Pattison, I.R., Pattison, D.S. and Alcock, N.W. (eds)(1992) *A Bibliography of Vernacular Architecture, Volume III: 1977–1989*, Aberystwyth: Vernacular Architecture Group.

Paul, B.K. (2003) 'Dwellings in Bangladesh', in R.G. Knapp (ed.) *Asia's Old Dwellings: Tradition, Resilience and Change*, New York: Oxford University Press.

Petherbridge, G.T. (1978) 'Vernacular architecture: The house and society', in G. Michell (ed.) *Architecture of the Islamic World: Its History and Social Meaning*, London: Thames and Hudson.

Petrie, F. (1990) *Decorative Patterns of the Ancient World*. London: Studio Editions.

Phaidon (2004) *The Phaidon Atlas of Contemporary World Architecture*, London: Phaidon.

Phleps, H. (1942) *Holzbaukunst: Der Blockbau*, Karlsruhe: Fachblattverlag Dr. Albert Bruder.

Pieper, R. (1999) 'Earthen architecture in the northern United States: European traditions in earthen construction', *Cultural Resource Management*, 22 (6): 30–33.

Pigou-Dennis, E. (2002) 'The Jamaican bungalow: Whose language?', in K.E.A. Monteith and G. Richards (eds) *Jamaica in Slavery and Freedom: History, Heritage and Culture*, Barbados/Jamaica/Trinidad and Tobago: University of the West Indies Press.

Piper, J. (1992) *Bamboos and Rattan: Traditional Uses and Beliefs*, Singapore: Oxford University Press.

Plattner, S. (1980) *Economic Anthropology*, Stanford: Stanford University Press.

Prasad, S. (1988) *The Havelis of North India: The Urban Courtyard House*, unpublished thesis, AA School of Architecture.

Pressouyre, L. (1996) *The World Heritage Convention, Twenty Years Later*, Paris: UNESCO Publishing.

Price, D.H. (1989) *Atlas of World Cultures: A Geographical Guide to Ethnographic Literature*, London: Sage.

Prizeman, J. (1975) *Your House: The Outside View*, London: Hutchinson.

Prussin, L. (1972) 'West African mud granaries', *Paideuma*, 18: 144–169.

Prussin, L. (1976) 'Sudanese architecture and the Manding', *African Arts*, 3 (1): 13–18 and 64–67.

Prussin, L. (1995) *African Nomadic Architecture: Space, Place and Gender*, Washington: Smithsonian Institution.

Radin, P. (1957) *Primitive Religion: Its Nature and Origin*, New York: Dover Publications.

Rapoport, A. (1969) *House, Form and Culture*, Englewood Cliffs: Prentice Hall.

Rapoport, A. (2006) 'Vernacular design as a model system', in L. Asquith and M. Vellinga (eds) *Vernacular Architecture in the Twenty-First Century: Theory, Education and Practice*, London: Taylor & Francis.

Reuter, T.A. (2002) *The House of our Ancestors: Precedence and Dualism in Highland Balinese Society*, Leiden: KITLV Press.

Reynolds, J. (1970) *Windmills and Watermills*, London: Hugh Evelyn.

Roaf, S. (1990) 'The traditional technology trap: Stereotypes of Middle Eastern traditional building types and technologies', *Trialog*, 25: 26–33.

Roaf, S. (1991) *The Wind-Catchers of the Middle East and Yazd*, Wisbech: MENAS Press.

Rooney, J.F., Zelinsky, W. and Louder, D.R. (1982) *This Remarkable Continent: An Atlas of United States and Canadian Society and Cultures*, College Station: A & M University Press.

Samizay, R. (2003) 'Traditional dwellings of Afghanistan: A multiple paradox', in R.G. Knapp (ed.) *Asia's Old Dwellings: Tradition, Resilience and Change*, New York: Oxford University Press.

Sather, C. (1993) 'Posts, hearth and thresholds: The Iban longhouse as a ritual structure', in J.J. Fox (ed.) *Inside Austronesian Houses: Perspectives on Domestic Designs for Living*, Canberra: Research School for Pacific and Asian Studies.

Schefold, R. (2003) 'The Southeast Asian-type house: Common features and local transformations of an ancient architectural tradition', in R. Schefold, P.J.M. Nas and G. Domenig (eds) *Indonesian Houses: Tradition and Transformation in Vernacular Architecture*, Leiden: KITLV Press.

Shadmon, A. (1996) *Stone: An Introduction*, London: Intermediate Technology Publications.

Shanin, T. (ed.)(1971) *Peasant and Peasant Societies*, Harmondsworth: Penguin Books.

Shurtleff, H.R. (1939) *The Log Cabin Myth: A Study of the Early Dwellings of the English Colonists in North America*, Cambridge, Mass.: Harvard University Press.

Singarimbun, M. (1975) *Kinship, Descent and Alliance among the Karo Batak*, Berkeley: University of California Press.

Sinha, S. (1994) 'The centre as void: Courtyard dwellings in India', *Open House International*, 19 (4): 28–35.

Slocum, T.A. (1999) *Thematic Cartography and Visualisation*, New Jersey: Prentice Hall.

Smith, A.D. (1995) *The Ethnic Origins of Nations*, Oxford: Blackwell.

Smith, J.T. (1975) 'Cruck distributions: An interpretation of some recent maps', *Vernacular Architecture*, 6: 3–18.

Sobti, M.P. (2003) 'Dwellings in the steppes and deserts of Inner Asia', in R.G. Knapp (ed.) *Asia's Old Dwellings: Tradition, Resilience and Change*, New York: Oxford University Press.

Solecki, R.S. (1978) 'Contemporary Kurdish winter-time inhabitants of Shanidar cave, Iraq', *World archaeology*, 10 (3): 318–330.

Sopher, D.E. (1967) *Geography of Religions*, Englewood Cliffs: Prentice-Hall.

Spence, R.J.S. and Cook, D.J. (1983) *Building Materials in Developing Countries*, Chichester: John Wiley and Sons.

Srivastava, Y. (2003) 'The bungalow: Symbol of Dominican sovereignty', *Contemporary Review*, 282 (1648): 301–304.

Steen, A., Steen, B. and Komatsu, E. (2003) *Built by Hand: Vernacular Buildings around the World*, Salt Lake City: Gibbs Smith.

Sumner, R. (1978) 'The tropical bungalow: The search for an indigenous Australian architecture', *Australian Journal of Art*, 1: 27–40.

Sunley, J. and Bedding, B. (eds) (1985) *Timber in Construction*, London: B.T. Batsford/TRADA.

Syson, L. (1965) *British Water-Mills*, London: Batsford.

Szabo, A. and Barfield, T.J. (1991) *Afghanistan: An Atlas of Indigenous Domestic Architecture*, Austin: University of Texas Press.

Talib, K. (1984) *Shelter in Saudi Arabia*, London: Academy Editions.

Taylor, M.R. (1999) 'Earthen architecture traditions in New Mexico', *Cultural Resource Management*, 22 (6): 21–27.

Thesiger, W. (1964) *The Marsh Arabs*, London: Longman.

Tufnell, R. (1982) *Building and Repairing Dry Stone Walls*, Stoneleigh Park: Dry Stone Walling Association of Great Britain.

Tufnell, R. (1991) *Better Dry Stone Walling*, Stoneleigh Park: Dry Stone Walling Association of Great Britain.

Tunnard, C. and Reed, H.H. (1956) *American Skyline*, New York: New American Library.

Tvedt, T. (ed.)(2006) *A History of Water*, London: Tauris.

Tyrwhitt, J. (1976) *The Mill*, Boston: New York Graphic Society.

Uhl, N.W. (1987) *Genera Palmarum: A Classification of Palms*, Lawrence: Allen Press.

Uldall, K. (1957) 'Open-air museums', *Museum*, 10 (1): 68–96.

UNESCO (2004) *World Heritage List*. Online. Available http://whc.unesco.org/en/list/ (accessed 20 July 2004).

United Nations (2004) *World Urbanization Prospects: The 2003 Revision*, New York: Department of Economic and Social Affairs.

United Nations (2005) *World Population Prospects: The 2004 Revision*, New York: Department of Economic and Social Affairs.

United Nations Centre for Human Settlements (1982) *Survey of Slum and Squatter Settlements*, Dublin: Tycooly.

United Nations Disaster Relief Organisation (1982) *Shelter after Disaster: Guidelines for Assistance*, New York: United Nations.

United Nations Human Settlements Programme (2003) *The Challenge of Slums*. Global Report on Human Settlements 2003, London: Earthscan.

United Nations Secretariat (1972) *The Use of Bamboos and Reed in Building Construction*, New York: UN Publications.

United Nations Statistic Division (2005) *Environmental Indicators: Forest Area*. Online. Available http://unstats.un.org/unsd/environment/forestarea.htm (accessed 1 March 2006).

United States Geological Survey Earthquake Hazards Program (2006) *Information on Significant Worldwide Earthquakes by Year*. Online. Available http://neic.usgs.gov/neis/eq_depot/ (accessed 21 March 2006).

Upton, D. and Vlach, J.M. (eds)(1986) *Common Places: Readings in American Vernacular Architecture*, Athens and London: University of Georgia Press.

Vegas, F. (1985) *Venezuelan Vernacular*, Princeton, N.J.: Princeton Architectural Press.

Vellinga, M. (2004) *Constituting Unity and Difference: Vernacular Architecture in a Minangkabau Village*, Leiden: KITLV Press.

Vischer, M. (2003) 'The two-faced Palu'é house: Multiple orientation and structural transformation in an eastern Indonesian dwelling', in R. Schefold, P.J.M. Nas and G. Domenig (eds), *Indonesian Houses: Tradition and Transformation in Vernacular Architecture*, Leiden: KITLV Press.

Vlach, J.M. (2003) *Barns*, New York and London: W.W. Norton & Company.

Volkman, T. (1985) *Feasts of Honour: Ritual and Change in the Toraja Highlands*, Urbana: University of Illinois Press.

Waldman, C. (1985) *Atlas of the North American Indian*, New York: Facts on File Publishers.

Walton, J. (1974) *Water-Mills, Windmills and Horse-Mills of South Africa*, Johannesburg: Struik Publishers.

Warren, K. (1990) *The British Iron and Steel Sheet Industry since 1840: An Economic Geography*, London: G. Bell and Sons.

Waterson, R. (1990) *The Living House: An Anthropology of Architecture in South-East Asia*, London: Thames and Hudson.

Waterson, R. (1993) 'Houses and the built environment in island Southeast Asia: Tracing some shared themes in the uses of space', in J.J. Fox (ed.) *Inside Austronesian Houses: Perspectives on Domestic Designs for Living*, Canberra: Research School of Pacific and Asian studies.

Weslager, C.A. (1969) *The Log Cabin in America: From Pioneer Days to the Present*, New Brunswick: Rutgers University Press.

West, R.C. (1974) 'The flat-roofed folk dwelling in rural Mexico', *Geoscience and Man*, 5: 129.

Westoby, J. (1989) *Introduction to World Forestry: People and their Trees*, Oxford: Blackwell.

Winberry, J.J. (1974) 'The log house in Mexico', *Annals of the Association of American Geographers*, 64: 54–69.

Winzeler, R.L. (ed.)(1998) *Indigenous Architecture in Borneo: Traditional Patterns and New Developments*, Philips, ME: Borneo Research Council.

Wittkower, R. (1977) *Allegory and the Migration of Symbols*, London: Thames and Hudson.

Wojciechowska, P. (2001) *Building with Earth: A Guide to Flexible-Form Earthbag Construction*, White River Junction: Chelsea Green.

Wonders, W.C. (1979) 'Log dwellings in Canadian folk architecture', *Annals of the Association of American Geographers*, 69 (2): 187–207.

Woodforde, J. (1976) *Bricks to Build a House*, London: Routledge and Kegan Paul.

Wright, A. (1991) *Craft Techniques for Traditional Buildings*, London: Batsford.

Wurm, S.A. (ed.)(1996; 2nd edn 2001) *Atlas of the World's Languages in Danger of Disappearing*, Paris: UNESCO.

Wyk, G.N. van (1998) *African Painted Houses: Basotho Dwellings of Southern Africa*, New York: Harry N. Abrams.

Xing, R. (2003) 'Pile-built dwellings in ethnic southern China: Type, myth and heterogeneity', in R.G. Knapp (ed.) *Asia's Old Dwellings: Tradition, Resilience and Change*, New York: Oxford University Press.

Yampolsky, M. (1993) *The Traditional Architecture of Mexico*, London: Thames and Hudson.

Yin, L.H. (2003) 'The kampong house: Evolutionary history of peninsular Malaysia's vernacular houseform', in R.G. Knapp (ed.) *Asia's Old Dwellings: Tradition, Resilience and Change*, New York: Oxford University Press.

Zippelius, A. (1974) *Handbuch der Europaischen Freilichtmuseen*, Cologne: Rheinland-Verlag.

Zook, N. (1971) *Museum Villages USA*, Barre: Barre Publishers.

Zurick, D. and Shrestha, N. (2003) 'Himalayan dwellings: A cultural-environmental perspective', in R.G. Knapp (ed.) *Asia's Old Dwellings: Tradition, Resilience and Change*, New York: Oxford University Press.

Index

In the following Index the Subjects of the Maps and those aspects that are represented therein, are followed by the Map Numbers in **Bold**. Items in the accompanying texts are also identified by the Map Numbers, but are not indicated in bold type. Entries in this Index that refer to the Introduction to the Atlas are in lower case Roman numerals (eg v, vi, vii,).